Informal Markets and Trade in Central Asia and the Caucasus

This edited book introduces new research on informal markets and trade in Central Asia and the Caucasus. The research presented in this volume is based on recent field research in Armenia, Georgia, Kazakhstan and Kyrgyzstan, as well as Beijing, Guangzhou, Yiwu and the Xinjiang Uyghur Autonomous Region in China. The nine chapters in this book illustrate how informal markets and trade in Central Asia and the Caucasus have provided space for millions of people across the region to negotiate changes in state and society in the three decades since the breakup of the Soviet Union and the emergence of successor states.

Collectively, the book suggests that informality should be seen as a normative order for polities in Central Asia and the Caucasus for three reasons: (1) The inability – or unwillingness – of the states to measure commercial transactions. (2) The highly personalized nature of small business operations that rest on networking and social relations, oral agreements and trust. (3) Markets and bazaars being embedded within states in which clientelism frequently thrives.

This book is a significant new contribution to the study of trade and informal markets in Central Asia and the Caucasus, and will be a great resource for academics, researchers and advanced students of Sociology, History, Politics, Business, Economics, Social Anthropology and Geography.

The chapters in this book were originally published as a special issue of the journal, *Central Asian Survey*.

Susanne Fehlings is Senior Researcher at the Frobenius Institute for Research in Cultural Anthropology, Frankfurt am Main. Her regional focus is the Caucasus. She specializes in urban and economic anthropology, the anthropology of the state, and research on bazaars, trade activity and entrepreneurship.

Hasan H. Karrar is Associate Professor and Department Chair, Department of Humanities and Social Sciences at the Lahore University of Management Sciences, Pakistan. He is a specialist of China and Central Asia with a special interest in new economic and political linkages since the Cold War.

Central Asian Studies

The Afghan-Central Asia Borderland
The State and Local Leaders
Suzanne Levi-Sanchez

Kyrgyzstan - Regime Security and Foreign Policy
Kemel Toktomushev

Legal Pluralism in Central Asia
Local Jurisdiction and Customary Practices
Mahabat Sadyrbek

Identity, History and Trans-Nationality in Central Asia
The Mountain Communities of Pamir
Edited by Carole Faucher and Dagikhudo Dagiev

Critical Approaches to Security in Central Asia
Edited by Edward Lemon

Russian Practices of Governance in Eurasia
Frontier Power Dynamics, 16–19th Century
Gulnar T. Kendirbai

Practices of Traditionalization in Central Asia
Edited by Judith Beyer and Peter Finke

Uzbekistan's International Relations
Oybek Madiyev

Parliamentary Representation in Central Asia
MPs Between Representing Their Voters and Serving an Authoritarian Regime
Esther Somfalvy

Socialist and Post-Socialist Mongolia
Nation, Identity, and Culture
Edited by Simon Wickhamsmith and Phillip P. Marzluf

Informal Markets and Trade in Central Asia and the Caucasus
Edited by Susanne Fehlings and Hasan H. Karrar

For more information about this series, please visit:
www.routledge.com/Central-Asian-Studies/book-series/CAS

Informal Markets and Trade in Central Asia and the Caucasus

Edited by
Susanne Fehlings and Hasan H. Karrar

LONDON AND NEW YORK

First published 2022
by Routledge
4 Park Square, Milton Park, Abingdon, Oxon OX14 4RN

and by Routledge
605 Third Avenue, New York, NY 10158

Routledge is an imprint of the Taylor & Francis Group, an informa business

Chapters 1–8 © 2022 Global South Ltd
Chapter 9 © 2020 Diana Ibañez-Tirado and Magnus Marsden. Originally published as Open Access.

With the exception of Chapter 9, no part of this book may be reprinted or reproduced or utilised in any form or by any electronic, mechanical, or other means, now known or hereafter invented, including photocopying and recording, or in any information storage or retrieval system, without permission in writing from the publishers. For details on the rights for Chapter 9, please see the chapter's Open Access footnote.

Trademark notice: Product or corporate names may be trademarks or registered trademarks, and are used only for identification and explanation without intent to infringe.

British Library Cataloguing in Publication Data
A catalogue record for this book is available from the British Library

ISBN: 978-1-032-19581-0 (hbk)
ISBN: 978-1-032-19582-7 (pbk)
ISBN: 978-1-003-25988-6 (ebk)

DOI: 10.4324/9781003259886

Typeset in Myriad Pro
by Newgen Publishing UK

Publisher's Note
The publisher accepts responsibility for any inconsistencies that may have arisen during the conversion of this book from journal articles to book chapters, namely the inclusion of journal terminology.

Disclaimer
Every effort has been made to contact copyright holders for their permission to reprint material in this book. The publishers would be grateful to hear from any copyright holder who is not here acknowledged and will undertake to rectify any errors or omissions in future editions of this book.

Contents

Citation Information vii
Notes on Contributors ix

1 Negotiating state and society: the normative informal economies of Central Asia and the Caucasus 1
   Susanne Fehlings and Hasan H. Karrar

2 Trading in Dordoi and Lilo bazaars: frontiers of formality, entrepreneurship and globalization 11
   Philippe Rudaz

3 The traders of Central Bazaar, Astana: motivation and networks 33
   Meiirzhan Baitas

4 The formal side of informality: non-state trading practices and local Uyghur ethnography 46
   Rune Steenberg

5 Markets at sacred sites: the globalized mobility and informality of the Armenian religious fairs 63
   Yulia Antonyan

6 The bazaar in ruins: rent and fire in Barakholka, Almaty 80
   Hasan H. Karrar

7 Doing business in Yabaolu Market, Beijing: (inter-)ethnic entrepreneurship, trust and friendship between Caucasian and Chinese traders 95
   Susanne Fehlings

8 Business 2.0: Kyrgyz middlemen in Guangzhou 116
   Philipp Schröder

9 Trade 'outside the law': Uzbek and Afghan transnational merchants between
   Yiwu and South-Central Asia   135
   Diana Ibañez-Tirado and Magnus Marsden

   Index   155

Citation Information

The chapters in this book were originally published in the journal *Central Asian Survey*, volume 39, issue 1 (2020). When citing this material, please use the original page numbering for each article, as follows:

Chapter 1
Negotiating state and society: the normative informal economies of Central Asia and the Caucasus
Susanne Fehlings and Hasan H. Karrar
Central Asian Survey, volume 39, issue 1 (2020), pp. 1–10

Chapter 2
Trading in Dordoi and Lilo bazaars: frontiers of formality, entrepreneurship and globalization
Philippe Rudaz
Central Asian Survey, volume 39, issue 1 (2020), pp. 11–32

Chapter 3
The traders of Central Bazaar, Astana: motivation and networks
Meiirzhan Baitas
Central Asian Survey, volume 39, issue 1 (2020), pp. 33–45

Chapter 4
The formal side of informality: non-state trading practices and local Uyghur ethnography
Rune Steenberg
Central Asian Survey, volume 39, issue 1 (2020), pp. 46–62

Chapter 5
Markets at sacred sites: the globalized mobility and informality of the Armenian religious fairs
Yulia Antonyan
Central Asian Survey, volume 39, issue 1 (2020), pp. 63–79

Chapter 6
The bazaar in ruins: rent and fire in Barakholka, Almaty
Hasan H. Karrar
Central Asian Survey, volume 39, issue 1 (2020), pp. 80–94

Chapter 7
Doing business in Yabaolu Market, Beijing: (inter-)ethnic entrepreneurship, trust and friendship between Caucasian and Chinese traders
Susanne Fehlings
Central Asian Survey, volume 39, issue 1 (2020), pp. 95–115

Chapter 8
Business 2.0: Kyrgyz middlemen in Guangzhou
Philipp Schröder
Central Asian Survey, volume 39, issue 1 (2020), pp. 116–134

Chapter 9
Trade 'outside the law': Uzbek and Afghan transnational merchants between Yiwu and South-Central Asia
Diana Ibañez-Tirado and Magnus Marsden
Central Asian Survey, volume 39, issue 1 (2020), pp. 135–154

For any permission-related enquiries please visit:
www.tandfonline.com/page/help/permissions

Notes on Contributors

Yulia Antonyan, Department of Cultural Studies, Faculty of History, Yerevan State University, Armenia.

Meiirzhan Baitas, Independent Scholar.

Susanne Fehlings, Department of Social and Cultural Anthropology, Goethe University, Frankfurt am Main, Germany.

Diana Ibañez-Tirado, Department of Anthropology, Sussex Asia Centre, University of Sussex, Brighton, UK.

Hasan H. Karrar, Department of Humanities and Social Sciences, Lahore University of Management Sciences, Pakistan.

Magnus Marsden, Department of Anthropology, Sussex Asia Centre, University of Sussex, Brighton, UK.

Philippe Rudaz, Entrepreneurship Section, United Nations Conference on Trade and Development, Geneva, Switzerland.

Philipp Schröder, Department of Social and Cultural Anthropology, Albert-Ludwigs-Universität Freiburg, Germany.

Rune Steenberg, Department of Asian Studies, Palacky University Olomouc, Czech Republic.

Negotiating state and society: the normative informal economies of Central Asia and the Caucasus

Susanne Fehlings and Hasan H. Karrar

ABSTRACT
This special issue introduces new research on informal markets and trade in Central Asia and the Caucasus. The research presented here was conducted in Armenia, Georgia, Kazakhstan and Kyrgyzstan, as well as Beijing, Guangzhou, Yiwu and the Xinjiang Uyghur Autonomous Region in China. The following eight articles illustrate how informal markets and trade in Central Asia and the Caucasus provided spaces for people across the region to negotiate state and society in the last three decades; the articles also suggest that informality should be seen as constitutive of a normative order for polities in Central Asia and the Caucasus. Informal markets and trade in Central Asia rest on three factors: the inability of the state to measure commercial transactions; markets and trade becoming places from which citizens built personalized networks that required individualized networking and oral agreements based on social relations, particularly trust; and markets being embedded within states in which clientelism frequently thrives.

In the nearly 30 years since the emergence of independent states in Central Asia and the Caucasus, informal practices have become central to how scholars understand the regional polities. The new research presented in this special issue identifies and describes ways in which informal markets and trade continue to animate not just the economy and politics, but also the social relations and ideas about culture and religion in Central Asia and the Caucasus, as well as the wider trading world in which people from the region operate. Building on rich empirical and theoretical contributions to the study of informality in our field, many of which have appeared in past issues of this journal, this special issue brings together new empirically informed research from Armenia, Georgia, Kazakhstan and Kyrgyzstan, as well as China (Beijing, Guangzhou, Yiwu and the Xinjiang Uyghur Autonomous Region).

The research we present enables cross-regional comparisons, and simultaneously points to the multitude of informal networks that stretch between Asia and Europe; although itinerant trader networks had existed across similar spaces through modern history (Aslanian 2011; Levi 2002), the following articles are illustrative of how contemporary globalization can take the form of grass-roots mobility, interpersonal networks and exchanges between individual traders. The research behind six of the eight articles was funded by the Volkswagen Foundation through two separate grants (Antonyan, Baitas, Fehlings, Karrar and Rudaz through one project; Schröder through a different call); the other two articles in the special issue were funded by the European Research Council under the European Union's Horizon 2020 research and innovation programme (Ibañez-Tirado and Marsden) and the Velux Foundation (Steenberg).

Two broad conclusions appear in the articles that follow. First, markets and trade in the region have been integral to how people negotiated state and society in the years since the breakup of the Soviet Union; as a corollary, here one could also include economic liberalization in China, especially that which took place in the 1980s (Karrar 2016). This trade was embedded in regional and global political economies, as well as in localized societal norms and values (which were often reflective of global trends). To study markets and trade includes acknowledging the myriad ways in which people approach borders, move goods and money between countries, and understand ownership, rent and urban property development. Simultaneously, studying informal markets and trade also mandates understanding relations between and within ethnic groups, networks that rest on local understandings of sociability, the role of memory and the place of nostalgia, as well as attitudes towards community and piety.

The second conclusion from this set of articles is that for Central Asia and the Caucasus, informal practices – while manifesting differently in the places we describe – is often not in opposition to a normative formality. We would posit, in fact, that informal practices are embedded in normative orders. Hence, the informal markets and trade we describe in the following articles are not shadow economies, nor are these illegal activities on the peripheries of an otherwise legible state. Rather, at the risk of overstatement, the informal markets and trade described in the following articles are at the core of regional circulation and consumption. For the last three decades or so, informal markets and trade could not be disaggregated from people's lived experience of society, and as an extension, the state. Consequently, in Central Asia and the Caucasus, the so-called informal markets and trade occupy a wider ambit than in the global North.

While these broad conclusions – the centrality of the economy and a normative informality – will not be surprising to regional specialists (Hardenberg and Fehlings 2016; Hayoz and Giordano 2013; Isaacs 2011; Isaacs and Frigerio 2019; Polese and Morris 2015; Radnitz 2011; Reeves 2014), they are worth foregrounding; beyond the absence or bypassing of regulatory mechanisms, informal markets and trade underscore the role of individual or collective agency. It is for this reason that we believe it is appropriate to describe people as 'negotiating' changes in state and society through markets and trade. Indeed, past scholarship on informal markets and trade serves as a timeline for how people – and strategies – have adapted to changing circumstances over 30 years (Alff 2014; Bobokhyan, Abrahamian, and Franklin 2014; Botoeva and Spector 2013; Dyatlov and Grigorichev 2015; Ledeneva 1998; Nasritdinov 2006; Rudaz 2017; Stefes 2008). Scholarship on markets and trade, including that presented here, is also a reflection of how citizens of the new republics connected with the world beyond (Stephan-Emmrich and Schröder 2018). To put it succinctly: informal markets and trade have evolved since the Soviet Union. While mobility and pragmatism remain fundamental to understanding informal markets and trade in Central Asia and the Caucasus – and the larger trading world of people from the region – new ideas have developed about community and cooperation, as well as new values and new possibilities for cooperation, and new competitiveness.

Although the markets and trade described in this collection differ, presenting them collectively in *Central Asian Survey* allows us to highlight common threads that have informed our research. Consequently, we suggest that informal markets and trade in Central Asia and the Caucasus – as well as the larger trading world of regional traders – rests on three factors: the widespread practice of commercial exchanges going undocumented; the building and maintaining of highly personalized commercial and support networks by the traders themselves; and a political economy in which clientelism thrives.

Parsing the informal economy

At a basic level, the informal economy in Central Asia and the Caucasus – of which the informal markets and trade are a part – can be considered that portion of the economy which does not appear in national statistics. Not only is it difficult to quantify informal markets and trade, but even agreeing on how many outlets there are, or how many people work in a particular market, is often difficult. For example, published estimates of the number of outlets and the number of traders in Bishkek's Dordoi bazaar vary considerably (Nasritdinov 2006; Özcan 2010; Spector 2017). This is not only a reflection that bazaars are continuously expanding and contracting, but also a question of methodology: do the estimates come from city officials, bazaar administration, unions, or traders themselves? How does one account for outlets that are open only part of the time? Are hawkers – such as those who climb aboard the *marshrutka* (minivans) to sell Band-Aids while it is filling up – included in the count? Put simply, the nature of informal commercial activity is such that it frequently defies easy quantification.

Similar methodological limitations then apply for the revenue that is generated in these marketplaces. That people make an income that is not known to the state is not surprising; indeed, Keith Hart's (1973) seminal study on the informal economy underscored the importance of income diversification as a safety mechanism. What is noteworthy in the case of Central Asia and the Caucasus is the amount of space these informal activities occupy. For example, upper estimates for the number of people who work in Dordoi bazaar, or Barakholka in Almaty – 60,000 and nearly 200,000, respectively – would have a substantial portion of either city's workforce toiling in the bazaar (Karrar 2017; Sholk 2018). Estimates by economists at the IMF corroborate these conclusions: a 2013 working paper estimates that Kyrgyzstan's informal economy was about 25% of its GDP; the figures for Armenia, Georgia and Kazakhstan were higher, at about 35% (Abdih and Medina 2013, 14). One may quarrel with how these figures were derived, but there is little doubt that a significant portion of the commerce in the region goes undocumented.

There is another consideration here, namely that the boundaries between formal and informal sometimes blur. Consider Georgia, where after the Rose Revolution and the anticorruption campaign initiated by Mikheil Saakashvili small traders were exposed to new regulations. Yet even as there was a tilt towards a more formal regulatory framework, new spaces for negotiating state regulation were appearing. Where formal regulation proves to be too rigid, norms are softened or adjusted. A similar blurring of boundaries between legal and illegal also occurs as goods move across the long-distance trading networks of regional traders (Fehlings 2020; Ibañez-Tirado and Marsden 2020).

Next, consider the centrality of networks as defining informal practices. Following the transition from communism, spaces appeared for citizens to establish independent commercial operations; although petty trading had begun under perestroika, after the emergence of the new states, this commercial activity increased sharply (Dyatlov and Grigorichev 2015; Fehlings and Karrar 2016; Mandel and Humphrey 2002; Rekhviashvili 2015). Across the former Soviet Union, millions of people took to shuttle trading and the sale of goods in ad hoc marketplaces, or what were frequently referred to as bazaars in local vernaculars (Fehlings 2017; Humphrey 2002). These bazaars have developed into re-export hubs in Central Asia and the Caucasus; at their widest, the trading networks could extend between China, Russia, Turkey and Ukraine (Alff 2015; Karrar 2017).

The widespread mobility of independent traders since the 1980s is well documented (Haugen 2018; Hung and Ngo 2018; Marsden 2016; Mathews 2017); our research affirms that the success of the independent traders depends on their ability to successfully network (Baitas 2020; Fehlings 2020; Steenberg 2020). These networks might span between Tbilisi and Beijing, Uzbekistan and Yiwu, Russia and Guangzhou (Fehlings 2020; Ibañez-Tirado and Marsden 2020; Schröder 2020), or be confined to neighbouring states or within the country (Antonyan 2020). At the same time, these networks need not be spatially expansive to be successful; many successful commercial networks operate within the communities within which people live (Steenberg 2020). Outside of familial, clan or ethnic associations between the people (Schatz 2004; Schröder 2020), networks are upheld by virtue of the fact that they are considered valuable, both because they generate a livelihood and also because it is a support mechanism in which the idea of what or who is benefited is not about the individual but the community (Baitas 2020; Rudaz 2020; Steenberg 2016).

Finally, markets and trade in Central Asia and the Caucasus are informal because they are situated within patrimonial states (Collins 2006; Cooley and Heathershaw 2017; McGlinchey 2011; Mostowlansky 2017), which perpetuate clientelism, although this may be more true of Central Asia than Armenia and Georgia or of the wider trading world in which the traders operate. Situated on rent-generating property, markets funnel rent to the elite through often opaque networks (Karrar 2020; Spector 2008). In the early 1990s, the new markets were sometimes places associated with extortion and racketeering (Holzlehner 2014; Melkumyan 2017). In the early years transition marketplaces became places of competition between the mafia, and occasionally sites of violent conflict. Hence, despite recent attempts to ascribe legibility through demolishing bazaars and building malls, the market embedded in a patrimonial state remains an informal institution (Karrar 2020).

A transnational research agenda

The articles in this special issue offer thick ethnographic descriptions of permanent and temporary marketplaces including wholesale markets in Yiwu and Guangzhou, Astana's Central Bazaar, Barakholka in Almaty, Dordoi bazaar in Bishkek, Yabaolu in Beijing, the Vernissage in Yerevan, and the Mshrali Khidi in Tbilisi. The articles also describe practices and values: the importance of mobility, the centrality of trust and networks, the negotiation of state regulation, and dealing with new ownership regimes.

The first article in this collection, by **Philippe Rudaz**, analyses quantitative data gathered from both Central Asia (from Dordoi bazaar in Bishkek) and the Caucasus (from

Lilo Bazroba in Tbilisi) and shows how trading activity in the bazaar presents along a continuum of informality, entrepreneurship and what he describes as globalization from below. The data illustrate that first, traders who (still) struggle to survive do not display entrepreneurial characteristics. Second, entrepreneurship and globalization from below do not necessarily overlap. Some traders in Dordoi who displayed 'entrepreneurial characteristics' run informal businesses, but may not be mobile. Finally, Rudaz illustrates how path-dependent processes created by uncertainty and survival manifest in bazaar trading. The different *modus operandi* of traders is indicative of deviation from a textbook path of economic development (Gustafson 1999; Robinson 2013; Vasileva 2018).

Meiirzhan Baitas argues that the type of personal networks traders maintain to organize their businesses cannot be disassociated from traders' motivation. Building on ethnography at Astana's Central Bazaar he describes how traders who are driven primarily by lifting themselves out of economic precarity tend to build strong social networks, while traders driven by ambition and goal attainment are less likely to establish and maintain strong social ties. In between these two extremes are traders who consciously maintain varied relationships with other traders and clients.

In his article, **Rune Steenberg** illustrates how Uyghur traders in Xinjiang and Kyrgyzstan are embedded in both complex state regulatory frameworks and strong social networks. But although social networks are not regulated by state institutions, they are still regular and predictable. Such networks are framed by notions of morality, pride and shame, which are applied to the economic sphere of trade. Among the Uyghurs, trade is associated with positive ideas and values also because social networks create a reliable and trusting environment.

The link between social and cultural values on the one hand and economic practice on the other has received extensive treatment in economic anthropology. In her contribution, **Yulia Antonyan** describes the informal commercial activities that appear in tandem with religious activity. In her study of mobile fairs in Armenia, Antonyan draws attention to the economy of consumption at religious and pilgrimage sites. At the same time, she reveals that objects, marketplace organization and consumption mirror social hierarchies, power relations, administrative concerns and ideological conflicts. Thus, the trade in religious objects reflects – and defines – the informal relationships between vendors and the Church, vendors and local authorities, and vendors and local elites, as well as vendors and buyers. The religious memorabilia on sale are reflective of the association between the local and the global in how localized religious traditions are contoured by global consumption trends.

The question of who decides what is sold in a market, who exercises power and how power is turned into profits is a fundamental one. In Antonyan's case, the Church, and its representatives, figure among the core interest groups. **Hasan Karrar's** article explores how Barakholka in Almaty has become a contested space, although in this case, the contestation is evidenced in the demolition of container bazaars, sometimes through fire. Following their demolition – which Karrar describes as a form of ruination – new malls are built in their stead, imposing new ownership structures on the bazaar.

Moving beyond trade that is confined to a particular country, or adjacent states, the remaining contributions in this special issue describe mobile traders who transgress regional and national boundaries.

Susanne Fehlings follows Georgian traders as they travel from Tbilisi to Beijing, where they purchase their merchandise in Yabaolu Market, the so-called Russian market, in the centre of Beijing. In their journeys Georgian traders build a set of relationships: with co-travellers from the Caucasus, traders from other post-Soviet countries, and Chinese businesspeople with whom they partner closely. Trust is key to these relationships. Trust presents as kinship-like, with strong undertones of friendship constituted as a Caucasian brotherhood. As Fehlings describes, in this transnational marketplace state regulatory mechanisms are almost absent. For these exchanges to continue, traders have to rely on personal contacts and, more generally, agree on a code of conduct that unites them in a shared business culture with predictable rules.

Trust is also an underlying theme in the transnational exchanges described by **Philipp Schröder,** who examines the role of Kyrgyz middlemen connecting Russian-speaking clients with Chinese suppliers. The job of the Kyrgyz middlemen is to organize their clients' buying trips, coordinate with manufacturers, translate, and oversee cargo shipments. Thus, one of their most important tasks is to negotiate and navigate between the formal and informal domains of local and cross-border economic transactions. They act as trustworthy brokers between individual traders from Russia or Central Asia and their Chinese counterparts, handle customs clearances, and assure the compliance of commodities with standards set by international bodies. To be successful, they need deep knowledge of the situation in China, as well as in Russia or other countries where their clients are from. Schröder argues that in contrast to the early bazaar or shuttle traders, who have been operating across Eurasia since the 1990s, the Kyrgyz middlemen are constitutive of a next generation of economic actors, who are more service-oriented and embedded within more formalized and diversified value chains across post-Socialist Eurasia. Schröder refers to this evolution as Business 2.0.

The ways in which traders organize their businesses and handle state regulations are manifold. Afghan and Uzbek traders are central to the analysis in **Diana Ibañez-Tirado and Magnus Marsden's** article. Ibañez-Tirado and Marsden describe the strategies Afghan and Uzbek traders use to circumvent formal regulatory frameworks and official control. Connecting trading hubs in China with places in Afghanistan, Pakistan, Tajikistan, Russia, Ukraine and Uzbekistan, this transnational trade blurs the boundaries between the formal and the informal, the legal and the illegal. Again, networks which transgress national borders and create new trading worlds are crucial for these traders, showing how informal practices are normative and conditional for the activities described in this special issue.

Acknowledgements: Building – and sustaining – transnational research and collaboration

This special issue is a collaborative effort between scholars variously based in Armenia, Georgia, Germany, Kazakhstan, Pakistan, Switzerland and the UK who come from anthropology, area studies, and economics. The research presented here is a result of conversations and observations, dialogue and critique in and beyond the field. Five of the eight articles in this special issue (Antonyan, Baitas, Fehlings, Karrar and Rudaz – in addition to Melkumyan, whose article on flea markets in Tbilisi and Yerevan is forthcoming in *Central Asian Survey*) are based on field research that was undertaken under the project 'Informal Markets and Trade in Central Asia in the Caucasus', which was supported by the Volkswagen

Foundation (2016–2019). Schröder's fieldwork in China was also funded by the Volkswagen Foundation (Grant no. Az.86870).

In 2018, support from the Volkswagen Foundation also enabled collaboration with Ibañez-Tirado and Marsden (whose research on independent trader networks in Yiwu has been supported by the European Research Council) and Steenberg (supported by the Velux Foundation). Between 2014 and 2018, this research was workshopped and presented at the University of Tübingen (2014), Ivane Javakhishvili Tbilisi State University (2016 and 2018), the annual conference of the Central Eurasian Studies Society (2017), a summer school in Astana (2017), and a Volkswagen Foundation status meeting in Almaty (2018).

Besides the present special issue, we have guest-edited a special issue of the *Caucasus Analytical Digest* (Rudaz and Fehlings 2017), guest-edited a special issue of *Anthropological Researches* that was published and distributed in the Caucasus (Fehlings and Melkumyan 2018), and launched a working paper series on informal markets and trade that is hosted at the University of Frankfurt library and is open-access and available for download (ISSN: 2510-2826). In collaboration with Fribourg University and Ilia State University we held a policy roundtable, 'Survival, Entrepreneurship and Innovation in the Caucasus', and curated a photo exhibition, 'Entrepreneurs on the New Silk Road: Photographs of Small Businesses in the Caucasus and Central Asia', both in Tbilisi, in 2019. Finally, as part of the project, we also conducted structured interviews of 1200 independent traders in Georgia, Kazakhstan and Kyrgyzstan, collecting quantitative data on trader demographics, motivations and informality. This data will be available for download in 2021.

We first approached *Central Asian Survey* in December 2017. Since that time, it has been our pleasure to work closely with Rico Isaacs, Raphael Jacquet and Madeleine Reeves; we are humbled at how much time they invested in helping us make this issue possible. We are also grateful to the peer reviewers for thoughtful, detailed commentaries on each of the articles. It is impossible not to be struck by the expertise in our scholarly community, and also the collegiality and support.

Across Central Asia and the Caucasus – and in field sites in China, and elsewhere – the people we spoke to or travelled with were instrumental in our building new research. The scholarship presented in the following pages rests on the generosity and kindness of people who in the short run have little if anything to gain from our academic preoccupations.

Finally, we are grateful for the opportunity to work closely with students in Georgia, Kazakhstan and Kyrgyzstan, whether they were accompanying us as research assistants in the field or were graduate students in the project on informal markets and trade in Central Asia and the Caucasus. Included in this special issue is an article by one of our junior colleagues, Meiirzhan Baitas, who received his MA at Nazarbayev University in 2017. Tragically, in 2018, Meiirzhan was diagnosed with cancer, and soon lost his life to it. Seeing his research in *Central Asian Survey*, the flagship journal of our field, is bittersweet: sadness at a life ending so early, yet also happiness at what he was able to accomplish at such a young age, which, we trust, also portends exciting scholarship on the region in the years to come.

Disclosure statement

No potential conflict of interest was reported by the author(s).

References

Abdih, Y., and L. Medina. 2013. "Measuring the Informal Economy in the Caucasus and Central Asia." IMF Working Paper WP/13/137.

Alff, H. 2014. "Post-Soviet Positionalities: Relations, Flows and the Transformation of Bishkek's Dordoy Bazaar." In *Tracing Connections: Explorations of Spaces and Places in Asian Contexts*, edited by H. Alff, and A. Benz, 71–90. Berlin: Wissenschaftlicher Verlag.

Alff, H. 2015. "Profiteers or Moral Entrepreneurs? Bazaars, Traders and Development Discourses in Almaty, Kazakhstan." *International Development Planning Review* 37 (3): 249–267. doi:10.3828/idpr.2014.28.

Antonyan, Y. 2020. "Markets at Sacred Sites: The Globalized Mobility and Informality of the Armenian Religious Fairs." *Central Asian Survey* 39 (1): 63–79. doi:10.1080/02634937.2020.1723490.

Aslanian, S. D. 2011. *From the Indian Ocean to the Mediterranean: The Global Trade Networks of Armenian Merchants from New Julfa*. Berkeley: University of California Press.

Baitas, M. 2020. "The Traders of Central Bazaar, Astana: Motivation and Networks." *Central Asian Survey* 39 (1): 33–45. doi:10.1080/02634937.2019.1697642.

Bobokhyan, A., L. Abrahamian, and K. Franklin, eds. 2014. *Market Beyond Economy*. Yerevan: NAS RA "Gitutyun".

Botoeva, A., and R. Spector. 2013. "Sewing to Satisfaction: Craft-based Entrepreneurs in Contemporary Kyrgyzstan." *Central Asian Survey* 32 (4): 487–500. doi:10.1080/02634937.2013.862963.

Collins, K. 2006. *Clan Politics and Regime Transition in Central Asia*. Cambridge: Cambridge University Press.

Cooley, A., and J. Heathershaw. 2017. *Dictators without Borders: Power and Modernity in Central Asia*. New Haven, CT: Yale University Press.

Dyatlov, V., and K. Grigorichev. 2015. *Ethnic Markets in Russia: Space of Bargaining and Place of Meeting*. Irkutsk: Publishing House of ISU.

Fehlings, S. 2017. "The Chinese Connection: Informal Trade Relations between the Caucasus and China Since the Early 1990s." *Caucasus Analytical Digest* 96: 2–5.

Fehlings, S. 2020. "Doing Business in Yabaolu Market, Beijing: (Inter-)Ethnic Entrepreneurship Trust and Friendship between Caucasian and Chinese Traders." *Central Asian Survey* 39 (1): 95–115. doi:10.1080/02634937.2019.1696281.

Fehlings, S., and H. H. Karrar. 2016. "Informal Markets and Trade in the Caucasus and Central Asia: A Preliminary Framework for Field Research." Working Paper no. 1 on Informal Markets and Trade.

Fehlings, S., and H. Melkumyan, eds. 2018. Transnational Trade, Trade Routes, and Local Marketplaces between the Caucasus and Central Asia. Special issue of *Anthropological Researches* 4, Association of Georgian Anthropologists.

Gustafson, T. 1999. *Capitalism: Russian-Style*. Cambridge: Cambridge University Press.

Hardenberg, R., and S. Fehlings. 2016. "Informality Reviewed: Everyday Experiences and the Study of Transformational Processes in Central Asia and the Caucasus." Working Paper no. 2 on Informal Markets and Trade.

Hart, K. 1973. "Informal Income Opportunities and Urban Employment in Ghana." *Journal of Modern African Studies* 11 (1): 61–89. doi:10.1017/S0022278X00008089.

Haugen, H. O. 2018. "China-Africa Exports: Governance through Mobility and Sojourning." *Journal of Contemporary Asia* 48 (2): 294–312. doi:10.1080/00472336.2018.1517897.

Hayoz, N., and C. Giordano. 2013. *Informality in Eastern Europe: Structures, Political Culture, and Social Practices*. Pieterlen: Peter Lang.

Holzlehner, T. 2014. *Shadow Networks: Border Economics, Informal Markets and Organized Crime in the Russian Far East*. Münster: LIT.

Humphrey, C. 2002. *The Unmaking of Soviet Life: Everyday Economies after Socialism*. Ithaca, NY: Cornell University Press.

Hung, E. P. W., and T.-W. Ngo. 2018. "Organized Informality and Suitcase Trading in the Pearl River Delta Region." *Journal of Contemporary Asia* 48 (2): 233–253.

Ibañez-Tirado, D., and M. Marsden. 2020. "Trade 'Outside the Law': Uzbek and Afghan Transnational Merchants between Yiwu and South-Central Asia." *Central Asian Survey* 39 (1): 135–154. doi:10.1080/02634937.2020.1716687.

Isaacs, R. 2011. *Party System Formation in Kazakhstan: Between Formal and Informal Politics.* London: Routledge.

Isaacs, R., and A. Frigerio. 2019. "Political Theory and Central Asia: An Introduction." In *Theorizing Central Asian Politics: The State, Ideology and Power*, edited by R. Isaacs and A. Frigerio, 1–13. Palgrave Macmillan.

Karrar, H. H. 2016. "The Resumption of Sino-Central Asian Trade, c. 1983–1994: Confidence Building and Reform along a Cold War Fault Line." *Central Asian Survey* 35 (3): 334–350. doi:10.1080/02634937.2016.1155384.

Karrar, H. H. 2017. "Kyrgyzstan's Dordoi and Kara-Suu Bazaars: Mobility, Globalization and Survival in two Central Asian Markets." *Globalizations* 14 (4): 643–657. doi:10.1080/14747731.2016.1201323.

Karrar, H. H. 2020. "The Bazaar in Ruins: Rent and Fire in the Barakholka, Almaty." *Central Asian Survey* 39 (1): 80–94. doi:0.1080/02634937.2020.1732299.

Ledeneva, A. 1998. *Russia's Economy of Favors: Blat, Networking and Informal Exchanges.* Cambridge: Cambridge University Press.

Levi, S. 2002. *The Indian Diaspora in Central Asia and its Trade, 1550–1900.* Leiden: Brill.

Mandel, R., and C. Humphrey. 2002. *Markets and Moralities: Ethnographies of Postsocialism.* Oxford: Berg.

Marsden, M. 2016. *Trading Worlds: Afghan Merchants across Modern Frontiers.* Oxford: Oxford University Press.

Mathews, G. 2017. *The World in Guangzhou: Africans and Other Foreigners in South China's Global Marketplace.* Chicago, IL: University of Chicago Press.

McGlinchey, E. 2011. *Chaos, Violence, Dynasty: Politics and Islam in Central Asia.* Pittsburgh, PA: University of Pittsburgh Press.

Melkumyan, H. 2017. "Informality, Politics and Mutual Support in Flea Markets in Post-Soviet Armenia." Working Paper no. 5 on Informal Markets and Trade.

Mostowlansky, T. 2017. *Azan on the Moon: Embedded Modernity along Tajikistan's Pamir Highway.* Pittsburgh, PA: University of Pittsburgh Press.

Nasritdinov, E. 2006. "Regional Change in Kyrgyzstan: Bazaars, Open-air Markets and Social Networks." Doctoral Dissertation, University of Melbourne, Australia.

Özcan, G. B. 2010. *Building States and Markets: Enterprise Development in Central Asia.* London: Palgrave Macmillan.

Polese, A., and J. Morris. 2015. "My Name is Legion: The Resilience and Endurance of Informality Beyond, or in Spite of, the State." In *Informal Economies in Post-Socialist Spaces: Practices, Institutions and Networks*, edited by J. Morris and A. Polese, 1–22. London: Palgrave Macmillan.

Radnitz, S. 2011. "Informal Politics and the State." *Comparative Politics* 43 (3): 351–371. doi:10.5129/001041511795274922.

Reeves, M. 2014. *Border Work: Spatial Lives of the State in Rural Central Asia.* Ithaca, NY: Cornell University Press.

Rekhviashvili, L. 2015. "Marketization and the Public-Private Divide: Contestations between the State and Petty Traders over the Access to Public Space in Tbilisi." *International Journal of Sociology and Social Policy* 35 (7/8): 478–496. doi:10.1108/IJSSP-10-2014-0091.

Robinson, N. 2013. "Economic and Political Hybridity: Patrimonial Capitalism in the Post-Soviet Sphere." *Journal of Eurasian Studies* 4: 136–145. doi:10.1016/j.euras.2013.03.003.

Rudaz, P. 2017. "The State of MSME Development in Kyrgyzstan." Working Paper no. 3 on Informal Markets and Trade.

Rudaz, P. 2020. "Trading in Dordoi and Lilo Bazaars: Frontiers of Formality, Entrepreneurship and Globalization." *Central Asian Survey* 39 (1): 11–32. doi:10.1080/02634937.2020.1732298.

Rudaz, P., and S. Fehlings, eds. 2017. Transborder Trade. Special issue of *Caucasus Analytical Digest* 96 (25 June).

Schatz, E. 2004. *Modern Clan Politics: The Power of "Blood" in Kazakhstan and Beyond.* Washington: University of Washington Press.

Schröder, P. 2020. "Business 2.0: Kyrgyz Middlemen in Guangzhou." *Central Asian Survey* 39 (1): 116–134.
Sholk, D. 2018. "Baraholka (Kazakhstan)." In *Global Encyclopedia of Informality, Vol. 2, Understanding Social and Cultural Complexity*, edited by A. Ledeneva, 125–129. London: UCL Press.
Spector, R. A. 2008. "Bazaar Politics: The Fate of Marketplaces in Kazakhstan." *Problems of Post-Communism* 55 (6): 42–53. doi:10.2753/PPC1075-8216550604.
Spector, R. A. 2017. *Order at the Bazaar: Power and Trade in Central Asia*. Ithaca, NY: Cornell University Press.
Steenberg, R. 2016. "Embedded Rubber Sandals: Trade and Gifts across the Sino-Kyrgyz Border." *Central Asian Survey* 35 (3): 405–420. doi:10.1080/02634937.2016.1221577.
Steenberg, R. 2020. "The Formal Side of Informality: Non-State Trading Practices and Local Uyghur Ethnography." *Central Asian Survey* 39 (1): 46–62. doi:10.1080/02634937.2019.1697207.
Stefes, C. H. 2008. "Governance, the State and Systematic Corruption: Armenia and Georgia in Comparison." *Caucasian Review of International Affairs* 2 (2): 73–83.
Stephan-Emmrich, M., and P. Schröder, eds. 2018. *Mobilities, Boundaries, and Travelling Ideas: Rethinking Translocality beyond Central Asia and the Caucasus*. Cambridge: Open Book.
Vasileva, A. 2018. "Trapped in Informality: The Big Role of Small Firms in Russia's Statist Patrimonial Capitalism." *New Political Economy* 23 (3): 314–330. doi:10.1080/13563467.2017.1349090.

Trading in Dordoi and Lilo bazaars: frontiers of formality, entrepreneurship and globalization

Philippe Rudaz

ABSTRACT
Cross-border trade is central to the socio-economic structure of the former Soviet republics and their integration in the world economy. In the Caucasus and Central Asia, bazaars have functioned as nodes that enable multi-directional, cross-border trade. While there have been studies on the bazaar trade in the Soviet successor states, few have used quantitative methods. Drawing from 600 structured interviews with traders in Dordoi (Bishkek) and Lilo (Tbilisi), the data from Dordoi highlight the relationship between informality and entrepreneurship, unlike Lilo, where there are clearer markers of formality, but where bazaar trade also seems to be less profitable. The data from the 600 interviews illustrate that Dordoi functions as a globalized trading hub, its transnational linkages forged by the bazaar traders and the buyers themselves. By contrast, trade in Lilo is more localized. Hence, 'globalization from below' presents itself differently across the post-Soviet space.

Introduction

One of the biggest political challenges – and economic experiments – of the last 25 years was the establishment of a free-market economy in the Soviet successor states, where central planning had been the main productive and distributive mechanism for about 70 years. The circuitous process of unravelling centralizing economic institutions, and reforming them under the framework of market reform, took the nondescript name of 'transition'. Efficient markets would emerge provided that people had the right economic incentives. Hence, economic orthodoxy created the illusion that the former planned economies could quickly and smoothly adopt a liberal market economy (Frye and Shleifer 1997). The complexity of building new economic systems was overlooked (Freeland 2000; North 2005).

The dismantling of centralizing economic institutions resulted in inflation, unemployment and underemployment, and scarcity, forcing people to turn to informal networks (Fehlings 2015; Hsu 2005; Karrar 2019; Ledeneva 1998; Van de Mortel 2002). These networks became essential for the non-elite to cope with sharply reduced purchasing power and the scarcity of day-to-day goods (Schatz 2004; Werner 1998). At the same time, these bottom-up informal practices – which relied on kin or familial networks – competed with top-down formal state regulation such as property rights, legal procedures, business registration, licences and formal contracts, some of which were rapidly changing as the 1990s progressed.

While the juxtaposition between ground-level precarity and formal state regulation in former Soviet economies has received considerable scholarly attention (Kaiser 1997; Ledeneva 1998; Morris and Polese 2014; Polese and Rodgers 2011; Rasanayagam 2011; Seabright 2000), appreciating the extent to which new economic actors relied – and continue to rely – on informal practices illustrates how privatization and entrepreneurship in Soviet successor states depended on institutional change at the micro level (Johnson, Smith, and Codling 2000). The dissolution of the USSR resulted not in transition per se but *recomposition* of economic, social, political and territorial structures. This recomposition produced multiple trajectories that deviated from the free-market model towards which 'transition' was expected to carry the nascent states. For example, in the new system, self-employment through farming and trade became the economic activity *par excellence* for economic survival; a quarter-century on, these remain the dominant occupations in the former Soviet economies. Trade plays a crucial role in poverty alleviation and social development (Bram 2017; Khutsishvili 2017; Sasunkevich 2014), and some *chelnoki* also became businessmen (Fehlings 2017), but the 'inbuilt inertia of informality, particularistic trust and network capital have created path-dependent processes' (Sik 2012, 68). This article shows the microfoundations of these path-dependent processes and sheds another light on the deviation from a textbook path of neoliberal economic development (Gustafson 1999; Puffer and McCarthy 2007; Robinson 2013; Vasileva 2018).

Besides the actual movement of goods across borders – which in the initial years after the Soviet Union was the domain of the *chelnoki,* or shuttle trader (Cieślewska 2014; Fehlings 2017; Holzlehner 2014) – the new commercial activity was centred in the bazaars, which grew in munber. Although bazaars have been carefully studied by area specialists (Alff 2014; Karrar 2017; Ozcan 2010; Spector 2008, 2017), quantitative data and analyses has been limited. Kaminski and Mitra's World Bank study (2012) sought to establish the importance of cross-border trade for commercial exchange, revenue and employment and was the first to build on empirical evidence, using a small sample of semi-structured interviews in 14 bazaars in Central Asia. The present article is the second study on the bazaar trade to make use of empirical evidence and compares one bazaar in the Caucasus and one in Central Asia. The analysis comes from 600 structured interviews with bazaar traders in the Lilo bazaar in Tbilisi, Georgia, home to approximately 6,000 shops,[1] and the larger Dordoi bazaar in Bishkek, Kyrgyzstan, which employs 60,000 individuals (Karrar 2017). The interviews were based on a set of 40 questions about demographic background, motivations for trade, trading practices and profitability.

This article contributes to Caucasus and Central Asian studies through a comparative analysis of the two bazaars based on a recently generated data set. The two bazaars – Dordoi being a trading hub in the middle of the 'new Silk Road' and Lilo, a much smaller bazaar in a frontier market with close economic ties to Turkey and the European Union – are sufficiently different to offer an interesting field of study to investigate the entrepreneurial potential of bazaar trading.

Bazaar trade, which still persists in spite of the advances of modern capitalism (Polese and Prigarin 2013), is largely unregistered by the state; here, I follow scholars who approach the informal economy as licit yet undocumented trade (Fehlings and Karrar

2016; Guha-Khasnobis, Kanbur, and Ostrom 2006; Hart 1992) and bazaars as markets where informal mechanisms of trust are necessary for individuals to conduct their business (Humphrey and Skvirskaja 2009), whether for economic survival or entrepreneurial reasons (Collins 2006; Karrar 2017; Werner 1998). Using the data collected, I will try to answer three questions: How embedded are informal practices in the two bazaars? How entrepreneurial are traders in these bazaars? And how global are they?

As I will show first, the bazaar is informal in how the day-to-day trading practices are carried out. This dimension is organizational, and the data set underscores a certain unpredictability of organizational behaviour. Second, I also show that entrepreneurship does not require formal organization. Data from Dordoi and Lilo allow us to see how trading activity in the bazaar presents along a continuum of informality, entrepreneurship, and globalization from below.

Overall, this article seeks to move beyond the scholarship on entrepreneurship in post-Soviet economies that tends to conflate survival and entrepreneurship (Aidis and Estrin 2006; Aidis, Estrin, and Mickiewicz 2008; Smallbone and Welter 2001). These questions have important policy implications for the countries of the Caucasus and Central Asia.

Methodology and its limitations

The analysis in this article uses a data set that was generated by a three-year project on informal markets and trade in Central Asia and the Caucasus funded by the Volkswagen Foundation. Three hundred traders from the Dordoi bazaar in Bishkek were interviewed in August 2016, and 300 traders from the Lilo bazaar outside Tbilisi were interviewed in February–March 2017. The structure of the questionnaire (displayed in Appendix) was developed to reflect general information about the traders, the organization of their businesses, and the performance of their business.

The questionnaires were tested before they were used in the field by graduate students. In both locations, students were supervised in the field by Hasan H. Karrar and Philippe Rudaz. As a sequential list of traders and trading outlets was unavailable, the survey sample could not be randomized. Though efforts were made to randomize the selection, and all sections of both bazaars were surveyed, selection bias cannot be ruled out. The present study is therefore an observational one, where the findings are not strictly representative of Dordoi and Lilo, and are not generalizable, but the data do allow associations between variables.

Semi-structured interviews, unlike in-depth interviews, are not conducive to longer conversations. Some of the questions posed, such as those about business performance and those related to living standards and reinvestment, are subjective and admittedly would have benefited from allowing respondents to elaborate. Finally, the questionnaire used closed-ended questions, with a list of examples constraining respondents' answers, although other answers were allowed. In spite of these disadvantages, the data still allow us to count frequencies, derive descriptive statistics and establish associations between variables.

The theoretical positioning of this paper is influenced by a meso-economic perspective grounded in institutional economics and political economy, which has an advantage in understanding processes and multidimensional phenomena such as entrepreneurial activities in the bazaar. This belongs to quantitative analytical tools, but qualitative approaches marked this study as well: the sample derived from constructed populations; and the analysis explored possible relations between different 'sets of cases' (informal traders, successful traders, globalized traders), as opposed to explaining dependent variables (Ragin 2008).

Table 1 summarizes the methodological discussion in the key areas identified by Caelli, Ray, and Mill (2003).

Entrepreneurship, informality and globalization from below: the analytical terrain

Although economists have long studied entrepreneurs, and sought to define them, as a field of research, entrepreneurship is relatively new. This article follows Shane and Venkataraman (2000, 218), who define entrepreneurship as a 'processes of discovery, evaluation and exploitation of opportunities'. According to this definition, entrepreneurship covers the ground between 'intending to' and the actual 'action of' creating and managing an enterprise or a business from the perspective of its becoming a lasting source of subsistence. At the same time, entrepreneurship is not a euphemism for self-employment. Self-employment, which is usually a part of the undocumented economy in developing countries, can be seen as either a form of incipient entrepreneurship (Albrecht, Navarro, and Vroman 2009; Bennett and Rablen 2015), which arguably is the case in most of the research on entrepreneurship (Naudé 2013; Parker 2004), or a form of precarious employment for the purpose of survival (Temkin 2009).

Separating entrepreneurs from survivalists is complicated because the continuum goes through the field of informality, whose heterogeneity and multiple dimensions has led to many different theories and schools of thought (Chen 2007). Far from a mere semantic concern, the failure to disaggregate entrepreneurship and survival leads to interpreting *any* kind of economic activity as entrepreneurial. The (debated) separation between the formal and informal economy (La Porta and Shleifer 2014) and/or the lack of entrepreneurial characteristics[2] of the self-employed (Rudaz 2017) could let one wonder whether the 'informal entrepreneur' is not an illusion. In this article, I follow Guha-Khasnobis, Kanbur, and Ostrom (2006) and view the informal sector in two dimensions, 'the reach of official governance and the degree of structuring' (5), and focus on the second one, 'the extent to which an activity and the interactions among its constituent individuals are structured according to a predictable framework' (6), to identify traders as formal or informal entrepreneurs.

The context of political uncertainty, in which restrictions on national and transborder commercial activities were eased, saw the rapid proliferation of bazaars in the former Soviet Union (Humphrey and Skvirskaja 2009; Karrar 2013). The post-Soviet bazaar in

Table 1. Key methodological pillars.

Theoretical positioning	Political economy / institutional economics
Research methodology	Survey
Research methods	Face-to-face structured questionnaires (15–20 min)
Knowledge generated	Descriptive/analytical
Interviewed sample	Constructed population (versus a given population)
Analytical lens	Set relations (versus correlations)

fact came to symbolize economic 'transition' – a concept of increasing vacuity as the transition becomes permanent – from a centralized economy to a market economy (Alff 2014; Fehlings and Karrar 2016; Ozcan 2010).

The post-Soviet bazaar is networked with other bazaars, both within the successor states and with countries such China and Turkey, where manufactured goods were being imported from, as reported by Ibanez Tirado and Fehlings in this issue. This is a form of grass-roots globalization, or globalization from below, described by Mathews and Yang (2012, 97) as 'the transnational flow of people and goods involving relatively small amounts of capital and informal, sometimes semi-legal or illegal transactions'. The grass-roots dimension is important not only because it is transnational but also because it allowed traders to place themselves along a spectrum of self-employment that stretched from survival to entrepreneurship. This non-hegemonic manifestation of 'globalization from below' (Appadurai 2000) relies on social capital and layered networks and is supported by more diverse socio-cultural influences than so-called globalization from above (Fonseca and Malheiros 2004). Self-employed bazaar (and shuttle) traders, small manufacturers, local authorities and grass-roots organizations became agents of such globalization practices (Fehlings and Karrar 2016).

In the scholarship on Central Asia, the unregistered dimension of this globalization has traditionally evaded state statistics, which leaves scholars to rely mostly on rich ethnographies of transnational mobility and exchange (Ibanez Tirado 2018; Marsden 2016; Mathews, Ribeiro, and Vega 2012; Schröder and Stephan Emmrich 2016; Steenberg 2016). But the bazaar, where thousands of traders conduct business through their transnational or local networks, also offers an opportunity for the unorthodox economist to explore the extent to which traders are informal, entrepreneurial and global.

Dordoi and Lilo: data-set demographics

In both bazaars, women account for more than half of the respondents interviewed; more than two-thirds are married. More than two-thirds of the traders surveyed in Dordoi are wholesale traders. In Lilo, wholesale traders account for 33% of those surveyed, retail for 32% (and since the questionnaire in Lilo allowed both answers, this last category accounts for the remaining 30%). More than half of the items sold in both markets are clothes (men's, women's and children's). The rest are household accessories, building materials, and electronics. The average age of the surveyed sellers was 38 in Dodoi and 41 in Lilo. Education was higher in Dordoi than in Lilo; about 20% more respondents have a university degree. In both bazaars, independence tests and logistic regressions show no association of gender, education or ethnicity with the practices or performance of traders.

In Kyrgyzstan, the decreasing number of small- and medium-sized enterprises (SMEs) and their shrinking contribution to GDP indicates that the self-employed are not entrepreneurs running growing, innovative firms (Rudaz 2017). The general lack of innovative growth invites closer scrutiny of bazaar traders, a trading demographic that was at the forefront of economic activity after the Soviet Union collapsed, and whose day-to-day activities are globalized (Fehlings and Karrar 2016; Ibanez Tirado 2018; Mathews and Yang 2012; Schröder and Stephan Emmrich 2016).

After the Soviet Union, re-export through bazaar intermediation has been pursued as an economic strategy and in Central Asia is unique to Kyrgyzstan, mainly due to a trade regime and regulatory environment that protect traders and bazaars (Alff 2016; Kaminski 2008), affirming that 'informal' trading frequently enjoys the support of the state (Karrar 2013). This support has given Kyrgyz traders a comparative advantage over bazaars and traders elsewhere in the region (Kaminski 2008). Early economic liberalization in Kyrgyzstan reduced state capacity – especially in comparison with Kazakhstan (Cummings and Nørgaard 2004) — which may also explain the tacit state support of bazaar trading. As a result, today the mountainous republic is home to two of Asia's largest bazaars, Dordoi and Kara-Suu, where about 75,000 people (total) work.[3] These bazaars represent a new market economy of transnational linkages. In Dordoi, retail and wholesale traders and clients of different ethnic backgrounds and nationalities deal with one another every day. It is a giant maze of containers, with alleys a kilometre long, run by carriers pushing goods on wooden carts through the crowd. There are facilities for some workers to compress the merchandise sold, which other workers cover with plastic. Other traders nearby sell duct tape and plastic bags. Next to the customs clearance administration, foreign exchange offices and shipping companies have their offices. Bazaar trading is enabled by an entire value chain of different services and places around the trading booth, including restaurants and a mosque, where social networks develop.[4]

Georgia followed a different path. In Georgia, self-employment has remained high (65% of total employment) for the last decade. After 2003 Georgia was eager to project an image of a modern liberal democracy the West could relate to. But capacity-building occurred amid contradictory policies as reforms directed at reducing state intervention were accompanied by the reversal of earlier privatization.[5] Simplified business regulations would have made Georgia an attractive place for foreign investors to do business, but were accompanied by a disregard for property rights.[6] Thus, while it sought foreign investment, post-revolutionary Georgia was not eager to support small-scale entrepreneurship or bazaar trade.[7] Yet, the bazaar of Lilo is home to approximately 6,000 shops and benefits from an enabling administrative infrastructure that employs 400 individuals. It also includes a medical centre, Lilo TV and Lilo Capital, which disburses microloans to Lilo traders. The full list of services is listed on the Lilo website[8] (see also Fehlings 2020).

While both Georgia and Kyrgyzstan are examples of transitions to a liberal market economy, the implementation of reforms and the state's role in supporting particular economic activities and not others illustrates the deviation from a textbook path of neoliberal economic development. These deviations have been analysed from a political-economy perspective, which led to labelling the former Soviet economies 'statist-patrimonial capitalism' (Vasileva 2018; see also Robinson 2013). In what follows, I illustrate these deviations from a bottom-up, institutional economic perspective.

Between formality and informality

The two dimensions of informality identified by Guha-Khasnobis, Kanbur, and Ostrom (2006) – the degree of structuring of enterprises, and the reach of official governance – help us approach informality in Dordoi and Lilo.[9]

As shown in Figures 1 and 2, two-thirds of the traders interviewed in both countries keep records of their transactions. The high degree of formality is due to the fact that

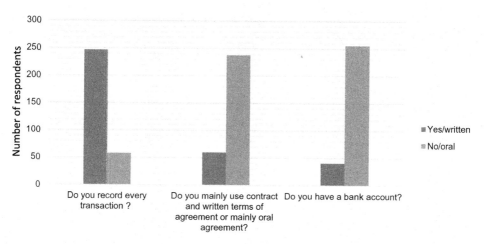

Figure 1. Informality levels in Dordoi (number of respondents). Source: Survey by the author and H. Karrar in August 2016 and February–March 2017.

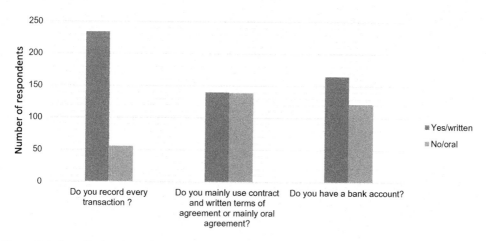

Figure 2. Informality levels in Lilo (number of respondents). Source: Survey by the author and H. Karrar in August 2016 and February–March 2017.

to curb tax evasion, authorities in Kyrgyzstan and Georgia started imposing cash registers in 2003 and 2006, respectively, which led to protest in both countries.[10] However, in Dordoi, more than 70% of those interviewed secure their transactions with oral agreements and do not have a bank account. This percentage drops to 50% in Lilo (Figure 2). In both markets, the traders reported that they trust each other; about 60% of those surveyed reported *always* trusting people they engage with. In contrast to the low levels of trust in public institutions (McKee et al. 2013; Schrader 2004), trust in the marketplace, which is considered a resource for entrepreneurs, is reportedly still very high among informal market participants in the former Soviet countries (Humphrey 2018; Yalçin-Heckmann and Aivazishvili 2012).

But in both markets, these different variables of informality are not necessarily connected. Cash register regulations might bring small businesses into the reach of state governance without affecting the informal practices structuring business organization. In Dordoi, as in Lilo, the different elements of a business that might signal formality from an organizational perspective – such as a written contract or depositing earnings in a bank at day's end – are not associated. Hence, the traders with bank accounts may not be the ones using written contracts. In particular, the Dordoi traders surveyed offer a good example of how informality can be hard to predict through organizational practices – those elements that make an organization informal cannot be coherently assembled, and therefore can easily be misconceived.[11] These data illustrate the fluidity of informality in the day-to-day operation of trading practices. In both markets, it is impossible to separate formal and informal practices into two neatly divided blocks or to ascribe them to a particular group of traders. This also illustrates the ambiguous role of the state with regard to its informal economy. The primary concern of state authorities is tax collection, not business stability. Official governance has reached the traders, but not the owners of the bazaars. Most traders in both markets register transactions and have complied with the reform introduced a decade ago, but as reported by Karrar in this issue, the ownership structure of the bazaar, at the sole advantage of the elite, is highly informal. Renting a container in Dordoi is quite expensive – a monthly average of USD 1000 according to our interviewees. 'You need money to make money', said one them. Moreover, a trader might own the container, but not the land on which it sits, and can be asked to move it away overnight, which illustrates the 'symbiotic relationship between formal constraints and informal behaviour' (Ledeneva 2018, 3), echoing the instability and exploitation *chelnoki* faced in the early days of transition (Cieślewska 2018).

Informal networks can substitute for institutions as a way to 'create order and reduce uncertainty' (North 1991, 97), and thus in these two bazaars informal networks can allow people to develop survival tactics to access goods and services (Karrar 2019). But these 'patterns of mutual help' (Ledeneva 2018, 490) might have evolved differently for the traders of Dordoi and Lilo. For instance, financial help from family members is significantly higher in Dordoi than in Lilo. When asked about the key to success, a group of traders responded with 'quality products, a good network and being able to trust'. The network is primarily used for the provision and distribution of goods, but does not appear as a mechanism to aid the organizational structure of a small business. Most traders in both markets (55% in Lilo and 75% in Dordoi) work alone. As Fehlings (this issue) has observed, Georgian traders travelling back and forth to China were not accompanied by family or kin. As estimated below, on average, trading at the bazaar usually generates barely enough revenue to sustain a household economy; these are not large businesses involving a multitude of workers.

Besides formality–informality, there is another continuum along which trading activity in Dordoi and Lilo can be placed: that which ranges from survival to entrepreneurship. Dordoi traders, given choices of the proxies for 'informality' and 'success', show that a bank account and written contracts are not necessarily preconditions for running a successful revenue-generating business.[12] This challenges fundamental assumptions of development economics; it also helps us begin to understand why, and how, economic development by itself does not lead to less informality. Put differently, bazaar practices illustrate the micro-foundations of the 'deviations' from a textbook path of neoliberal economic development.

Between survival and entrepreneurship

As a 'processes of discovery, evaluation and exploitation of opportunities' (Shane and Venkataraman 2000, 218), entrepreneurship covers the ground between intention and action; it is a multidimensional process. For the purpose of this article, these dimensions can be internal (motivations, psychological traits, behaviour, skills and competencies) or external (material and financial resources, legal and institutional structures). The realization of an entrepreneurial objective depends on these dimensions. Consequently, the movement from survival to entrepreneurship is contoured by the above internal and external variables. Trader responses help illustrate the interplay of these variables in Dordoi and Lilo. Motivation, business growth and revenue satisfaction are examples of variables that can be used as proxy for 'entrepreneurial characteristics'.

The major difference between Dordoi and Lilo lies in the percentage of respondents trading at the bazaar for lack of a better alternative. The proportion of these respondents is considerably higher in Lilo than in Dordoi. Very few of the respondents cite the exploitation of an opportunity as a motivation – they are, instead, driven by other reasons – in this way disregarding what is frequently seen as a yardstick for entrepreneurship.

Asking information about revenue is too difficult. But one can approximate average income with a back-of-the-envelope calculation. Kaminski and Mitra (2012) listed the total payment associated with the fixed costs of running sales outlets as USD 855 million for Dordoi in 2008. Labour income accounts for about 30% of the total fixed costs, or USD 256 million. According to Karrar (2017) there were about 60,000 people working in Dordoi in 2013. If this number was similar in 2008, we can estimate the income generated per individual at USD 4300 per year. This is a very rough approximation, which also does not take into consideration the extreme variation in earning between traders at the bazaar. But even taking margins of error into account, there is a considerable gap between the yearly GDP per capita of USD 1219 in 2017 (according to World Bank data) and the above estimate.

Drawing from the data set, we can likewise see that trading in Dordoi can be profitable, and considerably more so than in Lilo. As the revenue scale increases, so does the percentage of respondents in Dordoi, while the one in Lilo decreases (Figure 3). As GDP per capita in Lilo was USD 3853 in 2016,[13] traders have a much better chance in Dordoi than in Lilo to earn more than the national average.

Dordoi appears as a marketplace where traders can earn, on average, more than the average income; the data set confirms this finding with questions indirectly related to revenue. More than 60% declared that they were reinvesting revenues earned in their business, and 72% considered that their business had grown in 2015. The differences between Dordoi and Lilo in living standards, perception of growth and ability to reinvest are noteworthy. Respondents in Dordoi were clearly more optimistic than their counterparts in Lilo. The Dordoi bazaar is a transnational trading hub, with a larger volume of goods compared to Lilo.

One aspect in particular appears to stand apart in Lilo. Traders who travel (56%) also tend to be more successful. In Lilo, perception of business growth and having employees, the ability to reinvest, and satisfaction with generated revenue are all factors related to mobility and travelling. Travelling and the ability to reinvest in business are also related.

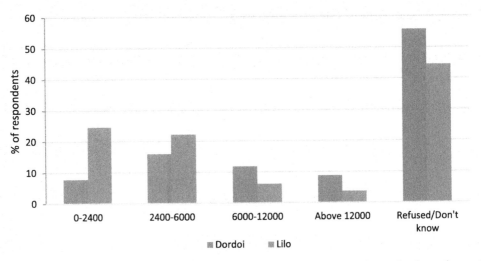

Figure 3. Revenue scale in Dordoi and Lilo in USD, % of respondents. Source: Survey by the author and H. Karrar in August 2016 and February–March 2017.

Finally, travelling is also related with having a bank account.[14] These appear to be the entrepreneurial businessmen and businesswomen well described by Fehlings (in this issue), who are engaged in more lucrative activities than the *chelnoki* and the rest of the traders in Lilo, who struggle with precariousness.

But in Dordoi, travel does not appear as a determining variable. Half of the traders surveyed are travelling for their business, but those who travel do not have higher living standards, nor do they perceive their business as growing more than those who do not travel. Thus, transnational linkages are important in both bazaars, but traders in Lilo seem to have to travel to exploit their transitional network, while the transnational networks of Dordoi materialize in Dordoi.

On the frontier of globalization from below

In both Dordoi and Lilo, trading is a transnational economic activity. Bazaar traders are exposed to globalization trends, which they negotiate through commercial networks or through kin, family, and clan networks (Steenberg; Ibanez Tirado; Fehlings, all in this issue). The exchanges that are structured in the bazaar contrast with formal, regulated, internationally standardized commercial exchanges.

There are different proxies for degrees of economic openness to trade. At the macroeconomic level, the ratio of trade to GDP conveys the percentage of import and export on which an economy is based. But this would not work for the bazaar, with its undocumented transactions; here, a different set of proxies is required to illustrate the embeddedness of bazaar trade in transnational flows. In the data set, transnational connections were identified through the country of origin of manufactured goods, the origin of buyers, and the number of foreign currencies used. These reflect the place of the bazaar in regional trade flows and indicate the mobility of traders.

Unsurprisingly, the origin of goods and buyers and the travel trajectories of the traders are related to the country's geographic location. Dordoi benefits from Kyrgyzstan's location between China and Russia. Lilo neighbours Turkey, which is also reflected in the data; in Lilo, 50% of the traders interviewed sell goods from Turkey, while 33% sell goods from China. Lilo Bazroba's administration, confirming this figure, indicates that 41% of the goods sold there come from China (Fehlings, this issue).

But Lilo appears as a local market, where almost all the buyers are from Georgia. Dordoi, on the other hand, is a regional hub. Hence, for Dordoi traders, travelling is not a necessary condition to trade in the market and the bazaar. When asked whether travelling is necessary for them to do their job, most traders – 60% in Dordoi and 45% in Lilo – said no. In Dordoi, for those who do travel, more than a third go to China, followed by Turkey and Russia. The corresponding destinations for traders in Lilo are Turkey, China and India.

Trading across borders implies dealing in multiple currencies, which can be taken as another indicator of the extent to which local traders are globalized. In Dordoi, the overwhelming majority deal with foreign currencies: only 18% of the traders interviewed deal only in Kyrgyz currency; half deal with one foreign currency (mainly the US dollar), and the rest with more than one, including the yuan, tenge, ruble, and euro. The fluctuation of these currencies is watched daily by more than a third of the traders. Some check exchange rates more than twice a day. These data show that Dordoi is a globalized place in itself, whereas the Lilo market is less exposed to foreign currency flows and fluctuations. More than 40% of the respondents in Lilo deal only in the Georgian lari, and a mere 6% deal with two foreign currencies.

The differences between these two post-Soviet bazaars sharpen as one digs further. The geographical position of a bazaar can influence the kinds of goods sold and their origin and ultimately is an important factor in determining its size and importance in the trading network as a hub or, as seems to be the case for the Lilo market, a national market. But trading in Dordoi and Lilo appears to be different in other ways, too. Another way globalization from below can manifest is in the source of information.

The main difference between Dordoi and Lilo relates to Internet usage versus relying on friends and family as sources of information (Figure 4). The sources of information for traders in Dordoi are first the Internet, and second clients and customers. This aligns well with Schröder's observation (in this issue) of Kyrgyz businessmen trading with China, for whom Internet access is important. These findings show the entrepreneurial aspect of trade, which tends to be weaker in Lilo. The use of the Internet to conduct business activities within a transnational network gives these businesses an informational advantage in ways that family and friends cannot.

Thus, compared to Lilo, the Dordoi bazaar is a hub of transnational trade. Dordoi is a highly organized place structured by small value chains. Southern Siberian traders come by bus, choose the merchandise they will resell, and return the same day. Shipping companies and foreign exchange brokers have small offices next to the customs clearance administration. This is evident not only in the origin of the goods sold and the origin of buyers, but also in the number of currencies traders have to deal with and their sources of information. But not all bazaars fulfil this function similarly, and trading in Dordoi is not the same as trading in Lilo. This itself is an important lesson, and one that is frequently overlooked in the economic development literature, which gravitates towards a one-size-fits-all view when it comes to the benefit of trade. The economic and social impact of re-exporting via the bazaar in Kyrgyzstan is important on multiple levels. Bazaars and

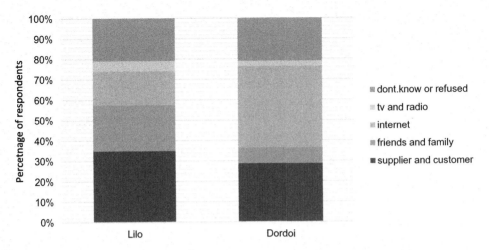

Figure 4. Main sources of information used for activities by traders in the Lilo and Dordoi markets. Source: Survey by the author and H. Karrar in August 2016 and February–March 2017.

cross-border trade alleviate poverty by reducing the cost of trade and thus providing products at lower prices. They also offer employment opportunities, especially for women, and play a central role in national and regional chains of production and distribution.

Trading, as new economic activities arising from the opportunities the transition brings, is often considered an entrepreneurial activity that allows people to escape poverty and grow businesses. Yet, trading can be a very different activity depending on where and how it is carried out. Schröder in this volume shows the evolution of Kyrgyz traders who in the 1990s were trading to survive. Now, in their trade with China, Kyrgyz intermediaries are making larger profits, and hence moving beyond precarious employment. Earlier *chelnoki* in Georgia became traders (Fehlings, this issue) for lack of a better means of livelihood, just as the *lomi* business in Hungary became more professional (Sik 2012). In the process, ethnic and interethnic networks allowed some traders to become entrepreneurs. But while trader mobility is one facet of globalization from below, similar tendencies are also manifest on the bazaar floor; traders can be globalized without having to move very far.

Conclusion

This article used data from 600 structured interviews in Dordoi and Lilo. The interviews posed questions related to daily trading activities, from which conclusions about organizational informality and entrepreneurship can be drawn. The data set generated from the interviews also illustrates that trade in these two bazaars is transnational and a globalized activity.

This article puts forward several findings. First, the traders in both bazaars who are on the spectrum towards precarious employment do not display entrepreneurial characteristics, as also noted by Cieślewska (2014). This is relevant on two levels. On a theoretical level, it questions the relevance of an occupational definition of entrepreneurship. These definitions of entrepreneurship tend to include everyone, from those who are self-employed by default, to ones who have been financially successful. The interplay of informality makes it even harder to determine the boundaries of entrepreneurship, which is already hard to define on its own. Studies of entrepreneurship in developing economies would therefore gain by adopting a theoretical approach to entrepreneurship focusing on the added value entrepreneurs generate rather than on its ability to be self-sustainable. The blurring of boundaries between survival and entrepreneurship also has important policy consequences. Those who took to trade by default and who are engaged in precarious employment might not be the most appropriate target for private-sector development, SMEs or entrepreneurship policy. The findings of this research confirm other scholars' conclusions (Cho, Robalino, and Watson 2016; Temkin 2009). A large amount of public resources risk being wasted on programmes and initiatives to increase economic opportunities for this segment of the population (e.g., business development services, entrepreneurship training and capacity building) where traders would in fact benefit more from risk reduction and revenue stabilization.

Second, informality, entrepreneurship and globalization (from below) do not necessarily overlap. Some traders with entrepreneurial characteristics also run informal businesses, but are not necessarily mobile. Lilo traders who travel have recorded better performance than those who do not (though Lilo appears more local than Dordoi). The profitability of cross-border trade depends on trading partners and on the level of economic development. As informal trade is a source of livelihood for many people it is important to evaluate its potential for revenue generation. This has implications for inclusive growth and economic inequality, given how few traders benefit from transnational mobility and connections. Also, informal networks are frequently considered an economic resource that allows people to cope with uncertainty (Humphrey 2018; Smallbone and Welter 2001). Yet our data set shows that in the two bazaars most traders tend to work and run their business alone, as also observed by Fehlings (in this issue). While there are kin and familial networks in the background (Steenberg 2016) that a quantitative survey would struggle to pick up, the data do allow distinguishing between 'network' as a means to cope with precariousness and 'network' as a component of an enterprise operation. Bearing this distinction in mind, the role of 'network' presents as being limited to a source of information in Lilo and a source of financial help in Dordoi, and not affecting day-to-day operations or the organizational platform on which a family

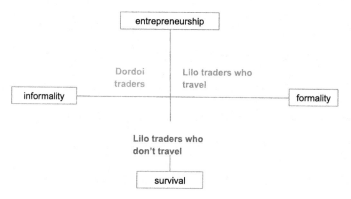

Figure 5. Graph of 'informality–formality' and 'survival–entrepreneurship' continuums.

businesses or cooperative is established. Also use of a personal network might come at the expense of economic efficiency (Menyashev and Polishchuk 2011). Social capital used for survival might not be easily recyclable to actually *run* businesses.

Methodological limitations notwithstanding, I shall risk categorizing the two bazaars along the dimension of informality and entrepreneurship (Figure 5). Although this illustration veers towards oversimplification, it is not presented to gloss over the complexity in bazaar trading; it is meant to illustrate that informality and entrepreneurship are present in both bazaars.

Finally, this article has tried to show how the path-dependent processes created by uncertainty and survival manifest themselves in bazaar trading. The different *modus operandi* of these economic actors sheds another light on the deviation from a textbook path of neoliberal economic development (Gustafson 1999; Puffer and McCarthy 2007; Robinson 2013; Vasileva 2018). In this way, this has article tried to illustrate how post-socialist informality has 'an important role to play in reinforcing the relevance of a multiple modernities perspective' (Morris and Polese 2014, 9).

Notes

1. According to the Lilo official administration in 2017.
2. Characteristics that relate to the motivations of the entrepreneur and their performance.
3. A wide range of manufactured goods are sold in Dordoi, most of them imported from China, and resold to Kazak, Russian, and Kyrgyz intermediaries or retail markets. The bazaar appears a giant maze, made of approximately 40,000 containers with alleys that can stretch up to a kilometre. Stacked upon another, the first container is used to display goods and the other one to store the merchandise. Dordoi bazaar provides employment to about 60,000 (Karrar 2017). Clients, retail and wholesale traders of different nationalities and ethnic background deal everyday with one another. People from southern Siberia are coming by bus. They choose the merchandise they will resell and return the same day.
4. The Dordoi Mosque is considered an important Islamic site in Kyrgyzstan (Berlioux and Paczai 2015).
5. This refers to the state redistribution of private property, taking back assets that had been already privatized to reprivatize them later (Papava 2009).
6. The country became the region's best performer according to the World Bank, ranking 9th in the world in ease of doing business, just after the UK and Norway, in 2018; but this increase in ranking was also part of a well-orchestrated public relations campaign (Schueth 2011).
7. The chosen course of economic policy, influenced by neoliberalism, got rid of government interference in the economic sphere and abolished the law on 'Small and Medium Enterprise Support' in 2006.
8. At https://lilomall.ge/; the semantic shift from 'bazaar' to 'mall' in the name of the website is also worth noting.
9. 'Degree of structuring' relates to the organization of an activity and the predictability of the framework according to which individuals in the organization act. 'Reach of official governance' underscores the interaction of this organization with the offices of the state.
10. As reported by Radio Free Europe Radio Liberty. Pannier B. (2003). Central Asia: Market Traders Registration Complaints Over New Regulations in Kyrgyzstan, Uzbekistan. Radio Free Europe Radio Liberty, 3 October. https://www.rferl.org/a/1104542.html and Radio Free Europe Radio Liberty. (2006) More Protest in Georgia Against Cash Register Law. 15 March. https://www.rferl.org/a/1066733.html.
11. To test the relationship between the different variables of 'informality' described above, chi-squared tests of independence and logistic regressions were conducted.

12. The minority of more formal traders in Dordoi are not the ones who report business growth or revenue satisfaction. Various chi-squared independence tests and logistic regressions showed that variables marking 'formality' are unrelated to variables marking 'performance'. Traders in Lilo tend to be more formal, but 'formality' and 'performance' are also unrelated in Lilo.
13. World Bank Data, https://data.worldbank.org/.
14. Chi-squared independence tests show that these variables are not independent.

Disclosure statement

No potential conflict of interest was reported by the author(s).

Disclaimer

This article represents the opinions of the author, and is the product of professional research. It is not meant to represent the position or opinions of UNCTAD or its Members, nor the official position of any staff members. Any errors are the fault of the author.

Funding

This work was supported by Volkswagen Foundation.

References

Aidis, R., and S. Estrin. 2006. Institutions, Networks and Entrepreneurship Development in Russia: An Exploration. Discussion Paper No. 2161, Institute for the Study of Labor.

Aidis, R., S. Estrin, and T. Mickiewicz. 2008. "Institutions and Entrepreneurship Development in Russia: A Comparative Perspective." *Journal of Business Venturing* 23: 656–672. doi:10.1016/j.jbusvent.2008.01.005

Albrecht, J., L. Navarro, and S. Vroman. 2009. "The Effects of Labour Market Policies in an Economy with an Informal Sector." *Economic Journal* 119 (539): 1105–1129. doi:10.1111/j.1468-0297.2009.02268.x

Alff, H. 2014. "Embracing Chinese Modernity? Articulation and Positioning in China–Kazakhstan Trade and Exchange Processes." Crossroads Asia, Working Paper 21.

Alff, H. 2016. "Flowing Goods, Hardening Borders? China's Commercial Expansion into Kyrgyzstan Re-examined." *Eurasian Geography and Economics* 57 (3): 433–456. doi:10.1080/15387216.2016.1200993

Appadurai, A. 2000. "Grassroots Globalization and the Research Imagination." *Public Culture* 12 (1): 1–19. doi:10.1215/08992363-12-1-1

Bennett, J., and M. D. Rablen. 2015. "Self-Employment, Wage Employment and Informality in a Developing Economy." *Oxford Economic Papers* 67 (2): 227–244. doi:10.1093/oep/gpu047

Berlioux, J., and T. Paczai. 2015. "Kyrgyzstan's Colossal Dordoi Bazaar: A Time of Opportunity and Change." *Eurasianet*. October 21, 2015. Accessed January 15, 2020. https://eurasianet.org/kyrgyzstans-colossal-dordoi-bazaar-a-time-of-opportunity-and-change.

Bram, C. 2017. "Moscow Azerbaijani-Juhuro 'Oligarchs' and the Eurasian Trade Networks." *Caucasus Analytical Digest* 96: 5–8.

Caelli, K., L. Ray, and J. Mill. 2003. "'Clear as Mud': Toward Greater Clarity in Generic Qualitative Research." *International Journal of Qualitative Methods* 2 (2): 1–13. doi:10.1177/160940690300200201

Chen, M. 2007. *Rethinking the Informal Economy: Linkages with the Formal Economy and the Formal Regulatory Environment*. DESA Working Paper No. 46.

Cho, Y., D. Robalino, and S. Watson. 2016. "Supporting Self-Employment Small-Scale Entrepreneurship: Potential Programs to Improve Livelihoods for Vulnerable Workers." *IZA Journal of Labor Policy* 5: 1–26.

Cieślewska, A. 2014. "From Shuttle Trader to Businesswomen: The Informal Bazaar Economy in Kyrgyzstan." In *The Informal Post-Socialist Economy: Embedded Practices and Livelihoods*, edited by J. Morris and A. Polese, 121–134. London: Routledge.

Cieślewska, A. 2018. "Chelnoki." In *The Global Encyclopaedia of Informality: Understanding Social and Cultural Complexity*, Vol. 2, edited by A. Ledeneva, 94–98. London: UCL.

Collins, K. 2006. *Clan Politics and Regime Transition in Central Asia*. Cambridge: Cambridge University Press.

Cummings, S. N., and O. Nørgaard. 2004. "Conceptualising State Capacity: Comparing Kazakhstan and Kyrgyzstan." *Political Studies* 52 (4): 685–708. doi:10.1111/j.1467-9248.2004.00503.x

Fehlings, S. 2015. "Intimacy and Exposure: The Armenian 'Tun' and Yerevan's Public Space." *International Journal of Sociology and Social Policy* 35 (7/8): 513–532. doi:10.1108/IJSSP-02-2015-0028

Fehlings, S. 2017. "From Chelnoki to Global Players: Encounters in the Context of Caucasian(-Chinese) Trade since the 1990s." *Paideuma* 63: 183–205.

Fehlings, S. 2020. "Traders, Trade and Local Markets between Tbilisi and Beijing." Habilitation (unpublished manuscript).

Fehlings, S., and H. Karrar. 2016. "Informal Markets and Trade in the Caucasus and Central Asia: A Preliminary Framework for Field Research." Working Paper Series on Informal Markets and Trade 1.

Fonseca, M. L., and J. Malheiros. 2004. "Immigration and Globalisation from Below: The Case of Ethnic Restaurants in Lisbon." *Finisterra* 39 (77): 129–156.

Freeland, C. 2000. *The Sale of the Century: Russia's Wild Ride from Communism to Capitalism*. New York: Crown Business.

Frye, T., and A. Shleifer. 1997. "The Invisible Hand and the Grabbing Hand." *American Economic Review: Papers and Proceedings* 87: 131–155.

Guha-Khasnobis, B., R. Kanbur, and E. Ostrom. 2006. "Linking the Formal and Informal Economy." UNU-Wider Studies in Development Economics.

Gustafson, T. 1999. *Capitalism Russian-Style*. Cambridge: Cambridge University Press.

Hart, K. 1992. "Market and State after the Cold War: The Informal Economy Reconsidered." In *Contesting Markets: A General Introduction to Market Ideology, Imagery and Discourse*, edited by R. Dilley, 214–227. Edinburgh: Edinburgh University Press.

Holzlehner, T. 2014. *Shadow Networks: Border Economics, Informal Markets and Organized Crime in the Russian Far East*. Münster: LIT.

Hsu, C. L. 2005. "Capitalism without Contracts versus Capitalists without Capitalism: Comparing the Influence of Chinese Guanxi and Russian Blat on Marketization." *Communist and Post-Communist Studies* 38: 309–327. doi:10.1016/j.postcomstud.2005.06.003

Humphrey, C., ed. 2018. *Trust and Mistrust in the Economies of the China–Russia Borderlands*. Amsterdam: Amsterdam University Press.

Humphrey, C., and V. Skvirskaja. 2009. "Trading Places: Post-Socialist Container Markets and the City." *Focaal: European Journal of Anthropology* 55: 61–73.

Ibanez Tirado, D. 2018. "Hierarchies of Trade in Yiwu and Dushanbe: The Case of an Uzbek Merchant Family from Tajikistan." *History and Anthropology* 29 (1): 31–47.

Johnson, G., S. Smith, and B. Codling. 2000. "Microprocesses of Institutional Change in the Context of Privatization." *Academy of Management Review* 25: 572–580. doi:10.5465/amr.2000.3363519

Kaiser, M. 1997. *Informal Sector Trade in Uzbekistan*. Bielefeld: Universität Bielefeld, Fakultät für Soziologie, Forschungsschwerpunkt Entwicklungssoziologie (Germany).

Kaminski, B. 2008. "How Kyrgyzstan has seized Opportunities offered by Central Asia's Economic Recovery." Background paper prepared for Kyrgyz Republic: Country Economic Memorandum 2008, ECA, World Bank, Washington.

Kaminski, B., and S. Mitra. 2012. *Borderless Bazaars and Regional Integration in Central Asia. Emerging Patterns of Trade and Cross-Border Cooperation*. Direction in Development Series. Washington, DC: World Bank.

Karrar, H. 2013. "Merchants, Markets, and the State: Informality, Transnationality and Spatial Imaginaries in the Revival of Central Eurasian Trade." *Critical Asian Studies* 45 (3): 459–480. doi:10.1080/14672715.2013.829315

Karrar, H. 2017. "Kyrgyzstan's Dordoi and Kara-Suu Bazaars: Mobility, Globalization and Survival in Two Central Asian Markets." *Globalizations* 14 (4): 643–657. doi:10.1080/14747731.2016.1201323

Karrar, H. 2019. "Between Border and Bazaar: Central Asia's Informal Economy." *Journal of Contemporary Asia* 49 (2): 272–293. doi:10.1080/00472336.2018.1532017

Khutsishvili, K. 2017. "Suddenly a Border: Hazelnut Trade across the De Facto Border between Abkhazia and the Zugdidi Municipal Region of Georgia." *Caucasus Analytical Digest* 96: 9–12.

La Porta, R., and A. Shleifer. 2014. "Informality and Development." *Journal of Economic Perspectives* 28: 109–126. doi:10.1257/jep.28.3.109

Ledeneva, A. V. 1998. *Russia's Economy of Favours*. Cambridge: Cambridge University Press.

Ledeneva, A. 2018. "The Functional Ambivalence of Informal Strategies: Supportive or Subversive? Preface." In *The Global Encyclopaedia of Informality: Understanding Social and Cultural Complexity, Vol. 2*, edited by A. Ledeneva, 3–6. London: UCL Press.

Marsden, M. 2016. *Trading Worlds: Afghan Merchants across Modern Frontiers*. London: Hurst.

Mathews, G., G. L. Ribeiro, and C. A. Vega. 2012. *Globalization from Below: The World's Other Economy*. London: Routledge.

Mathews, G., and Y. Yang. 2012. "How Africans Pursue Low-End Globalization in Hong Kong and Mainland China." *Journal of Current Chinese Affairs* 41 (2): 95–120. doi:10.1177/186810261204100205

McKee, R., A. Murphy, E. Richardson, R. Bayard, C. Haerpfer, and M. McKee. 2013. "Do Citizens of the Former Soviet Union Trust State Institutions, and Why?" *East European Politics* 29 (4): 377–396. doi:10.1080/21599165.2013.821981

Menyashev, R., and L. Polishchuk. 2011. *Bridging or Bonding: Economic Payoff to Social Capital, with an Application to Russia*. Working Paper, Moscow Center for Institutional Studies at the Higher School of Economics.

Morris, J., and A. Polese, eds. 2014. *The Informal Post-Socialist Economy: Embedded Practices and Livelihoods*. London: Routledge.

Naudé, W. 2013. *Entrepreneurship and Economic Development: Theory, Evidence and Policy*. Discussion Paper No. 7507, Institute for the Study of Labor (IZA).

North, D. 1991. "Institutions." *Journal of Economic Perspectives* 5: 97–112. doi:10.1257/jep.5.1.97

North, D. 2005. "The Contribution of New Institutional Economics to an Understanding of the Transition Problem." In *Wider Perspectives on Global Development*, edited by A. B. Atkinson, 1–15. New York: Palgrave Macmillan.

Ozcan, G. B. 2010. *Building States and Markets: Enterprise Development in Central Asia*. London: Palgrave Macmillan.

Papava, V. 2009. "Georgia's Economy: Post-Revolutionary Development and Post-War Difficulties." *Central Asian Survey* 28 (2): 199–213. doi:10.1080/02634930903043717

Parker, S. C. 2004. *The Economics of Self-Employment and Entrepreneurship*. Cambridge: Cambridge University Press.

Polese, A., and A. Prigarin. 2013. "On the Persistence of Bazaars in the Newly Capitalist World: Reflections From Odessa." *Anthropology of East Europe Review* 31 (1): 110–136.

Polese, A., and P. Rodgers. 2011. "Surviving Post-Socialism: the Role of Informal Economic Practices." *International Journal of Sociology and Social Policy* 31 (11/12): 612–618. doi:10.1108/01443331111177896

Puffer, M. S., and D. McCarthy. 2007. "Can Russia's State-Managed, Network Capitalism be Competitive? Institutional Pull versus Institutional Push." *Journal of World Business* 42: 1–13. doi:10.1016/j.jwb.2006.08.008

Ragin, C. 2008. *Redesigning Social Inquiry: Fuzzy Sets and Beyond*. Chicago, IL: University of Chicago Press.

Rasanayagam, J. 2011. "Informal Economy, Informal State: The Case of Uzbekistan." *International Journal of Sociology and Social Policy* 31 (11/12): 681–696. doi:10.1108/01443331111177878

Robinson, N. 2013. "Economic and Political Hybridity: Patrimonial Capitalism in the Post-Soviet Sphere." *Journal of Eurasian Studies* 4: 136–145. doi:10.1016/j.euras.2013.03.003

Rudaz, P. 2017. "The State of MSME in Kyrgyzstan." Informal Market and Trades in Central Asia and the Caucasus Research Project, Working Paper No. 3.

Sasunkevich, O. 2014. "'Business as Casual': Shuttle Trade on the Belarus–Lithuania Border." In *The Informal Post-Socialist Economy*, edited by J. Morris and A. Polese, 135–151. London: Routledge.

Schatz, E. 2004. *Modern Clan Politics: The Power of Blood in Kazakhstan and Beyond*. Washington: University of Washington Press.

Schrader, H. 2004. "Social Capital and Social Transformation in Russia." *Journal of East European Management Studies* 9 (4): 392–411. doi:10.5771/0949-6181-2004-4-392

Schröder, P., and M. Stephan Emmrich. 2016. "The Institutionalization of Mobility: Well-Being and Social Hierarchies in Central Asian Translocal Livelihoods." *Mobilities* 11 (3): 420–443. doi:10.1080/17450101.2014.984939

Schueth, S. 2011. "Assembling International Competitiveness: The Republic of Georgia, USAID, and the Doing Business Project." *Economic Geography* 87: 51–77. doi:10.1111/j.1944-8287.2010.01103.x

Seabright, P., ed. 2000. *The Vanishing Ruble: Barter Networks and Non-Monetary Transactions in Post-Soviet Societies*. Cambridge: Cambridge University Press.

Shane, S., and S. Venkataraman. 2000. "The Promise of Entrepreneurship as a Field of Research." *Academy of Management Review* 25: 217–226.

Sik, A. 2012. "Trust, Network Capital, and Informality: Cross-Border Entrepreneurship in the First Two Decades of Post-Communism." *Review of Sociology* 4: 53–72.

Smallbone, D., and F. Welter. 2001. "The Distinctiveness of Entrepreneurship in Transition Economies." *Small Business Economics* 16: 249–262. doi:10.1023/A:1011159216578

Spector, R. 2008. "Securing Property in Contemporary Kyrgyzstan." *Post-Soviet Affairs* 24 (2): 149–176. doi:10.2747/1060-586X.24.2.149

Spector, R. 2017. *Order at the Bazaar: Power and Trade in Central Asia*. Ithaca, NY: Cornell University Press.

Steenberg, R. 2016. "Embedded Rubber Sandals: Trade and Gifts across the Sino-Kyrgyz Border." *Central Asian Survey* 35 (3): 405–420. doi:10.1080/02634937.2016.1221577

Temkin, B. 2009. "Informal Self-Employment in Developing Countries: Entrepreneurship or Survivalist Strategy? Some Implications for Public Policy" *Analyses of Social Issues and Public Policy* 9 (1): 135–156. doi:10.1111/j.1530-2415.2009.01174.x

Van de Mortel, E. 2002. *An Institutional Approach to Transition Processes*. Burlington: Ashgate.

Vasileva, A. 2018. "Trapped in Informality: The Big Role of Small Firms in Russia's Statist-Patrimonial Capitalism." *New Political Economy* 23 (3): 314–330. doi:10.1080/13563467.2017.1349090

Werner, C. 1998. "Household Networks and the Security of Mutual Indebtedness in Rural Kazakhstan." *Central Asian Survey* 17 (4): 597–612. doi:10.1080/02634939808401058

Yalçın-Heckmann, L., and N. Aivazishvili. 2012. "Scales of Trade, Informal Economy and Citizenship at Georgian–Azerbaijani Borderlands." In *Subverting Borders: Doing Research on Smuggling and Small-Scale Trade*, edited by B. Bruns and J. Miggelbrink, 193–212. Wiesbaden: Verlag für Sozialwissenschaft.

Appendix: Informal Markets and Trade in the Caucasus and Central Asia

A. CONTROL INFORMATION
(1) Language of the interview
(2) Country
(3) Name of city/town/village
(4) City with population of: less than 20,000 / 20,000–50,000 / 100,000–500,000
(5) Gender
(6) Age
(7) Marital status
(8) Number of children
(9) What is your level of education?

General education
Professional education
University degree
Don't know / Refused

B. GENERAL INFORMATION ON BUSINESS
(10) What is your activity, or the activity of your enterprise? DESCRIBE IN A FEW WORDS
(11) Is that a retail or a wholesale business?
　　Retail
　　Wholesale
　　Both
　　Don't know / Refused

(12) When did you start your business?
(13) What are you selling? WRITE DOWN THE 3 ITEMS MOST SOLD IN THE SHOP
(14) Where are the goods coming from? WRITE DOWN 3 COUNTRY OF ORIGIN
(15) Where are the buyers coming from? WRITE DOWN 3 COUNTRY OF ORIGIN
(16) Is this the first business activity for you?
　　Yes, the first one
　　No, had other business experiences
　　Don't know / Refused

(17) If not, then what happened to the previous business?
　　It failed mostly because of insufficient sales
　　It failed mostly because of lack of finance
　　It failed mostly because of taxes and government intervention
　　Don't know / refused

C. ORGANIZATION OF BUSINESS

(18) Do you work alone or do you employ regular employee, and if so how many?
(19) Do you sometimes get help from …
　　Friends
　　Family members at home
　　Family members abroad
　　Colleagues/people living from the same activities
　　State-run organization or foreign development aid
　　I don't get help

(20) Many people may give you advice on your business. Have you received advice from the following (CHOOSE 2 OF THE ANSWERS FROM BELOW)
　　Your spouse or life companion, parents, family relatives
　　Partners or former boss
　　Somebody in another country or somebody who has come from abroad
　　Somebody with much business experience
　　A bank, development agency, possible investor
　　A customer, supplier, another firm
　　I don't receive advice
　　Don't know / refused

(21) What are the main sources of information you use for your activity? (CHOOSE 2 OF THE ANSWERS FROM BELOW)
　　Friends and family
　　TV and radio
　　Suppliers and customers
　　Don't know / refused

(22) Do you feel that you have the knowledge, skills and experience required to start a business different from the one you are running now?
Yes
No
Don't know / refused

(23) Do you use what you learnt at school for your business?
No, not anything
Yes, to some extent
Yes, it helps very much
Don't know / refused

D. INFORMALITY

(24) Do you know someone personally who started a business in the past two years?
Yes
No
Don't know / refused

(25) At this time, do you have a bank account?
Yes
No
Don't know / refused

(26) Do you record every transaction?
Yes
No
Don't know / refused

(27) Do you mainly use contract and written terms of transaction or mainly oral agreement?
Mainly oral
Mainly with written terms and contract
Don't know / refused

(28) Do you think that moral and honest behaviour is rewarded in business or on the contrary one has to learn to cheat sometimes?
Moral and honest behaviour is rewarded
There are no rules in business
Don't know / refused

(29) In general, do you trust your partner, clients and suppliers?
Yes, always
I like to deal with people recommended by others
No, never
Don't know / refused

E. MOTIVATIONS

F. What is the motivation for doing what you do? (CHOOSE 3 OF THE ANSWERS FROM BELOW)
To take advantage of a business opportunity
No better choice for work
To be my own boss
To increase my income
To provide jobs for family members
My own satisfaction and growth
To build a business to pass on
To be closer to my family
Don't know / refused

G. Would you stop doing what you do for the same fixed salary as an employee
   Yes
   No
   Don't know / refused

H. How did you choose the sector of your business?
   You heard about someone doing the same thing
   It is an activity that you were already doing in the past as an employee
   Because some people asked you to
   Because you did not have any other employment opportunity
   Don't know / refused

I. Do you think that the state supports business such as yours?
   Yes, the state supports businesses such as mine
   No, the state favours big business
   Don't know / refused

F. PERFORMANCE AND MOBILITY

(30) How many foreign currencies do you use for your business
   1 only
   2 currencies
   3 currencies
   Don't know / refused

(31) Specify which foreign currencies please
(32) How often do you watch the exchange rate of these currencies
   More than once a day
   Daily
   Weekly
   I don't watch the exchange rate of foreign currencies
   Don't know / refused

(33) Do you have to travel for your business, and if so how far
(34) What, in your opinion, are the necessary elements of a successful business (CHOOSE THE MOST IMPORTANT ONE)
   Material resources (truck, land plot, etc.)
   Financial resources
   To know people – to have a good network
   To be motivated
   To be organized
   To be able to take risks
   Don't know / refused

(35) Do you think that you earn enough revenue from your business?
   To live comfortably
   To live normally
   To live very simply
   To survive
   Don't know / refused

(36) Do you think that business conditions are improving?
   Yes
   No
   Don't know / refused

(37) Has your business grown since its creation?
    No, it has decreased
    It has remained stable
    Yes, it grew
    Don't know / refused

(38) If you suddenly win the lottery, would you
    Buy a piece of land
    Buy an apartment (real estate)
    Keep the money in cash in ARM
    Keep the money in cash in USD
    Buy other material resources useful to run my business
    Don't know / refused

(39) Could you give us an approximate idea of the revenue that your activity is generating per year?
    USD 0–200
    USD 201–500
    USD 501–1000
    USD 1001–2000
    USD 2001–10,000
    USD 10,001–20,0000
    More than USD 20,0000
    Don't know / refused

(40) Do you reinvest any profit in the business, and if so what percentage?

The traders of Central Bazaar, Astana: motivation and networks

Meiirzhan Baitas[†]

ABSTRACT
Trading in Astana's Central Bazaar rests on mutually beneficial people-to-people contacts, or personal networks. Twenty-five years after the Soviet collapse, personal networks are pivotal in whether one succeeds in an informal market economy. I argue that networks cannot be disassociated from trader motivation, which serves as a measure of how these networks evolve over time. I describe how those traders who were driven primarily by lifting themselves out of economic precarity tended to build strong social networks; these strong social networks sometimes evolved into 'unconditional' social networks, by which I mean a trader supporting others even though doing so has no commercial benefit. At the other extreme were traders driven by ambition and goal attainment. I argue that such traders are less likely to establish and maintain social networks. Between these two extremes is a middle ground, where traders alternate between strong and weak social networks.

When I was in primary school, my family moved to Astana. We took up residence with a family near the city's main bazaar, which at that time was at the intersection of Seifullin and Ualikhanov Streets. I would cross the bazaar on the way to school and back, six times a week. Hence, quite by chance, I began walking past this bazaar, which exposed me to day-to-day trading activities.

In the years that followed, I would observe activity in the bazaar daily; I was particularly struck by the early-morning bustle. Regardless of the weather, traders would be hauling goods using metal pushcarts, unpacking bags, and setting up their displays on metal stalls. As they engaged in these activities, the traders were shielded from neither wind nor cold – and in summer, they toiled under the sun. Bazaar work impressed me as

---

[†]This article is based on Meiirzhan Baitas's MA thesis, Traders of the Central Bazaar in Astana: A Perspective on Motives and Social Networks, which he had successfully submitted to the School of Humanities and Social Sciences at Nazarbayev University in 2017 for his MA in Eurasian Studies. As an MA student, Baitas was one of our junior colleagues in the project on Informal Markets and Trade in Central Asia and the Caucasus, which was supported by the Volkswagen Foundation. Baitas's thesis was supervised by John Schoeberlein (Alima Bissenova was the second reader; Hasan Karrar was the external examiner). The following year, Baitas was diagnosed with cancer. Shortly before his untimely passing, he gave us permission to edit his thesis and submit his findings to *Central Asian Survey* in article form, where it underwent peer review similar to the other articles in this collection. Baitas had graduated with honours, winning the Zakharova Prize for best Eurasian Studies thesis. We were impressed by the promise Baitas showed so early in his scholarly career and hope that scholars will engage with and build on his important contribution to the study of markets and trade in Central Asia. —Susanne Fehlings and Hasan H. Karrar.

being hard – even more so during the extremes of cold or hot weather – and I remember asking myself why traders had chosen this line of work. Observing the very same individuals day after day, year after year, I wondered why they hadn't moved on to something else. After my family moved to another part of Astana, my exposure to the bazaar was limited. Then, in 2008, the Central Bazaar was shifted to the outskirts of the city. But although my exposure to the bazaar decreased, my interest in it continued.

With the collapse of the Soviet Union, citizens experienced deterioration in living conditions, rising unemployment, downward social mobility and acute shortages of goods (Volkov 2002; Oushakine 2009; Shevchenko 2009). Across the Soviet Union, tens of millions took to petty trading; this precarious employment took the form of shuttling goods between cities and across international borders, and selling them in ad hoc marketplaces. This was an undocumented informal economy in which the newly unemployed and underemployed sought economic refuge (Kaiser 1997; Werner 1998; Humphrey 2000; Fehlings and Karrar 2016).

In the wake of the Soviet collapse, this informal economy operated outside of a formal regulatory framework and rested on mutually beneficial people-to-people contacts, or what I describe as personal networks. Although it may be tempting to consider the personal network as a safety mechanism of a long-past, tumultuous transition decade, my study of the Central Bazaar shows that 25 years later, personal networks continue to play a pivotal role in whether one succeeds in an informal market economy.

States frequently project their modernization efforts teleologically, where forward movement is based on the past being left behind. In the case of the bazaar, the march of modernity assumes that with overall economic development, petty trading (which in post-Soviet Central Asia took the form of shuttle trading and bazaar trading) will become part of the regulated economy. In scholarship on bazaars, this view was famously articulated by Clifford Geertz (1963), who saw the bazaar-to-market transition as a transition out of a so-called traditional economy. In Central Asia, this teleology was assumed to transform undocumented (and sometimes unregulated) informal markets; these markets would become regulated and documented formal markets (Vidritskaya 2006). But in Kazakhstan, despite protracted efforts by city officials to modernize marketplaces (Spector 2008; Alff 2015), hundreds of thousands continue to engage in petty trade. This trade remains undocumented, and sometimes sidesteps regulation. This article attempts to answer why this is so. How do we understand the continuity of bazaar trade? Considering the professional trajectories of three traders, as they told it to me over multiple meetings, I asked why these traders chose informal employment, how they positioned themselves in the market, and to what extent they considered themselves successful.

In this article, I approach these questions through inquiring about trader motivation. As I illustrate in this article, motivation determines the social network a trader will use.[1] Put differently, I discovered that social networks – or in extreme cases, the lack thereof – cannot be disassociated from motivation; likewise, these same motivations are also a measure of how social networks will evolve over time. Among the traders I describe, those who were driven primarily by lifting themselves out of economic precarity tended to favour strong social networks; these strong social networks sometimes evolved into 'unconditional' social networks, by which I mean a trader supporting others even though doing so has no commercial benefit. For such traders, strong social networks were an affirmation of a moral economy, or what might be described as a security-first ethos. That being said, over time, such social *networks* tend to become less complex, now functioning more as social *relationships* among friends.

At the other extreme are traders who are driven by ambition and goal attainment. I argue that such traders are less likely to establish and maintain social networks. They take an individualistic approach which translates to limited cooperation with other traders in the bazaar, and a limited commitment to networks. As I also demonstrate, between these two extremes is a broad middle ground, where traders alternate between strong and weak social networks.

Field site and field methods

The Central Bazaar in Astana is at Alash tas zholy.[2] A large signboard reading 'Central Bazaar' (Kazakh: *Ortalyq Bazar*; Russian: *Tsentral'nyy Rynok*) greets visitors. It is the largest marketplace in the city. As in other bazaars in Central Asia (such as the Barakholka in Almaty, and Dordoi in Bishkek), the businesses are run by independent traders. The bazaar has both retail and wholesale outlets that operate out of shipping containers. While a range of manufactured goods are sold, for personal and household consumption, most of the outlets are for clothing and shoes.[3] Although covered from the outside, this is a container bazaar.

Besides the container outlets, there are also peddlers who display their merchandise on metal stalls. Trading outlets are arranged in long rows. Two perpendicular rows intersect the bazaar; these perpendicular rows are also used for trading, although there are no container outlets here; instead, the space is used by smaller traders who display their goods on racks. Besides the lack of outlets in these horizontal rows, there is also no roof on this portion of the bazaar, an illustration of their marginal position within the bazaar.

There are two parking lots, to the front and to the left. Behind the parking lot are two two-storey buildings, where the bazaar begins. The outlets at the front of the bazaar, which are close to the entrance and which sees the heaviest traffic, sell a variety of goods: here apparel, bags and luggage, household accessories, mobile phones and accessories, as well as food are sold next to each other; there are also outlets selling *1000 mclochey*, or '1000 trinkets').

Past the bazaar entrance, the merchandise tends to be clustered: clothes, linens and food, for example, are sold in different areas. Although there is some retailing, this portion of the bazaar is geared towards wholesale trade. Clustering allows traders to position themselves within their own niche; it also increases the visibility of their wares, allowing customers to find them more easily. Finally, clustering also allows a relatively legible spatial layout, with different parts of the bazaar identified (and hence locatable) based on the merchandise sold there.

This article is based on fieldwork at the Central Bazaar in Astana throughout the fall of 2016. Besides shorter interviews with traders across the bazaar, which helped me understand bazaar work and organization, I was able to conduct a series of in-depth, semi-structured interviews with business owners (as opposed to employees).

I conducted my interviews in Russian or Kazakh. Most of my respondents were women, ranging in age from 25 to 65. Broadly, age maps onto when they started trading. There is an elder demographic cluster that began trading during *perestroika*; despite their advancing age, they can still be found working at the bazaar, although their numbers have declined in recent years (Karrar 2017). The second demographic cluster started trading after 2002, and range in age from 25 to 40. Seen sequentially, the date of entry into the bazaar serves as an arc of recent history, from perestroika or pre-independence, to independence and finally post-independence. Perhaps more relevant to my argument is that when people started trading also affects organization and social networks.

In this article, I describe Saltanat, Ruslan and Bota. I describe why they started trading, whether they benefited from social networks, and whether they consider themselves successful. I selected these three traders in part because I was able to do follow-up interviews after work in an informal setting. These three traders are also illustrative because their success and failure correspond to theoretical writing on bazaar trade, which I describe below. As a result, although my ethnography is limited to Astana's Central Bazaar, I believe that my observations and conclusions can be generalized to other bazaars in Central Asia, and broadly speak to the scholarship on informal markets and trade in the global South.

Traders' motivation: theory and praxis

Scholars have identified various motivations for why people might start trading: the pursuit of extrinsic and intrinsic rewards (Boyd and Gumpert 1983; Langan-Fox and Roth 1995; Stewart et al. 2003; Benzing, Chu, and Callanan 2005); push and pull factors (Alstete 2002; Werner 2004; Ipek 2007; Yalcin and Kapu 2008; Cieslewska 2014; Polese 2014; Sasunkevich 2014); willing and unwilling motives (Ageev, Gratchev, and Hisrich 1995; Botoeva and Spector 2013). There is considerable overlap in these theoretical perspectives. My engagement with theory is to provide a framework with which we can begin to disaggregate trader motivation, which in turn offers a window into the importance of social networks in the informal economy. My purpose is not so much to classify behaviour but to use theory to deepen our understanding.

First, *extrinsic* rewards. Scholarship on extrinsic rewards sees trading as an activity that is driven primarily by monetary needs and monetary benefit (Boyd and Gumpert 1983; Langan-Fox and Roth 1995). Newfound capital, which can be acquired through trading, is beneficial in that it can be used for goals that are possible only with a certain amount of capital. These are immediate needs, such as providing for one's family. *Intrinsic* rewards are different; these are motives that drive entrepreneurs to achieve their personal goals. These often appear intangible, in that they defy an empirical classification or measurable benchmark (Stewart et al. 2003; Benzing, Chu, and Callanan 2005): the shedding of dependency, for example, or public recognition. In general, traders in developing economies – and specifically in Kazakhstan, where private trade emerged in the wake of transition from the Soviet Union – will be driven by extrinsic rewards, which will tangibly improve a trader's material conditions.[4] The extrinsic and intrinsic rewards framework is similar to what others have described as push and pull factors.[5]

But why enter the informal market to achieve these goals? As is now well understood, following the collapse of the Soviet Union – which was accompanied by the collapse of the command economy and rising under- and unemployment – professionals were forced to look for alternative sources of income. People sought vocations where they perceived the lowest barriers to entry; trade – either shuttling goods, or selling goods in newly emerging markets – was one of the most popular options.[6] It is important to keep in mind that there was a spectrum of attitudes to trading, from those who were reluctant to leave their previous jobs, the 'unwilling traders' (Ageev, Gratchev, and Hisrich 1995; Botoeva and Spector 2013; Karrar 2017), to those who were not actually forced out of a contracting labour market but were still seeking new opportunities. The latter were individuals who took an intrinsic interest in business, in some instances leaving permanent employment for more lucrative opportunities (Ageev, Gratchev, and Hisrich 1995, 372; see also Taalaibekova 2018). These willing and unwilling motives map onto intrinsic and extrinsic factors. Hence extrinsic and extrinsic rewards, push and pull factors, and willing and unwilling attitudes are constitutive of motivation for bazaar traders.

These theoretical moorings are useful in understanding trading in an informal economy. When I asked traders in the Central Bazaar why and how they started trading, they would respond with a story. While each story was unique, they shared themes, such as the need to escape poverty, the necessity of supporting family and children, the wish enrich oneself – sometimes in a short time. Invariably, these stories correspond to an analytical frame.

As I noted earlier, there is a temporal divide between people who started trading in the late Soviet period, during perestroika, versus those who began trading later. Those who had started during perestroika, or in the years immediately after the Soviet collapse, claimed to have been forced by financial hardship (although some of the first-generation traders did well financially, they were the unwilling traders, driven initially by extrinsic factors). Economic reforms under perestroika reduced the role of the state in people's everyday life (Kaiser 1997; Cieslewska 2014; Fehlings 2017; Taalaibekova 2018). While it did constitute economic freedom, perestroika also reduced job security, and people were laid off. Severance pay, or pension – when it did exist – was either inadequate or slow in coming. Often, when people were laid off, they struggled to find new employment, especially the middle-aged who had a limited skill set. This required people to look for alternative sources of income. In the absence of formal employment, those who had been made economically vulnerable found themselves looking for work in the informal economy.[7] The informal economy became a fall-back mechanism (Niyozov and Shamatov 2007; Cieslewska 2014; Fehlings 2017).

While 1991 serves as a temporal divide, there are limits to how much can be read into it as a transitionary moment. For example, many of the traders in Central Asia, who *started* trading in the early 2000s – that is, more than a *decade* after the breakup of the Soviet Union – also claim they took up trading because of personal financial constraints. This may seem paradoxical: the labour market was stable in the early 2000s, and this second generation of traders had permanent jobs and a stable income. But these traders say that they were unable to provide for their family on their salaries. For this trading demographic, the motivation behind establishing a business was independence from low-paying occupations, which could be considered an extrinsic factor. At the same time, we can also discern intrinsic motivation in the form of wanting to be independent. Consider Ruslan, who left a job in the civil service to begin trading. While I discuss Ruslan in detail below, for now let us note that Ruslan found working in the civil service prestigious, and there was potential for long-term growth. But Ruslan could not see himself working year after year without a promotion. He wanted to escape the rigid hierarchy of the bureaucracy and be independent of his superiors. His was not a financially precarious existence per se, but he did want to realize his potential and become more successful financially.

Motivation and social networks

Bazaar trade is usually accompanied by the growth of ethnic, kin, family and friendship networks. There are two reasons. First, the proclivities of traders shape their interaction with other people, which initially takes the form of social capital. Second, in an informal economy, networks are important for success; a shifting economic terrain and changing regulations – in which traders may not be able to seek protection in official regulation – require traders to rely on networks. Using the examples of Saltanat, Ruslan and Bota, I offer three variations on how trade networks in Astana's Central Bazaar might function. In this section, I examine the relationship between success or failure and social networks.

Saltanat: extrinsic motives and social networks

As I noted, during the twilight of the Soviet Union, people experienced dire living conditions and unemployment that emerged from volatility in the economy; bazaar trade presented as an opportunity on which to build a family economy (Shevchenko 2009). As we also discussed, in Kazakhstan, the unpredictability of the economy and diminished purchasing power meant that people continued to join the informal sector well into the second decade after independence.

I begin with Saltanat's life story, as she related it to me. Sultanate sells garments in the Central Bazaar. She has been a trader for about three decades. Her story is of someone who, motivated by extrinsic factors, built a strong social network to mitigate the uncertainty and unpredictability she experienced as a trader.

In the final years of perestroika, Saltanat suddenly found herself out of a job (what it was she used to do, we never talked about). Trade seemed like the only option to compensate for the loss of a salary. She began by importing clothes from Russia, although she soon switched to Kyrgyzstan, as clothing from Russia was considered too expensive by local buyers.

By the mid-1990s, Bishkek's Dordoi Bazaar was emerging as a regional trading hub for locally manufactured garments and also for re-export of Chinese and Turkish goods (sometimes under local labels). Saltanat found herself travelling to Bishkek, gradually building close ties with the same Kyrgyz sellers in the Dordoi Bazaar. Eventually, she had developed a close enough relationship with sellers that she could acquire goods on credit. Saltanat described the Dordoi traders she acquired goods from as friends, but was quick to point out that she too was a good friend to them: she paid her dues on time, repaid the money if she was ever forced to borrow while in Bishkek, lent money to her Kyrgyz friends if they needed help, and reciprocated the favours of Kyrgyz traders (which, according to her, also included sharing information on new fashion trends and connecting Kyrgyz traders with traders in the Central Bazaar). The result was a professional-personal network that also served as a safety net.

But in my conversations with Saltanat it also became apparent that professional networks that are predicated on close friendships have a ceiling in terms of how much they can grow, partly because they need continuous affirmation. While Saltanat speaks warmly of the traders in Dordoi with whom she works closely, she has not expressed a desire to extend this network. In this respect, Saltanat's social network is less of a web – or a multidirectional social network – and more about one-on-one mutual help, support and risk mitigation. Like family relationships, Saltanat's network has become one that she unconditionally accepts without wondering about the monitory reward.

The profitability ceiling that Saltanat has reached does not bother her. This is because her ambitions are modest: to earn a stable income and retain financial security. Interestingly, this had been Saltanat's first impulse in trade: to earn an income and minimize her vulnerability when she found herself unemployed. This was a time when she lost trust in institutions and formal employment, which she has sought to find in informal and highly personalized networks. This mindset permeates Saltanat's actions up to this date.

Saltanat insists that her business network serves her well; it is predictable, and it has yielded a steady income. New, more lucrative possibilities, such as switching to Turkish products or selling winter coats, do not interest her. Saltanat prioritizes stability, reliable connections with suppliers, predictability and security over constant growth. She told me that she would consider a fluctuating income a failure, even if it resulted in a high net profit, while currently she considers herself a successful businessperson.

Intrinsic motives and social networks

Saltanat's motivation was extrinsic: she had material needs which she was able to address through a limited but strong network. Such extrinsic motives are usually associated with developing economies. By comparison, intrinsic rewards are mostly associated with strong and stable economies that provide favourable conditions for business establishments (Bernabè 2002; Aziz et al. 2013). While examples of intrinsic motivations are unusual in Kazakhstan, a transitional economy allows leveraging new opportunities, where an intrinsically driven trader might seek independence, self-realization, personal development or other personal goals (Stewart et al. 2003; Benzing, Chu, and Callanan 2005). Let us consider Ruslan, who I introduced earlier, in more detail. Here too motivation is important in the cultivation of relations that can then be leveraged for professional gain.

When I met Ruslan he had been a trader for four years (he started in 2012). He specializes in men's jeans, which he buys in the Barakholka in Almaty. Before he started selling jeans, Ruslan had worked as a civil servant. But he found the hierarchy overbearing, promotions rare and the salary limited, all of which led him to quit his job and work for himself. In doing so, Ruslan was defying what Keith Hart (1973) identified as the importance of long-term security over everything else. Ruslan wants material benefits through self-realization, which, he told me, naturally follows when people lead their own lives and have their own businesses; this self-realization had not been possible for him as a civil servant.

In my visits to his shop, I noticed that Ruslan liked to work alone. He told me he did not need help from others – including other traders in the bazaar – and claimed to not receive help from family or kin members either. Like Saltanat, whose motivation for entry into the bazaar continued to influence her business practice three decades later, Ruslan's attitude appeared to be a result of why he had started trading. He had accumulated the initial capital with which he started trading by himself; he had not received help from family or kin. For him, the market is not a place where relations need to be cultivated; as he described, when he travels to Barakholka, Ruslan buys from the suppliers who give him the best price. He does not have a sense of loyalty to his suppliers and makes no effort to build a regular clientele.

For Ruslan, the matter of trust does not arise. He describes himself as self-sufficient and independent; he sees the cultivation of social ties as a form of indebtedness. He works alone and reaps the benefits alone. He is not worried about not having a support system in the bazaar. Inevitably, the lack of interaction in the bazaar means that Ruslan does not follow opportunities that are available to other traders. But he claims not to be interested. For example, he does not acquire garments from Dordoi Bazaar in Bishkek, unlike many other bulk traders around him. He dismisses this option by saying that shipments from Dordoi take too long – more than a week – and are costly. He does not know, or at least claims not to know, of cargo services such as Abdi, Natasha and Zamira, which can deliver goods from Dordoi to Astana in two or three days. How do we explain this?

Given how freely information circulates in the market, it is not possible to say that Ruslan is unaware of such possibilities. Rather, I would suggest that Ruslan is an example of success being measured through a different matrix: independence, self-realization and material gains through labour. He finds himself in a conflicted position because although he did achieve independence, the material gains have not materialized. He confessed to me that he wants to buy a flat for his family, but at this point, his limited income makes that impossible; his extreme individualism has imposed a growth ceiling. We can conjecture that individualism has led to a limited social network, and a wide-ranging network could have been more lucrative. A robust social network leads to assistance in times of need; at the very least it can lead to a steady and reliable source of information, which is valuable in an informal market.

Mixed motives and flexible social networks

While Saltanat and Ruslan could be said to occupy two extremes in their reliance on social networks in the bazaar, there is, of course, a broad middle ground. I describe this middle ground through a third trader, Bota. Unlike Saltanat and Ruslan, Bota is motivated by both extrinsic and intrinsic rewards. Bota is ambitious, and clear in her mind that she wants to be financially independent; she does realize, however, that success will depend on tapping into social networks, asking for help, and reciprocating this assistance from time to time. She is content with this. For Bota, social networks need to be balanced with profitability. In this respect, she would be in the middle of the motivation continuum, with Saltanat and Ruslan at the two extremes.

Bota has been trading since 2009. She has an outlet in the Central Bazaar, where she sells winter coats and women's dresses. Before she started trading, Bota worked at the Ministry of Justice; she quit that job because it had limited prospects for growth. From her initial forays into trading, Bota has carefully cultivated connections with other traders. She immediately perceived that networks were valuable social capital if she wanted to succeed in trade. As she described, when she started trading, she had limited knowledge of the trading world; buying, price setting and shipping logistics were all unknown to her. It was only through interacting with other traders that Bota learned about running a business. But within a few years, she had made and saved enough money to finance her own container in Astana.

For Bota, connections with fellow traders are important because Bota's family was unable to support her financially or otherwise in her new vocation. Bota realized that to have a successful professional network in the bazaar, trust needed to be cultivated (Geertz 1978). Initially she relied on 'thin' or generalized trust, in the form of a person's reputation in the bazaar. If she perceived a trader as trustworthy based on thin trust, Bota increased her interaction with that trader. With more personal interaction Bota built 'thick' trust, personalized trust, which deepened as she cultivated business relations with these traders. For her, these networks were particularly important because they were channels for information, which is particularly important in an informal market. Bota also shares information about prices and traders who can make discounts to reciprocate other traders as well as reciprocating through mutual financial help.

Bota describes her connections in the bazaar as flexible. She does not believe in cultivating relationships that do not provide safety nets or a sense of mutual indebtedness. But instead of completely abandoning them, Bota preserves them as weak connections. She wants to benefit from double safety nets: from both weak and strong social networks. In this respect, she follows what Nasritdinov (2006, 21–22) observed in his study of traders in Kyrgyzstan: there is utility in weak social networks, which can be imagined as secondary mechanisms. The primary safety net, however, is bound to strong networks that have a strong sense of obligation for mutual help among their members.

Bota understands success as constant improvement, development and growth, which has a material dimension, such as buying a container or a flat. Bota also claims that traders in the Central Bazaar have well-defined career ladders that they wish to climb for personal and professional growth. The first step in the hierarchy is to bring goods from Almaty. The next step is to trade goods from Kyrgyzstan. The next step, according to Bota, is to sell Chinese, Russian or Turkish products. The final step is to deal in fur and leather; a trader who can do this is no longer a petty trader but has established herself as a successful businessperson who can now confidently seek partnerships and move out of the bazaar.

On every rung of this ladder, the business grows larger, inventories and risks increase, and traders require more social capital to act as a safety net. A successful trader also needs to keep moving up the ladder. Bota describes a successful trader as upwardly mobile, and failure not just in financial loss but in stagnation, too. According to her own assessment, Bota is a successful trader; she has been able to buy a container and a flat. And she has switched from Kyrgyz products to selling only Turkish products of higher quality. In future Bota wants to sell expensive furs and establish her own shop in the city.

Saltanat, Ruslan and Bota illustrate how different attitudes to trade shape social networks. In particular, highly extrinsically driven traders tend to focus on establishing strong social networks that might evolve into unconditional social networks through high trust, mutual reciprocity and indebtedness, and the provision of safety nets in the case of need. Here social networks tend to lose their complex nature and turn into bilateral agreements that do not necessarily yield the best profits. But rigid social networks reduce unpredictability and provide a sense of stability and security to the members of the network. Highly intrinsically driven traders often cannot establish meaningful social networks due to the lack of trust and commitment to help others, and thus cannot count on mutual help. In the last case, where traders are driven by a combination of intrinsic and extrinsic motives, social networks tend to be flexible, alternating between strong and weak ones based on thick or thin trust, and urgency to help as well as to mutually reciprocate. And in the mixed-motives case traders get double safety nets through having strong social networks along with preserving weak social networks for safety.

Conclusion

I began this paper by describing how, walking past the old Central Bazaar as a child, I would wonder why people chose to trade. I have attempted to identify some of the motivations behind trade, including why people became traders in the first place, and the extent to which they built and used social networks. While one needs to be cautious of generalizing, the behaviour of the three traders I describe can illustrate trends, variations of which appear readily in the bazaar. At their broadest, these trends illustrate how people negotiate the largely unknown terrain of the informal economy. The informal economy tends to be localized in places like this bazaar; in its day-to-day functioning, the informal economy here appears removed from the macro-economy and the world of politics at the state level, although these do impinge on the day-to-day transactions in local marketplaces through shifting trade regimes and border regulations.

I have argued that in the informal economy, the role of social networks can be crucial. This is evident where traders choose to build, and enjoy the benefits of, a ground-level support mechanism. Based on the cases I presented, one might conclude that traders tend to alternate between weak and strong social networks; traders can strategically choose to have weaker or stronger social networks depending on the network members' capabilities in terms of capital and information. In addition, traders might reverse their social networks, that is, intensify weak social networks and weaken previously strong social networks with respect to economic conditions and context in general. For instance, if traders observe that economic conditions are not suitable for larger scales of trade, they might choose to weaken social networks to avoid losses.

Traders might also disperse strong social networks when their customers' income shrinks, or their preferences and tastes shift over time. Alternatively, traders could choose to intensify networks in the case of positive economic developments, adoption of policies that promote trade, or buyers' increased interest in purchasing particular types of goods. In such positive developments traders might use their social networks to raise more capital for investment in increasing scales of trade or in trying more risky behaviour to reap more benefits, compensating for the risks by strong social networks that provide safety nets.

The intensifying or loosening up of social networks could also be connected with the fact that social networks become weaker over time due to their limited functionality for business growth. That is, there might be limits to some social networks in the case of asymmetrical capital accumulation by their members. For instance, Bota switched from Kyrgyz to Turkish apparel once she acquired enough capital. Thus, Bota has chosen to weaken her previous social networks. Still, she did not completely withdraw from them, because they represented sunk costs, and because they still might provide safety nets, because some members still need to reciprocate help previously received.

Notes

1. I approach social networks as an individual's web of connections to others, which act alternatively as safety nets, mutual reciprocity obligations and support mechanisms. These were particularly important for traders who were shuttling goods domestically or internationally, given how mobility between two points added to their vulnerability. For the itinerant traders, cultivation of trust, establishment of reciprocity among members of the network, and the provision of safety nets were essential. I would argue that the establishment of social networks and the

evolution of social networks over time cannot be disassociated from the motivation behind trading.
2. Until 2008 the bazaar was at the intersection of Ualikhanov and Seifullin Streets. The old bazaar remains idle for the most part, except for some street vendors outside the area of the old bazaar. In late April 2017, the company Constructive-A is planning to start construction of a residential complex on the territory of the old bazaar.
3. For example, I counted 34 rows in which only apparel was being sold. Interestingly, these were not subdivided into men's, women's and children's clothes. Clothing gives way to shoes, which extend across 15 rows. Although clothes and shoes occupy the largest segment of the bazaar, there are other, smaller clusters too: jewelry, toys, carpets.
4. Conversely, entrepreneurs in developed economies might emphasize intrinsic rewards to a greater degree to realize personal potential, sometimes by avoiding taxation and regulations posed by the state (Bernabè 2002; Aziz et al. 2013).
5. In scholarship on independent traders, push factors are described as financial motives, such as increasing income, that come about through contractions in the labor market which incentivize people to look for their own employment (Yalcin and Kapu 2008, 188). Pull factors – similar to the intrinsic rewards described above – refer to the desire to elevate one's own reputation and independence (Yalcin and Kapu 2008, 189). In reality, the combination of push and pull factors affects entrepreneurs' economic and social behaviour, rather than each affecting behaviour in isolation (Alstete 2002). Although extrinsic and intrinsic and push and pull factors largely echo each other, one difference is that in the literature on push and pull factors, the emphasis is on flexibility of activities. The advantage of such flexibility, I think, lies in researching the role of family-based networks and motivations, in contrast to the frame of the literature on extrinsic and intrinsic rewards.
6. As a corollary, some people tried to use their existing skills for new employment opportunities. This explains, for example, the crafts industry in Kyrgyzstan, in which craftspeople have successfully used their artisanal skills (Botoeva and Spector 2013, 489–490).
7. Of course, the so-called second economy had always been present in the Soviet Union (Kaiser 1997; Ledeneva 2006; Spector 2009). But the magnitude of informal activity now increased because of declining state control over the economy; the other consequence of declining state control was rapid liberalization and privatization across the former Soviet Union (Chen 2007; Mogilevski 2012; Sik and Wallace 1999, 697–698).

Disclosure statement

No potential conflict of interest was reported by the author.

References

Ageev, A., M. Gratchev, and R. Hisrich. 1995. "Entrepreneurship in the Soviet Union and Post-Socialist Russia." *Small Business Economics* 7 (5): 365–376. doi:10.1007/BF01302737

Alff, H. 2015. "Profiteers or Moral Entrepreneurs? Bazaars, Traders and Development Discourses in Almaty, Kazakhstan." *International Development Planning Review* 37 (3): 249–267. doi:10.3828/idpr.2014.28

Alstete, J. 2002. "On Becoming an Entrepreneur: An Evolving Typology." *International Journal of Entrepreneurial Behavior and Research* 8 (5): 222–234. doi:10.1108/13552550210436521

Aziz, N., B. A. Friedman, A. Bopieva, and I. Keles. 2013. "Entrepreneurial Motives and Perceived Problems: An Empirical Study of Entrepreneurs in Kyrgyzstan." *International Journal of Business* 18 (2): 163–176.

Benzing, C., H. Chu, and G. Callanan. 2005. "A Regional Comparison of the Motivation and Problems of Vietnamese Entrepreneurs." *Journal of Developmental Entrepreneurship* 10 (1): 3–27. doi:10.1142/S1084946705000033

Bernabè, S. 2002. "Informal Employment in Countries in Transition: A Conceptual Framework." *Centre for Analysis of Social Exclusion*, paper 56: 1–64.

Botoeva, A., and R. A. Spector. 2013. "Sewing to Satisfaction: Craft-Based Entrepreneurs in Contemporary Kyrgyzstan." *Central Asian Survey* 32 (4): 487–500. doi:10.1080/02634937.2013.862963

Boyd, D., and D. Gumpert. 1983. "Coping with Entrepreneurial Stress." *Harvard Business Review*, March-April, 44–64.

Cieslewska, A. 2014. "From Shuttle Trader to Businesswomen: The Informal Bazaar Economy in Kyrgyzstan." In *The Informal Post-Socialist Economy: Embedded Practices and Livelihoods*, edited by J. Morris and A. Polese, 121–134. New York: Routledge.

Chen, M. A. 2007. "Rethinking the Informal Economy: Linkages with the Formal Economy and the Formal Regulatory Environment." DESA Working Paper No. 46. *Economic & Social Affairs*, 2007.

Fehlings, S. 2017. "From Chelnoki to Global Players: Encounters in the Context of Caucasian(-Chinese) Trade Since the 1990s." *Paideuma* 63: 183–205.

Fehlings, S., and H. H. Karrar. 2016. "Informal Markets and Trade in the Caucasus and Central Asia: A Preliminary Framework for Field Research." *Informal Markets and Trade Working Paper Series* 1. Frankfurt am Main: Goethe Universitat.

Geertz, C. 1963. *Peddlers and Princes: Social Development and Economic Change in Two Indonesian Towns*. Chicago: University of Chicago Press.

Geertz, C. 1978. "The Bazaar Economy: Information and Search in Peasant Marketing." *American Economic Review* 68 (2): 28–32.

Humphrey, C. 2000. *The Unmaking of Soviet Life: Everyday Economies after Socialism*. Ithaca: Cornell University Press.

Ipek, P. 2007. "New Trade Routes and New Traders of Energy Resources in Central Asia and the Caspian Sea Region." *Toronto Studies in Central and Inner Asia* 8 (Traders and Trade Routes of Central and Inner Asia: The 'Silk Road', Then and Now): 255–272.

Kaiser, M. 1997. "Informal Sector Trade in Uzbekistan." Working Paper No. 281. Universität Bielefeld, Fakultät für Soziologie, Forschungsschwerpunkt Entwicklungssoziologie.

Karrar, H. H. 2017. "Do Bazaars Die? Notes on Failure in the Central Asian Bazaar." *Informal Markets and Trade Working Paper Series*, 4.

Keith, H. 1973. "Informal Income Opportunities and Urban Employment in Ghana." *Journal of Modern African Studies* 11 (1): 61–89. doi:10.1017/S0022278X00008089

Langan-Fox, J., and S. Roth. 1995. "Achievement Motivation and Female Entrepreneurs." *Journal of Occupational and Organizational Psychology* 68: 209–218. doi:10.1111/j.2044-8325.1995.tb00582.x

Ledeneva, A. 2006. *How Russia Really Works: The Informal Practices That Shaped Post-Soviet Politics and Business*. Ithaca: Cornell University Press.

Mogilevski, R. 2012. "Re-export Activities in Kyrgyzstan." Issues and Prospects, Institute of Public Policy and Administration, Working paper No. 9.

Nasritdinov, E. 2006. *Regional Change in Kyrgyzstan: Bazaars, Open-air Markets and Social Networks*. Doctoral Dissertation. University of Melbourne, Australia.

Niyozov, S., and D. Shamatov. 2007. "Teaching and Trading: Local Voices and Global Issues From Central Asia." *Toronto Studies in Central and Inner Asia* 8: 281–300.

Oushakine, S. 2009. *The Patriotism of Despair: Nation, War, and Loss in Russia*. Ithaca: Cornell University Press.

Polese, A. 2014. "Drinking with Vova: An Individual Entrepreneur between Illegality and Informality." In *The Informal Post-Socialist Economy: Embedded Practices and Livelihoods*, edited by J. Morris and A. Polese, 85–101. New York: Routledge.

Sasunkevich, O. 2014. "'Business as Casual': Shuttle Trade on the Belarus-Lithuania Border." In *The Informal Post-Socialist Economy: Embedded Practices and Livelihoods*, edited by J. Morris and A. Polese, 135–151. New York: Routledge.

Shevchenko, O. 2009. *Crisis and the Everyday in Postsocialist Moscow*. Bloomington: Indiana University Press.

Sik, E., and C. Wallace. 1999. "The Development of Open-Air Markets in East-Central Europe." *International Journal of Urban and Regional Research* 23 (4): 697–714. doi:10.1111/1468-2427.00223

Spector, R. 2008. "Bazaar Politics: The Fate of Marketplaces in Kazakhstan." *Problems of Post-Communism* 55 (6): 42–53. doi:10.2753/PPC1075-8216550604

Spector, R. A. 2009. *Protecting Property: The Politics of Bazaars in Kyrgyzstan*. Doctoral Dissertation. University of California, Berkeley.

Stewart, W., W. Watson, J. Carland, and J. Carland. 2003. "A Proclivity for Entrepreneurship: A Comparative Study of Entrepreneurs, Small Business Owners, and Corporate Managers." *Journal of Business Venturing* 14 (20): 189–214.

Taalaibekova, G. 2018. "The Changing Perception of Trade as 'Real' Work: The Unmaking of Soviet Workers at the Vernissage in Armenia." *Informal Markets and Trade Working Paper Series*, 8.

Vidritskaya, N. 2006. Neformal'naya Ekonomika v Sisteme Natsional'nogo Vosproizvodstva (Dissertatsiya Kandidatskoy Stepeni Ekonomicheskikh Nauk). Karagandinskiy ekonomicheskiy Universitet Kazpotrebsoyuza: Karaganda.

Volkov, V. 2002. *Violent Entrepreneurs: The Use of Force in the Making of Russian Capitalism*. Ithaca: Cornell University Press.

Werner, C. 1998. "Household Networks and the Security of Mutual Indebtedness in Rural Kazakhstan." *Central Asian Survey* 17 (4): 597–612. doi:10.1080/02634939808401058

Werner, C. 2004. "Feminizing the New Silk Road: Women Traders in Rural Kazakhstan." In *Post-Soviet Women Encountering Transition: Nation-Building, Economic Survival, and Civic Activism*, edited by C. Nechemias and K. Kuehnast, 105–126. Baltimore, MD: Johns Hopkins University Press.

Yalcin, S., and H. Kapu. 2008. "Entrepreneurial Dimensions in Transitional Economies: A Review of Relevant Literature and the Case of Kyrgyzstan." *Journal of Developmental Entrepreneurship* 13 (2): 185–204. doi:10.1142/S1084946708000922

The formal side of informality: non-state trading practices and local Uyghur ethnography

Rune Steenberg

ABSTRACT
This article approaches 'informal' modes of organization among Uyghur bazaar traders in Xinjiang and Kyrgyzstan in a complex context of increasing state regulatory measures and strong social networks. It captures this organization as a 'formal side of informality'. The practices comprising it are deemed 'informal' from a state-centred perspective, as they are not regulated by the state law or bureaucracy, but they still display a non-state formalization in the sense of being codified, regular and predictable to the traders. The article explores areas and examples of such 'informal' formality in the bazaar trade that are built around notions of morality, piousness, pride and shame. It pays special attention to oral contracts, purchase on credit, go-betweens and the status of profit. The article draws on participant observation and interviews in Xinjiang and Kyrgyzstan as well as on descriptions of trade morals and trade customs in ethnographic and folkloristic publications by local Uyghur scholars in Xinjiang.

Our people make up the most ancient trading nation. They value trading and practice it along a clean, halal path. They do trade that benefits people that doesn't hurt people. Money from such trade brings no happiness, it brings disaster. They have developed their own long-standing, advanced trade and business ethics.[1]
— Yarmuhemmet Tahir Tughluq, *Our Customs* (2009), 61

Don't make too much profit.[2]
Kifaytulla Rehmitulla, *Jewels of Moral and Custom* (2015), 157

Introduction

Traders were among those groups of the Uyghur population in Xinjiang that benefitted most from China's reform policies and the ensuing opening-up of the economy after 1979. They started bringing cheap consumer products from eastern China to Xinjiang and after the fall of the Soviet Union ventured into the newly independent Central Asian states to export Chinese commodities. This reinvigorated trade routes that had been out of use since the 1930s (Kreutzmann 1998, 292) and provided possibilities for economic success to Uyghurs, including those not well integrated into the Han-Chinese-dominated state and economy. The border trade flourished in the 1990s and 2000s, with a peak in the late 2000s and early 2010s. Uyghur traders' opportunities were curbed by strengthened regulation and securitization of Xinjiang in the wake of policy changes in 2009 and again in 2014 (Steenberg 2016a, 2018). With limited access to formal infrastructure the Uyghur traders rely on 'informal institutions', including networks of trust (Tilly 2005) and mutual support systems, in much of their trade. These are informal in the sense of not being regulated by the state law or bureaucracy (Graeber 2016; Hart 1973; Pfeffer 2016). They largely evade codified law and its execution by state actors such as police and tax collectors (Hardenberg and Fehlings 2016; Scott 2009). Yet, approaching these institutions from a less state-centred perspective, they can also be said to be quite formalized in the sense of being regular, predictable and sanctioned following more or less explicit social obligations and moral norms and customs.

This article draws on two kinds of material that are combined to approach this non-bureaucratic trading order. The first set of data is taken from ethnographic fieldwork among Uyghur trading communities in southern Xinjiang and Kyrgyzstan between 2010 and 2016 and more recent interviews with traders from these communities living abroad.[3] The second set of data derives from published Uyghur-language literature on customs and morals in Uyghur communities in Xinjiang, in which trade, bazaars and moral conduct are described by local intellectuals. Trading customs and morals have become much-revered elements of Uyghur intellectuals' depiction of local ethnic (民族 minzu, millet[4]) traditions, often covered in their own chapter in ethnographic publications. Unlike in most of the post-Soviet neighbouring states (Fehlings 2017; Humphrey 2002; Spector 2017; Taalaibekova 2018), in southern Xinjiang trading is immensely popular, and traders enjoy high prestige. Uyghur traders are known across the region for their skills in trade and their tightly knit and well-functioning networks of trust. These two sets of data are treated as different perspectives onto the same complex reality, each calling for different epistemological cautions.[5] After introducing the shifting political and economic context through two Uyghur traders' stories in 2013 and 2016, respectively, I briefly discuss my notions of informality and formality. Thereafter I present some institutions, moral codes and norms of the traders that constitute non-state (informal) ways of organizing the trade in an orderly, predictable (formalized) fashion.

Yüsüpjan

Yüsüpjan sat across from me on the padded platform before a streetside restaurant in Kashgar telling me of his last two years in Ürümchi (2011–2012). He, a friend and the friend's brother had pooled their funds and had managed to establish themselves in small-scale wholesaling of packaged food products, which they purchased from factories in the region and inland China to distribute to retailers in Ürümchi. Yüsüpjan had recently returned to Kashgar to look after his grandmother. He was eager to start his own business and shared his plans with me. He had a number of ideas, and we discussed them in detail. This was 2013; the economy in southern Xinjiang was still growing (see Table 1). Despite political tensions after the violence in Ürümchi in 2009 (Bovingdon 2010), attitudes among the growing numbers of middle-class and lower-middle-class Uyghurs in Kashgar were cautiously optimistic. Business opportunities were expanding, and while Uyghurs were clearly at a disadvantage on the job market for both government and private-sector employment, traders and other businesspeople from Uyghur communities were creating niches for themselves and prospering.

Table 1. GDP and value of exports for Xinjiang (2009–2016)

Year	GDP for Xinjiang (in billions of yuan)	Total value of exports from Xinjiang (in USD billions)
2009	427.7	10.9
2010	543.7	12.9
2011	661.0	16.8
2012	750.5	19.3
2013	844.3	22.2
2014	927.3	23.4
2015	932.4	17.4
2016	964.9	15.5

Source: National Bureau of Statistics of China. (http://data.stas.gov.cn, accessed 27 August 2018.)

Opportunities presented themselves as trickle-down effects from the massive government investment in Xinjiang in the wake of the first Xinjiang Meeting in May 2010 (Klimeš 2018), when the Develop the Great West economic strategy was expanded, including new pairing assistance programmes, and a special economic zone was established in Kashgar (Guo 2015, 39). Local Uyghurs employed their wide networks to take advantage of these opportunities in tourism, restaurant business and trade. It was difficult for Yüsüpjan to comprehend that I was merely academically interested in trade and didn't want to pursue my own business. Business and trade (*tijaret*) was all he thought about, he conceded. The same was the case for many of his peers, young men both urban and rural. When I asked my friends' children what they wanted to be when they grew up, 'tijaretchi' and 'sodiger' (businessman, trader) were common answers.

There were several good reasons for Uyghurs in Kashgar and Atush to want to pursue trade in 2013. Though the border trade with Kyrgyzstan no longer was as profitable as before 2011, it still gave access to both profit and freedoms not available to government workers. It provided the pride of being your own master and more freedom to practice your religion, which many of the traders explored with great enthusiasm during this time. Also, between 2010 and 2014 I was often told that a cadre's salary, though it had been raised to around 4000 yuan per month in 2014, was not enough to provide the kind of living standard that middle-class Uyghurs sought, including owning a house and a car.

Abduwéli

Three years later, in an apartment in Ürümchi, Abduwéli poured tea into delicate, gold-brimmed earless china cups. We were sitting on a cream-coloured couch in his living room, which was ornamented in the Uyghur style. He had moved here from Atush when his wife started university. He himself was a trader and had made good money selling baby products bought in Fujian in the early 2010s. He had gone abroad to Kyrgyzstan and Turkey before but now focussed his business on Xinjiang. The afternoon sun of late summer 2016 shone past the heavy curtains onto the low sofa table and the factory-produced carpet. Business had been difficult for a good two years now, and all of his profits were being eaten by advertising. Since my conversation with Yüsüpjan, both the political and the economic situations in southern Xinjiang had deteriorated significantly. At the Second Xinjiang Meeting in May 2014 (Klimeš 2018), the economic policies established in 2010 were given up and hard security prioritized, in the so-called People's War on Terror (Byler and Zolin 2017). The mobility of Uyghurs in south Xinjiang was seriously restricted, which damaged the local economy, including trade. After having grown at over 10% annually from 2009 to 2014, Xinjiang's GDP all but halted after 2014, and the total value of exports, which had more than doubled between 2009 and 2014, had fallen to below 2011 levels two years later (see Figure 1). Growing ethnic tension and suspicion of Uyghurs further complicated both business and employment.

Yet, real businessmen, Abduwéli proudly claimed, can go without profit for extended periods, waiting for their chance. If in need, he could draw funds from his peers, who trusted him completely to pay them back. This trust was necessary, as transactions on credit (*nisi*), on the basis of oral agreement, was the most common way of trading in Abduwéli's circles. He attributed the trust in some part to the rise in religiosity in the past two decades. Fear of God helps keep one's record straight, he said, though some had gone too far in their piousness, claiming it to be *haram* to trade with Han Chinese and isolating themselves. He found this wrong and problematic. At times like these, he admitted, when the economy suffers and profit is scarce, some will cheat and lie to secure short-term profits. Some even display piety as a cover for their deceit. In the stable and prosperous business environment before 2014, such people were kept out of the business circles or quickly found out, but in the past two years it had become more difficult (see Schröder, this issue).

My conversations with Abduwéli and Yüsüpjan were two of many I had on business, trust and religion with Uyghur traders in Xinjiang and Kyrgyzstan between 2010 and 2016. The strong ties of trust between Uyghur traders were also mentioned by the Han, Uzbeks and Kyrgyz I talked to. These relations provide the basis for trading networks across China to the bazaars in Xinjiang and Central Asia and trade at the small local bazaars, such as the Sunday Bazaar of Atush, where Abduwéli started his trading career. Here most of the trade is small-scale and goes unregistered, though a fee is paid to register and set up a stall cart. The business of these traders takes place within or in relation to the formal state economy, using state-sanctioned markets, state money and to some extent registration, but many of the transactions are informal in the sense that they are not bureaucratically accounted for or registered by state organs (Karrar and Fehlings 2016). Instead, as Abduwéli's examples illustrate, transactions are largely based on personal connections, a moral code of conduct tacitly accepted by the traders and a partly religious symbolic language to communicate adherence to this order. Many of the traders have poor Mandarin skills and are better integrated into their Uyghur social communities, networks and kinship groups than into formal systems of schooling, bureaucracy and banking. Much can be done through social relations and thus they do not require much access to formal infrastructure or the Chinese bureaucracy. Social networking, at which many of the traders from Kashgar and Atush excel and which is seen as a value in itself, is essential. It is formalized in rules of reciprocity and gift giving as well as kinship obligation.

Informality

The importance of informal political and economic practices in Central Asian has been widely recognized (Alff 2014; Humphrey 2012; Werner 1999), and much scholarly attention has been devoted to the areas in which formal and informal structures overlap and influence each other (Massicard and Trevisani 2003; Rasanayagam 2002, 2011). The analytical utility of the term has been questioned by several scholars (Polese and Morris 2015; Reeves 2009; Sindzingre 2006; Steenberg 2016b), and various different attempts at a definition have been made. The broad consensus and approach adopted here is that the term generically defines practices outside the control and regulation of state law and bureaucracy (Grzymala-Busse 2010, 312, 313; Polese and Morris 2015, 3). These very diverse practices are not very adequately or productively described by the same term, and this makes an attempt at a positive general theory of informal practices rather futile. Anthropology and other social sciences have long since developed sophisticated analytical approaches to different aspects of non-state social organization, including kinship or relatedness (Carsten 2000; Kuper 2008; Parkin and Stone 2004), gift giving and reciprocity (Gregory 1982; Sahlins 1972; Strathern 1992), trust networks (Tilly 2005) and community (Raport 2002). In contrast to the insights provided by such studies, practices deemed 'informal' are often seen as disorderly, unorganized, intransparent and unpredictable (Kanbur 2009, 4; Sindzingre 2006, 61). Such attributions express an implicit state bias, as the institutions and practices are primarily unpredictable and disorderly from a state-bureaucratic perspective (Steenberg 2016b; Spector 2017), while from the local perspective of those participating they are not. The strength of most informal institutions – and arguably a big part of why they persevere – is precisely that they are not disorderly or random. 'Informal' institutions have their own type of regularity, their own kind of *formality*. It is defined not by the state but by moral rules governing social relations more generally. They are therefore deeply embedded in local communities' customs and best approached with analytical tools provided by kinship anthropology, network sociology, moral philosophy and other subdisciplines concerned with different aspects of non-state forms of organization. These practices sometimes evade the state, sometimes copy it and sometimes co-opt it; the relation to the state can be of competition, contradiction or complementarity.

In this article I therefore use the term 'formal' or 'informal' (no italics) to differentiate whether a practice is regulated by the state and bureaucracy, while I use the term *formal* (in *italics*) to signify that a practice is regular, organized, predictable and orderly from the perspective of its practitioners. To call this type of non-state regularity, regulation and predictability *formality* may seem unnecessarily confusing, as it invokes two different meanings of the same word differentiated only by the italics. But this confusion, or Derridean *différance*, serves a specific purpose: It allows me to call into question the implicit and unquestioned primacy of the state as sole legitimate provider of and measure of order, inherent in the term 'informality'. By calling non-state, non-bureaucratic 'informal' organization *formal*, I seek to, at least temporarily, question and counter the hierarchy between state organization and non-state organization and plead for more systematic attention to the various non-state types.

Non-state *formality*

Abdulla's story gives us some insight into this regularity of non-state, non-bureaucratic organization of bazaar trade. The credit arrangements and oral agreements he mentions rest on notions of social obligations, religious morality and self-respect rather than on laws and state regulations. In an earlier article, I showed how the trust networks of Atush traders are often created around concrete relations between households from a single locality and their close relatives, whose members uphold gift-giving relations with each other (Steenberg 2016a). Such relations between the household members and relatives of the traders provide a foundation upon which personal trust between the traders can be established and developed. Helping and supporting each other in business becomes part of the gift-giving obligations between the households and thus easily sanctionable and institutionalized in the village *habitus*. Often traders from the same locality thus connected will explore new markets and businesses together, providing each other with full information and sharing their available infrastructure, contacts and funding. Personal loyalty and social obligation are central values in this. They figure as superior to striving for profit and sometimes to commitment to the law. In this sense they can be said to formulate a structural counterpoint to discourses condemning corruption, tribalism, regionalism and nepotism (Collins 2006; Gulette 2010; Luong-Jones 2002), as they invert the value hierarchy between commitment to the law and commitment to the community or specific individuals. This is important, as most practices we find in bazaars in Xinjiang and Central Asia relate to state regulations and institutions as well as to social networks and other non-state organization (Massicard and Trevisani 2003; Rasanayagam 2002; Spector 2017).

Informal trade and trust building does not stop at the boundaries of close social relations. Trust can be extended and built beyond these local networks. This is often done through relations forged in the trade that draw on the symbolism of long-standing social ties and that may develop into intertwined multidimensional involvement between the actors' families and wider network over time but that don't spring from these. The informal organization may also draw on other symbolisms, such as local or ethnic identity, religion, or even the logics of bureaucratic structures, as Regine Spector (2017) attests to at the Dordoi Market in Bishkek. Here, self-organized trade unions copied structures known to them from Soviet state organization. Regardless of the particular symbolism, and regardless of whether a direct or indirect option for sanctioning exists, a main prerequisite for these practices to be upheld is their framing recourse to morality: a sense of right and wrong, of what to do and what not to do. According to Uyghur social scientist Enwer Semet Qorghan (2007, 319), Uyghurs see trading as something great or holy (*ulugh*), and their conduct is influenced by trade morals and norms (*tijaret exlaq, mizanliri*), with a bit of superstition (*xurapiyliq*) mixed in. As in the adherence to law, here too there is a recourse to a higher authority in the form of God, fate, tradition or a notion of human decency.

In Uyghur such moral imperatives are primarily expressed in three idioms, each conveying a sense of prohibition or taboo: *ubal, yaman bolidu* and *haram*. *Yaman bolidu* refers to practices that are against custom and tradition. In some cases they are believed to lead to bad fortune. *Haram* is the Islamic notion of religiously prohibited behaviour that will have negative consequences in the afterlife. *Haram* is stronger than *yaman bolidu*, and most things deemed *haram* by the traders have connections to Islamic legislation, though not always in a straightforward or direct way. *Ubal* is based in local tradition, not Islam. But it has a similar severity as *haram* in the sense that actions so deemed are wrong in a spiritual or quasi-religious sense. This includes deep traditional taboos such as stepping on bread. *Ubal* is rarely used for practices related to trading, but the other two show up repeatedly both in oral discourse and in Uyghur publications on customs and traditions. Though *haram* is explicitly religious and *yaman bolidu* refers to traditional prohibitions, their use belongs to the same system of understandings of right and wrong among the traders, who generally see their moral conduct as both religious in type and traditionally Uyghur.

Enwer Semet Qorghan (2007, 321) recounts nine practices from a Uyghur trading *risala*[6] that are *haram* to Uyghur traders and seven things that are bad (*yaman*). The *haram*:

- Usury, exploitation.
- Fraud, disloyalty (not to honour an agreement).
- Eating at the house of someone who is in debt.
- Taking the possessions of orphans.
- Lying while trading.
- Manipulating the scales.
- Swearing in Allah's name while trading.
- Selling things whose price was settled to someone else for higher price.
- Swearing something untrue.

The seven *yaman* behaviours refer mainly to hygiene but also include 'speaking harshly to others'.

Kifaytulla Rehmitulla (2015, 157) mentions two rules that seem to have similar roots in Islamic law, though he does not use the word *haram*, most likely with a nod to censorship.

- Don't trade things that don't exist.
- Don't trade with trade (do not trade options).

He goes on to add two further rules that stand out as they do not seem to be connected to religious legislation but rather, like Enwer Semet Qorghan's rule of not speaking harshly, to considerateness in social conduct:

- Don't make too much profit.
- Both partners have to be satisfied with a deal.

These rules embed the commodity exchange within a logic of social obligations similar to gift-giving practices, where attention to the sentiments of the other side is crucial and a pure striving for profit is deemed inappropriate. Yarmuhemmet Tahir Tughluq (2009, 61–63) sums it up in a moral imperative: 'Trade must be fair; this is a vow of the Uyghur traders; both parties need to benefit, no one may wilfully cause losses to the other side.'

These are not merely principles of organization abstracted by scientific analysis. They display a degree of *formalization*, of standardization and fixation in rules and codes formulated among the traders. The principles are explicated through what Bourdieu (1977, 38) calls 'officializing strategies' and are formulated rules rather than merely regularities (22, 29). They constitute what Geertz (1973, 93) calls 'models for' and not just 'models of' social practice. In these quotes they are further fixed in text by intellectuals in a special form of abstraction, but their *formalization* exists in oral discourse too, in the representations and self-representations of the traders. Not everybody adheres to these rules, as Abduwéli attested, but neither does everyone to the state laws, and in both cases sanctions are in place, though they are of a very different form. While the state sanctions through fines and imprisonment, traders not honouring the moral code may be ostracized and lose their reputation, credibility and trustworthiness and thus their network and infrastructure for business – or, as importantly, be haunted by shame and loss of self-worth. Defaulted debt can be claimed from their relatives, or the business partner simply accepts that this investment has failed and produced loss. Either way, it brings shame and loss of face to the individual among the people most central to this individual's further success in business, as in life. This was demonstrated to me most tragically by a Uyghur trader now living in Europe. He had lost all his investment in Kyrgyzstan in the late 1990s and had been too ashamed to return to Kashgar.

Agreements – *kélishish*

By far the most deals among traders were struck on the basis of trust, Abduwéli said: by handshake and oral agreement, not by written contract. Both parties respect the agreement, neither backing out afterwards, he recounted, echoing Qorhgan's second and eighth *haram* items above. Yarmuhemmet Tahir Tughluq (2009, 63) writes that 'in all common transactions' (*lewzige hörmet qilidu*) the traders honour their word (see also Enwer Semet Qorghan 2007, 320). According to Abduwéli, demanding a written contract from a long-term contact would be an affront to most traders, who would feel their integrity insulted. In case one felt it necessary to draw up a contract, one would have to go about it very carefully and with 'reassuring words' (*chirayliq gep*). Among Uyghurs doing large and small business in Kashgar and Atush I often saw deals being struck, and deliverances given on credit (*nisi*), without any written evidence. This ranged from large, regular transactions, such as vacuum-packed, compressed bales of clothes and the weekly deliveries of meat for a restaurant, to smaller, irregularly timed transactions such as a shoemaker's service of cutting and sewing of 100 sheets of soft leather into leather socks (*meyza*) and the delivery of four bags of charcoal to a restaurant for grilling meat skewers on the night market. In all of these cases I saw goods being delivered and payment following later without any written contract. In the clothing trade both sides kept book of the exact number of shirts and sandals shipped, but the books were not compared or written in sight of the other. The charcoal producer wrote down his deliveries in a small booklet after returning home in the evening. In both cases the writing down served as an aid to memory and to keep track of earnings to calculate *sadaqa* in Ramadan. They were deliberately not done in sight of the business partner; this would have been an insult, insinuating that the other could not be trusted.

The preference for oral agreements does not result from a lack of written tradition or unfamiliarity with contracts in Xinjiang.[7] As Ildikó Bellér-Hann (2000) and Rian Thum (2014) both convincingly show, the oral and written traditions in Xinjiang do not contradict each other but expand on and complement each other. In some cases, a common written record is kept. The Atush traders I visited in Kadamjay in southern Kyrgyzstan in 2013 sold a large percentage of their goods to female Uzbek traders, who took them across the nearby border to sell privately in Uzbekistan. Lacking funds to invest, these women usually paid for the commodities only after they had been sold on. All purchases were written down and signed by both parties in both partner's notebooks. The Atush traders stayed together in shared apartments during their periods of trade in Kadamjay. Here too, all expenses were kept book of in written form. In both these cases, the type of trust display achieved by forgoing a common written record is not deemed necessary or appropriate, while in many business deals it is. In the case of the Uzbek female traders, the level of familiarity was low. No display of trust was expected, so it was deemed appropriate to demand a signature as proof of the transaction. Regarding household expenses, the trust between the traders living together is self-evident, and the written record as a memory aid poses no risk of insult and can thus be conducted openly and shared. This, I contend, is the defining difference: the oral contract is a symbolic performance of trust. It is used in situations where such a display is needed or appropriate.

Credit – *nisi*

Among the traders themselves, almost everything is purchased on credit (*nisi*), to be paid later. Each individual is personally responsible for repaying his debts and should strive to do this on their own account. As in many other contexts, repaying your debt is seen as a moral imperative with spiritual implications, as Kifaytulla Rehimtulla (2015, 157) and Enwer Semet Qorghan (2007, 320) note (see also Graeber 2011). This is expressed in the local notion of reciprocity as a value. Bellér-Hann (2008a, 2008b) has repeatedly pointed to reciprocity as a central ordering principle in pre-PRC Uyghur society, and my own research confirms its importance today. Uyghur scholar Ibrahim Rehimi (2014, 144) writes that the first phrase Uyghur children learn to spell in school is *élip ber* (take and give).

> Thereby they learn the customary rule [*qa'ide*] that every taking has a giving [*almaqning bermiki bar*]: if one has borrowed or in another way taken money or another keepsake [*amanet*] from people, it is a duty [*shert*] to give it back in time.

While this may not be a fact about the state educational system, it shows the importance given to this principle in Uyghur discourse. It smooths bazaar trade, as it allows the delays between agreement, delivery and payment necessary for both long-distance trade from coastal China to Kyrgyzstan and the sale of agricultural products on local markets. Sale on credit usually takes place between individuals with established connections or with a person of trust mediating between them. Among the Uyghur traders of Atush and Kashgar, I saw two forms of *nisi* trade: one in which the commodities were delivered first and the payment was to follow at a specified or unspecified later time, and one in which the payment was to follow when the acquired commodities had been sold on. The former was usually practised in the long-distance trade, including by the Atush traders in Kyrgyzstan and in Abduwéli's dealings in Ürümchi and Kucha. The reasons were in part organizational, to not hamper the flow of commodities and to collect and balance debts, saving transaction costs; but the practice also entailed a symbolic level on which trust was communicated and thereby built. Like a written contract, immediate payment suggests an anonymous relation of distrust and detachment. In cases where everything is formally registered and easily claimable before the law, trust is mainly of affective importance, but within informal, unregistered arrangements the trust and the social connections are essential for the system to function. This is also preferred by many of the traders.[8] As the earlier quotes by Enwer Semet Qorghan (2007, 321) and Rehimtulla (2015, 157) support, social harmony, positive sentiments and relations both have important functions and are viewed as values in themselves.

The second type of *nisi* arrangement, where the commodities are paid only after they have been sold on, was usually connected to a lack of liquidity and funds. The female Uzbek traders walking across the border in Kadamjay to buy small amounts of clothes and sandals from Uyghur traders did not pay till after they had sold their stock. Similarly, in 2013 several newly opened restaurants trying to become established had their charcoal delivered on *nisi* during phases with slumping business, paying after the next big holiday or in the tourist season. This type of *nisi* was seen by the traders involved as a form of money lending and expressed in the same idioms as direct borrowing. Abduwéli cited a Uyghur saying among traders: 'Séning bir mu tien pulingmu mende qalmisun, méningmu bir mu tien pulum sende qalmisun' (May not one cent of your money stay with me, and may not one cent of mine stay with you). This applies both to money lending and to credit sales. Here the tangibility of the money is played down and the transaction presented as a relation between specific, earmarked money and a person – the person to whom it rightfully belongs: the creditor. The connection between the given and the giver is discursively retained, much like in gift giving, which, in contrast to commodity exchange, has classically been defined as entailing the 'inalienability' of the given from the giver (Gregory 1982). This symbolically cements the obligation to return the given as a natural and moral imperative (compare Graeber 2011). For most of the small-scale Uyghur traders and other businessmen in Kashgar and Atush, amassing funds is done not through banks but through their social networks. Abdurahman from Atush, who in spring 2014 had just opened a *lengmen* restaurant in Kashgar at age 24, told me that his starting capital of 25,000 yuan had come from his father and uncles and that it was still their money, and thus the shop would remain in part theirs until he had paid back the entire loan. The idiomatic expression for lending money is *bérip turush* (lit.: to continue to give), which implies that the loan must be continuously given and renewed while it automatically (or shall we say morally) strives to return to its giver and owner.

Similarly, Yüsüpjan lent parts of the profit he had made in Ürümchi to his friends in trade. His money was working, Yüsüpjan laughed – it would be a waste if it just sat around idly. The money 'is working' both in the sense that it creates liquidity for traders in his network and thus also may be of help to him some day, but also in the sense that it 'works' at constituting his relations to those he lends the money to and to the network more generally through the social connections he thus builds and the reputation he acquires. The loans are paid back to the exact amount. No interest is taken. This would be usury (*jazanxorluq*), which is prohibited by Islamic tradition and, according to Yarmuhemmet Tahir Tughluq (2009, 63–64), 'one of the practices most hated by our people'.

Go-between – *bédik*

When doing business in an unregulated space (or when lacking confidence in the regulators), credit is tied to personal trust. This is built on the basis of showing moral integrity, often including some display of piousness, and – beyond personal acquaintance – with reference and reputation. Such a reference can be given by a common friend or some kind of mediator. The mediator in important ways connects personal relations and trust with the anonymous commodity economy by making a more secure (social) connection to the unfamiliar and unknown.[9] One of the central figures in Uyghur trade is the go-between (*dellal, bédik*), who mediates between buyer and seller. The professional *bédik* is mentioned by several Uyghur intellectuals as essential to the trade and as a carrier of Uyghur national or ethnic (*milliy*) tradition (Abdukérim, Hemdulla, and Xushtar 2008, 16). This figure has played an essential role in historical bazaars (Bellér-Hann 2008a, 97) and is today prominently found in animal markets (Ablet Nurdun 2009, 2; Eli 2010). In 2011 the Sunday Market near Döletbagh, slightly outside Kashgar, featured several square kilometres of gravel parking ground that was used for used car sales. Young men bought used cars in Gansu and Qinghai, drove them to southern Xinjiang and sold them in this huge market. Here, most trade was done with the help of a *bédik* who knew cars and prices, including the daily variations in the market, and could thus provide valuable information not accessible elsewhere. The high prices of cars meant handsome fees for the *bédik*, who crowded the market, actively approaching potential customers. At Kashgar's largest used mobile phone bazaar, at Güze across from the old potter's quarters, much younger men offered their brokering services. They generally expected no fee, hoping rather to learn about prices, preferences and the market to later establish themselves as mobile phone traders.

Abdukérim, Hemdulla, and Xushtar (2008, 16) describe two arrangements for sales through a *bédik*. In the first, seller and *bédik* agree on a price. The *bédik* then sells the commodity for any price for which he can find a buyer and keeps the difference. The original seller does not interfere. In the second, the *bédik* makes a connection between seller and buyer and moves back and forth between them; this is called *yeng sodisi* (sleeve trade), as the *bédik* tugs on the sleeves of seller and buyer in turn. When a deal is agreed on, the *bédik* witnesses the two shaking hands to seal the deal and receives a fee for his services, most often paid by the seller according to his profit. The latter practice is prevalent in long-distance trade, and many *bédik* in Ürümchi, Kashgar and Osh also act as interpreters, guides and cultural brokers for foreign traders (see Schröder, this issue; Mathews 2015). They approach potential customers in the markets or hotels, and their services are requested by retail traders buying stock in wholesale markets with which they are little familiar (Fehlings; Ibanez-Tirada and Marsden, this issue). In Kyrgyzstan some of the Uyghur traders needed go-betweens (here mostly called *dellal*) to deal with the state authorities or bazaar authorities or to connect with local Uzbek or Kyrgyz traders. The go-between in these cases functions as a guarantee for the other side until sufficient trust and entanglement has been established.

Go-betweens (not always professional) are widespread in all types of business in Xinjiang. Whether to secure a delivery contract for a restaurant or just to buy a new pair of shoes for the daughter, acquaintances with knowledge of these fields, good contacts or merely affinity with the market and good bargaining skills are asked to intermediate. After having spent a good year in Kashgar in 2010–2011 and having built up my own social network, I too was approached quite matter-of-factly for shoe purchases and train tickets. I was well acquainted with the shoe traders, selling look-alike Italian brands from Guangzhou and Wenzhou on Renmin Xilu, near the Chinese part of central Kashgar, and had become close with a family whose members worked in the Kashgar tourism department and had frequent dealings with the ticket offices.

A fee may be offered to intermediaries, even if they are not professionals, but usually in these cases the money is seen as a gift, a token of gratitude and fulfilling of reciprocity. This is the case at weddings, where the logic of a go-between is similar in many ways: here the bride's and groom's sides have the delicate marriage negotiations led by an intermediary or broker (*elchi*, *dellal*), usually an older woman from the neighbourhood of the groom's family (Bellér-Hann 2008a, 238; Dautcher 2009, 115–116; Enwer Semet Qorghan 2007, 122–123). She smooths out differences in expectations and makes sure nobody loses face or feels insulted, thus reducing risk, much like the *bédik*.

Accessing the market through an acquaintance introduces a personal relation into the anonymous commercial transaction. It invokes rules of social conduct and moral obligations and copies their symbolism to render the market transactions more predictable and trustworthy. There is a gradual slide from a marriage broker to a well-connected acquaintance helping with a purchase, to a professional go-between for price negotiations over livestock or cars. It ranges from the far social to the far commercial poles of exchange. For the professional *bédik* it is important to allude to these social relations and the trust in them, but also to keep in mind that the market works according to the principles of commercial exchange, the direct exchange of alienable commodities, without further obligations arising between the partners. The delicate distinction between social obligations connected to gift giving and the detached nature of commodity exchange (Gregory 1982) must be cautiously kept. Uyghur scholar Yarmuhemmet Tahir Tughluq (2009, 63) therefore stresses that a *bédik* may never portray it as an obligation to buy or sell. Both have to choose freely, or else it counts as force. In the context of trade, commercial striving is given primacy over the pressures of social and moral obligations. This is also reflected in a rule or superstition mentioned by Enwer Semet Qorghan (2007, 322): The first trade of the day should not be given on credit (*nisi*). The money made from this trade should not be given to anyone as loan or used to pay off debt, and before the first trade of the day is completed, one should not give *sadaqa* or other charity.

Profit and value

Profit (*payda*) is one of the central topics talked about by the Atush traders in southern Kyrgyzstan. Everybody is there to make profit. It is a main motivation for embarking on the trade endeavour, but as I have argued in a previous article (Steenberg 2016a), it is not the only motivation, nor the only aim pursued. Monetary profit is balanced against other values, and the price of profit is also considered. In 2013, I saw large numbers of Atush traders in Kyrgyzstan stay in business even after profitability had dropped significantly and many were incurring losses. Like Abduwéli in Ürümchi, they were willing to continue business without profit for long stretches of time. This was in part due to the social benefits in terms of consolidating and expanding their trust networks. Cultivating relations and fulfilling social obligations were viewed as more important than maximizing profit. Also, reputation, personal self-respect and 'fear of God' (religious adherence) often take priority over the monetary value of profit gains.

In his book *Jewels of Conduct and Customs* (Edep-qa'ide Jewherliri), Kifaytulla Rehimtulla (2015, 157), describes it as morally commendable for traders to 'not make too much profit' (*bek köp payda almasliq*), to ensure that both partners in a deal are satisfied and not to monopolize streets when peddling (*ushshaq tijaret*). The command not to make too much profit fits well with the conduct of the Atush traders sharing business niches or even leaving them to the others. One of the first shoe traders at the bazaar in Kadamjay had left the business. He said that he had made enough money to build a house for his son and pay for the wedding of his daughter, so he was happy to give others the opportunity. Some, coming from a more formal economic understanding, see this attitude as lacking in ambition and bad for Uyghurs' opportunities. A young professional who had lived abroad for many years and was now working for a Chinese firm in Ürümchi complained that many Uyghur businessmen retire early to commit themselves to religious practice and charity instead of seeking to expand their business, thus robbing the field of much needed experience and skill.

Conclusion

The institutions described here rely on values beyond those of a *homo œconomicus,* who strives to maximize profit while adhering only to state law. In the areas of trading practice not strictly regulated and sanctioned by a state, predictability and reliability are founded rather on reputation, pride, shame, self-respect, identity and religious piety. This is all evidenced in the examples above of Uyghur traders' preference for oral agreements, their credit arrangements, the institution of a go-between and the place of profit in the social value hierarchy. Social relations and their symbolism are central to the functioning of this kind of non-state *formality*, but at the same time the commercial realm is given a legitimate if limited primacy.

This article has shown the *formal* side of some of the informal elements, but we must keep in mind that these practices play out in a context that is not just structured along communities and kinship networks but also observed by the state. Most undertakings are hybrid practices, including some elements registered and controlled by the state and others following a social or religious moral order (Rasanayagam 2002, 2011). These practices in their current form would also not be possible without some state regulation, including measures against various kinds of violence, domination and exploitation. The Chinese state laws and police provide certain forms of protection, as Uyghur traders came to realize when trading in Kyrgyzstan in the 1990s, where the state was hardly present and the environment was considered dangerous. On the other hand, state laws are also sometimes used as weapons to hurt certain groups or suppress the competition. This has been experienced by Uyghur traders both in Kyrgyzstan, where the local competitors use their closer ties to the authorities, and in southern Xinjiang, where Han Chinese business elites have profited from a similar situation, especially in the wake of the Pairing Assistance programme and clamp-downs on minority cadres (Cliff 2016).

Outlook: state violence in Xinjiang

Informal practices and non-state organization in trade has been a two-edged sword for many Uyghurs. It has provided access to fields otherwise not accessible, and created basic security for traders without privileged access to government and formal infrastructure, but it has also become a liability for some, who have been increasingly targeted and criminalized by the authorities. Since 2017, many Uyghur traders and several of the authors I quoted have been detained, held for months in indoctrination facilities and received prison sentences. The excesses of violence against minorities in Xinjiang in the past three years can in part be seen as the forceful attempt by the Chinese state to end all informal practices and close any space not regulated by the state. This targets the very social relations, local traditions and notions of honour and piety that these communities are built on. The massive internments and intense surveillance are guaranteed to affect the informal *formalities* of Uyghur trade and society. How precisely, and which elements prove resilient or transformable, remains to be seen. Fieldwork in the region is currently neither feasible nor ethically defendable, which is one of the reasons I have turned my attention towards current Uyghur texts and the diaspora.

Notes

1. 'Xelqimiz eng qedemki soda milliti. Ular sodani qedirleydu, sodini halal, pak yol bilen qilidu, insanlargha paydisi tégidighan mehsulatlarning sodisini qilidu. Insanlargha ziyan yetküzidighan sodini qilmaydu. Bundaq sodida tapqan pulning berikiti bolmaydu, bala-qaza élip kélidu dep qaraydu. Ular uzaq esirlik soda-tijaret dawamida özige xas nahayiti ilghar soda-tijaret exlaqini barliqqa keltürgen.'
2. 'Bek köp payda almasliq.'
3. Between 2010 and 2016 I spent around 20 months in Xinjiang, with occasional trips to Kyrgyzstan and eastern China. During these visits I spent much time with traders and at bazaars in the region.
4. *Minzu* (in Uyghur, *millet*) means both nation and ethnic group. In China the term often connotes minorities, and in Uyghur the adjective *milliy* is used to mean 'Uyghur' and 'traditional' and has a positive connotation. For useful and comprehensive discussions of the term see Bovingdon (2010) and Mullaney (2011).
5. The traders' expression and employment of knowledge of trade practices as observed by me during fieldwork is aimed at reproduction and consolidation of the practices themselves, but also at their construction of a positive self-identity. The publications offer more generalized formulated information aimed more broadly at the construction of a positive Uyghur identity. This includes a tendency to idealize the practices, which I have tried to balance by comparison with my field observations. Authors, editors and readers are often intimately familiar with Uyghur business worlds, which raises their trustworthiness. Some books were mentioned by friends of mine engaged in business, and several traders expressed the wish to write about it themselves. I have later discussed the books with Uyghur businesspeople outside of China.
6. *Risalas* are crafts manuals passed from master to apprentice used all over Central Asia for centuries (Bellér-Hann 2008a, 325; Dağyeli 2011). Enwer Semet Qorghan does not say when this *risala* is from, but *risalas* were in use in Kashgar at least into the 2000s. I collected several photocopied manuals in 2011.
7. Legal documents, including contracts for money lending and sales, from the nineteenth century have provided the basis for much historical research on Xinjiang (Bellér-Hann 2008a; Thum 2014). Adil Muhemmet (2012, 280) mentions sale documents for land and water rights in Xinjiang from the seventeenth century, and Ibrahim Rehimi (2014, 12) accounts similar documents in the thirteenth century (see also Yarmuhemmet Tahir Tughluq 2009, 63).
8. To some degree, the two systems, adherence to formal regulations on the one side and following social conduct on the other, exclude each other or at least function as alternatives, not unlike Mauss's (1990) understanding of gift giving as a precursor for – or, if we remove the evolutionist undertones of his time's social theory, an alternative to – a formal legal system (see also Parry 1986).
9. In a well-regulated, fully available, non-discriminatory system, this function can be fulfilled by the law and bureaucratic institutions.

Disclosure statement

No potential conflict of interest was reported by the author.

Funding

This work was supported by Velux Fonden [Grant no. 111687]. This work was supported by the European Regional Development Fund [Sinophone Borderlands – Interaction at the Edges] Project number: CZ.02.1.01/0.0/0.0/16_019/0000791.

References

Abdukérim, R., R. Hemdulla, and S. Xushtar. 2008. *Uyghur Örp-Adetliri*. Ürümchi: Shinjang Yashlar Ösümler Neshriyati.

Ablet Nurdun. 2009. *Xinjiang soda-bazar tarixi toghrisida tetqiqat*. Ürümchi: Shinjang Universitéti Neshriyati.
Adil Muhemmet. 2012. *Qeshqer Medeniyeti*. Ürümchi: Shinjang Universitéti Neshriyati.
Alff, H. 2014. *Embracing Chinese Modernity? Articulation and Positioning in China-Kazakhstan Trade and Exchange Processes*. Working Paper Series 21. Bonn: Crossroads Asia Network.
Bellér-Hann, I. 2000. *The Written and the Spoken: Literacy and Oral Transmission among the Uyghur*. Berlin: ANOR.
Bellér-Hann, I. 2008a. *Community Matters in Xinjiang, 1880–1949: Towards a Historical Anthropology of the Uyghurs*. Leiden: Brill.
Bellér-Hann, I. 2008b. "Strangers Guests and Beggars in Xinjiang: The Ambiguities of Hospitality among the Uyghurs." *Etudes Orientales* 25 (1): 145–164.
Bourdieu, P. 1977. *Outline of a Theory of Practice*. Cambridge: Cambridge University Press.
Bovingdon, G. E. 2010. *The Uyghurs: Strangers in Their Own Land*. New York: Columbia University Press.
Byler, D., and N. Zolin. 2017. "Uyghur Migrant Life in the City during the People's War on Terror." Accessed 27 August 2018. http://www.youthcirculations.com/blog/2017/10/22/uyghur-migrant-life-in-the-city-during-the-peoples-war.
Carsten, J. 2000. *Cultures of Relatedness: New Approaches to the Study of Kinship*. Cambridge: Cambridge University Press.
Cliff, T. 2016. *Oil and Water: Being Han in Xinjiang*. Chicago, IL: University of Chicago Press.
Collins, K. 2006. *Clan Politics and Regime Transition in Central Asia*. Cambridge, MA: Cambridge University Press.
Dağyeli, J. E. 2011. *"Gott liebt das Handwerk": Moral, Identität und religiöse Legitimierung in der mittelasiatischen Handwerks-risāla*. Wiesbaden: Reichert Verlag.
Dautcher, J. 2009. *Down a Narrow Road: Identity and Masculinity in a Uyghur Community in Xinjiang, China*. Boston: Harvard University Asia Center.
Eli, A. 2010. "Donkey Bazaar, a Bazaar of Hell: An Investigation into Donkeys and Donkey Trading in Kashgar, Xinjiang, China." In *Economic Action in Theory and Practice: Anthropological Investigations*, edited by D. C. Wood, 159–185.
Enwer Semet Qorghan. 2007. *Uyghurlarda Perhiz*. Ürümchi: Shinjang Xelq Neshriyiti.
Fehlings, S. 2017. "From Chelnoki to Global Players: Encounters in the Context of Caucasian(-Chinese) Trade Since the 1990s." *Paideuma* 63: 183–205.
Geertz, C. 1973. *The Interpretation of Cultures: Selected Essays*. New York: Basic Books.
Graeber, D. 2011. *Debt: The First 5000 Years*. New York: Melville House.
Graeber, D. 2016. *The Utopia of Rules: On Technology, Stupidity, and the Secret Joys of Bureaucracy*. New York: Melville House.
Gregory, C. A. 1982. *Gifts and Commodities*. London: Academic Press.
Grzymala-Busse, A. 2010. "The Best Laid Plans: The Impact of Informal Rules on Formal Institutions in Transitional Regimes." *Studies in Comparative International Development* 45 (3): 311–333.
Guo, R. 2015. *China's Spatial (Dis) Integration: Political Economy of the Interethnic Unrest in Xinjiang*. Waltham: Chandos.
Gulette, D. 2010. *The Genealogical Construction of the Kyrgyz Republic: Kinship, State and Tribalism*. Leiden: Brill.
Hardenberg & Fehlings. 2016. *Informality Reviewed: Everyday Experiences and the Study of Transformational Processes in Central Asia and the Caucasus*. Working Paper Series on Informal Markets and Trade 2.
Hart, K. 1973. "Informal Income Opportunities and Urban Employment in Ghana." *Journal of Modern African Studies* 11 (1): 61–89.
Humphrey, C. 2002. *The Unmaking of Soviet Life: Everyday Economics after Socialism*. Ithaca: Cornell University Press.
Humphrey, C. 2012. "Favors and 'Normal Heroes.' The Case of Postsocialist Higher Education." *HAU: Journal of Ethnographic Theory* 2 (2): 22–41.
Ibrahim Rehimi. 2014. *Uyghur en'eniwi örp-adetliri*. Ürümchi: Shinjang Xelq Neshriyati.

Kanbur, R. 2009. *Conceptualising Informality: Regulation and Enforcement*. V.V. Giri Memorial Lecture, delivered at Lucknow on 13 December, 2008, to the Golden Jubilee Conference of the Indian Society of Labour Economics. www.people.cornell.edu/pages/sk145.

Karrar, H., and S. Fehlings. 2016. *Informal Markets and Trade in the Caucasus and Central Asia: A Preliminary Framework for Field Research*, Working Paper Series on Informal Markets and Trade 1.

Kifaytulla Rehmitulla. 2015. *Edep-qa'ide Jewherliri*. Ürümchi: Shinjang Xelq Bash Neshriyiti, Shinjang Xelq Sehiye Neshriyati.

Klimeš, O. 2018. "Advancing 'Ethnic Unity' and 'De-Extremization': Ideational Governance in Xinjiang under 'New Circumstances' (2012–2017)." *Journal of Chinese Political Science* 1–24. doi:10.1007/s11366-018-9537-8.

Kreutzmann, H. 1998. "The Chitral Triangle." *Asien Afrika Lateinamerika* 26: 289–327.

Kuper, A. 2008. "Changing the Subject: About Cousin Marriage, among Other Things." *Journal of the Royal Anthropological Institute* 14 (4): 717–735.

Luong-Jones, P. 2002. *Institutional Change and Continuity in Post-Soviet Central Asia*. Cambridge: Cambridge University Press.

Massicard, E., and T. Trevisani. 2003. "The Uzbek Mahalla: Between State and Society." In *Central Asia: Aspects of Transition*, edited by T. Everett-Heath, 205–219. London: Routledge.

Mathews, G. 2015. "African Logistics Agents and Middlemen as Cultural Brokers in Guangzhou." *Journal of Current Chinese Affairs* 44 (4): 117–144.

Mauss, M. [1950] 1990. *The Gift: The Form and Reason for Exchange in Archaic Societies*. London: Routledge.

Mullaney, T. 2011. *Coming to Terms with the Nation: Ethnic Classification in Modern China*. Berkeley: University of California Press.

National Bureau of Statistics of China. 2009–2016. http://data.stats.gov.cn, accessed 27 August 2018.

Parry, J. 1986. "The Gift, the Indian Gift and the 'Indian Gift'." *Man* 21 (3): 453–473. doi:10.2307/2803096.

Parkin, R., and L. Stone. 2004. *Kinship and Family: An Anthropological Reader*. Oxford: Wiley-Blackwell.

Pfeffer, G. 2016. *Verwandtschaft als Verfassung: Unbürokratische Muster öffentlicher Ordnung*. Baden-Baden: Nomos.

Polese, A., and J. Morris. 2015. "Introduction: My Name is Legion. The Resilience and Endurance of Informality beyond, or in Spite of, the State." In *Informal Economies in Post-socialist Spaces. Practices, Institutions and Networks*, edited by J. Morris and A. Polese, 1–21. New York: Palgrave Macmillan.

Raport, N. 2002. "Community." In *Encyclopedia of Social and Cultural Anthropology*, edited by A. Barnard and J. Spencer, 173–177. London: Routledge.

Rasanayagam, J. 2002. "Spheres of Communal Participation: Placing the State within Local Modes of Interaction in Rural Uzbekistan." *Central Asian Survey* 21 (1): 55–70. doi:10.1080/02634930220127946.

Rasanayagam, J. 2011. "Informal Economy, Informal State: The Case of Uzbekistan." *International Journal of Sociology and Social Policy* 31 (11–12): 681–696.

Reeves, M. 2009. "Beyond Economic Determinism: Microdynamics of Migration from Rural Kyrgyzstan." *Neprikosnovennyi zapas* 66 (4): 262–280.

Sahlins, M. D. 1972. *Stone Age Economics*. Chicago: Aldine-Atherton.

Scott, J. C. 2009. *The Art of Not Being Governed: An Anarchist History of Upland Southeast Asia*. New Haven: Yale University Press.

Sindzingre, A. 2006. "The Relevance of the Concepts of Formality and Informality: A Theoretical Appraisal." In *Linking the Formal and Informal Economy: Concepts and Policies*, edited by B. Guha-Khasnobis, R. Kanbur, and E. Ostrom, 58–74. Oxford: Oxford University Press.

Spector, R. A. 2017. *Order at the Bazaar: Power and Trade in Central Asia*. Ithaca: Cornell University Press.

Steenberg, R. 2016a. "Embedded Rubber Sandals: Trade and Gifts across the Sino–Kyrgyz Border." *Central Asian Survey* 35 (3): 405–420.

Steenberg, R. 2016b. "The Art of Not Seeing Like a State: On the Ideology of 'Informality'." *Journal of Contemporary Central and Eastern Europe* 24 (3): 293–306.

Steenberg, R. 2018. "Accumulating Trust: Uyghur Traders in the Sino–Kyrgyz Border Trade After 1991." In *Routledge Handbook on Asian Borderlands,* edited by A. Horstmann, A. Rippa, and R. B. Bennike, 294–303. London: Routledge.
Strathern, M. 1992. "Qualified Value: The Perspective of Gift Exchange." In *Barter, Exchange and Value: An Anthropological Approach*, edited by S. Hugh-Jones and C. Humphrey, 169–191. Cambridge: Cambridge University Press.
Taalaibekova, G. 2018. "The Changing Perception of Trade as 'Real' Work: The Unmaking of Soviet Workers at the Vernissage in Armenia." *Informal Markets and Trade Working Paper Series*, 8.
Thum, R. 2014. *The Sacred Routes of Uyghur History*. Cambridge, MA: Harvard University Press.
Tilly, C. 2005. *Trust and Rule*. New York: Cambridge University Press.
Werner, C. A. 1999. "The Dynamics of Gift Exchange in Rural Kazakstan." In *Contemporary Kazaks: Cultural and Social Perspectives*, edited by I. Svanberg, 47–72. Richmond: Curzon.
Yarmuhemmet Tahir Tughluq. 2009. *Qa'ide yosunlirimiz*. Ürümchi: Qeshqer Uyghur Neshriyati; Shinjang Güzel Sen'et-foto Süret Neshriyati.

Markets at sacred sites: the globalized mobility and informality of the Armenian religious fairs

Yulia Antonyan

ABSTRACT
Along with other globalizing forces such as migration and proselytism, religious markets have played a key role in the transformation of religious practices in Armenia. This article focuses on the intersection of mobility and markets through mobile fairs, which are temporarily organized at shrines on pilgrimage days. Market vendors tend to travel from shrine to shrine across Armenia throughout the year, each following his or her own trajectory. In this article I examine how such markets are organized, how and by whom they are run and controlled, how small-scale mono-confessional markets become part of transnational globalization processes, and how the marketplace is embedded in the pilgrimage ritual, changing and modernizing its traditional meanings and structure.

Introduction

This article seeks to answer two questions. First, what impact have the new market economy and informal commercial practices had on religious practices in Armenia? And second, how have new forms of mobility that have taken shape since the Soviet Union – coupled with recent globalizing processes – changed ritual and iconography, and transformed ideas of piety, spirituality and religious morality?

The breakup of the Soviet Union led to the collapse of political and economic systems, and a de-secularization of the post-Soviet space. In Armenia, it also led to a reconfiguration of how religion was practised through the creation of markets for religious goods at pilgrimage sites. Since the early 1990s, these markets have proliferated rapidly. The items sold in these markets – amulets, candles, crosses, plaster figurines – are produced in Armenia or imported from outside, from countries such as China, Turkey, Iran, or Lebanon. Today, these markets have become integral to the practice of religion in Armenia, in particular on the pilgrimage circuit.

I use 'religious market' as shorthand for both the market in religious artefacts, and marketplaces in the vicinity of churches and pilgrimage sites. Based on new empirical evidence I collected through fieldwork, I illustrate how in Armenia, informality was an essential component of the post-Soviet religious market. The religious market became one of the ways through which citizens negotiated the new state.

At a basic level, informality is evident in the networks that underlie commercial transactions in religious markets, not dissimilar to bazaar trade by independent traders in the Caucasus and Central Asia (Fehlings and Karrar 2016). The importing of goods, and the revenue generated through the sale of merchandise, are also largely undocumented and outside the state regulatory mechanism, again, not unlike independent commercial practices elsewhere in the former Soviet Union (Yalçin-Heckmann 2007; Özcan 2010; Karrar 2017).

As a result of the itinerant nature of the market, religious markets at pilgrimage sites tend to be less structured than a regular market (Tocheva 2014; Kormina 2017). Unlike in regular retail markets, relations between the sellers and the local or church authorities, as well as relations amongst the sellers, and between sellers and purchasers, must be continuously negotiated, sometimes through discreet means. But the formal and the informal are not disparate categories (Fanselow 1990); in fact, a characteristic of the informal market in religious merchandise, as we shall see, is that it is frequently embedded in regular markets. The difference between religious and non-religious goods also blurs, as religious artefacts (amulets, crosses, or figurines) are frequently sold alongside non-religious items, such as food, toys, or sunglasses. Hence, the market not only has different characteristics, but is an assemblage of representations (Coleman and Eade 2018, 8).

Religious markets have characteristics that differentiate them from other markets in consumer goods. Religious markets are inextricably associated with questions of identity and morality and often speak to issues of purity and impurity, power and miracles (Starrett 1995; Coleman and Eade 2018). The commodification of religion usually means the diversified reification of power and practice (Weller 2008). Here, the market plays a key, mediating role between the secular and religious interpretations of the same phenomena. For instance, desire for profit may be impeded by moral or ideological restrictions imposed by religion (Starrett 1995), just as nationalism and identity may be commodified through symbolic form (Muzakki 2008; Melkumyan 2009; Kormina 2017). Thus, the market, as a primarily secular phenomenon, has a tendency to 'secularize' people's approaches to the religious by imposing a transactional price and consumer form (Askew 2008). At the same time, the market enlarges the space in which the religious operates, blurs the boundaries between the religious and the secular, and diversifies the forms, imaginary or not, of the religious and the sacred (Eade and Sallnow 1991).

The market*place* is a socially constructed site. While the organization and the ascribed meanings of religious markets may appear similar to those of non-religious markets (Watson 2009), I argue that concepts of charity, purity and morality are *informally* ascribed (Sinha 2008; Gudeman and Hann 2015; Kapustina 2016; Kormina 2017). The spatial layout of the market is influenced by social hierarchies among the participants, where the place of each individual may be determined, in particular, by the degree of his or her association with the sacred (Gell 1982; Zaidman and Lowengart 2001; Zaidman 2003).

By focusing on the pilgrimage economy, I follow recent scholarship that has begun to pay attention to the economic dimensions of pilgrimage. While some early scholars of pilgrimage saw a bifurcation in the structural, ideological, semantic, social, political and economic aspects of pilgrimage (Eade and Sallnow 1991; Morinis 1992; Coleman and Eade 2004), others refute such a dichotomy, arguing that modern pilgrimage is semantically and practically merged with consumption practices (Askew 2008; Sinha 2008; Reader 2014). There is also a tendency to see pilgrimage as a part of transnational economic processes (Coleman and Eade 2018). The pilgrimage economy builds infrastructure to provide pilgrims with shelter, food and souvenirs, and creates spaces where the exchange is twofold: goods and money on one side, and religious values, forms and ideas on the other. Pilgrimage transforms the economic, political and social lives of villages, towns and cities near churches and shrines (McKevitt 1991; Cohen 1992; Reader 2014).

Finally, note that the pilgrimage economy is, by its very nature, a globalized market. Mobility – in the form of pilgrimage and proselytism, as well as religious tourism – mediates the exchange process in the religious market (Beyer 2007; Coleman and Eade 2018). Here there is utility in thinking about globalization as processes that can either be top-down, 'from above' (formal market regulation and control in the religious sphere), or grass-roots globalization, 'from below' (Portes 1996; Mathews and Alba Vega 2012). Like formal/informal and religious/secular, the two globalizations are meshed. Combined, these lead to the dissemination of new ideas and forms, the emergence of new trade routes, new contacts and new 'centres', and new consumption patterns (Coleman and Eade 2018). In this article, I deepen our understanding of the nature of interactions between religion, market and modern globalized consumption by focusing on specific cases of itinerant pilgrimage markets and illustrating how they are woven into the act of religious pilgrimage, changing and modernizing its earlier meaning and structure.

This article is based on fieldwork over a three-year period (2016–2018), primarily in the neighbouring regions of Kotaik, Aragatsotn, Gegharkunik and Yerevan. It was qualitative research based on methods of participant observation and unstructured/semistructured short interviews, as well as occasional conversations (with up to several tens of people per field visit), accompanied by photography and voice/video recording, when possible. Sampling was random, categorized by function, gender and age. Such a methodology is justified by the specifics of the field: most markets lasted for just one whole day and acted as whole organisms; the constant mobility and determination of pilgrims, as well as the busyness of sellers, made it difficult to conduct long interviews (half an hour being a good result); some could be acquired only through participant observation, by engaging in activities fitting the context (buying things, participating in the ritual, asking for advice and guidelines, etc.). Some participants were not easily interviewed at the shrines themselves (e.g., priests). I filled this gap by speaking with them on other occasions.

Seven shrines—the Amenaprkich (All Savior) of Nor Gyugh, the Getargel monastery near Arinj Village, the Poghos-Petros shrine (St. Paul and Peter) near Akunk Village, Surb Gevork (St. George) of Aramus Village, Surb Nshan (St. Sign) of Kotaik village, the Surb Hovhannes (St. John) of Mayakovski Village, and Tsaghkevank (Monastery of Flowers) of Mount Ara, all in the Kotaik or Aragatsotn region—are particularly central to this research. They form a chain of traditional annual post-Easter pilgrimages that occurs every Sunday for a period seven weeks (except for Tsaghkevank's pilgrimage, which is on Thursdays). The pilgrimage is widely known in Armenia and attended by locals and outside visitors alike (Abrahamian et al. 2018, 70–71).

Religions markets in Armenia

Armenia is dotted with hundreds of monasteries, churches and shrines.[1] Many of these function as pilgrimage sites. While they are visited year-round, on the set pilgrimage days the number of visitors can rise sharply, from several hundred to several thousand. On these days, informal mobile fairs selling religious paraphernalia (e.g., icons, amulets, religious souvenirs) and other goods (e.g., food, drinks, toys, jewellery) are organized in the vicinity.

Such periodic religious markets have existed in Armenia at least since the early 1980s.[2] Many elderly sellers I spoke with told me they began the trade in religious artefacts during the final decade of the Soviet Union (indeed, my childhood memories include sellers, mostly women, of 'evil eye amulets' and home-made sweets at Geghard Monastery in Kotayk Province). While some artefacts, such as religious souvenirs, were manufactured in Armenia, others, such as divine images and icons, were imported from other countries (e.g., China, Russia, Turkey, Iran, Lebanon) and distributed through informal networks. One of my informants told me that since the late 1970s he had been using his personal family network to import religious iconography from Greece.

The years preceding and following the Soviet collapse saw a sharp increase in public religious activity in Soviet and the subsequent post-Soviet societies (Steinberg and Wanner 2008; Pelkmans 2009; Hann 2010). In Armenia, this resulted in the re-institutionalization of traditional churches (the Armenian Apostolic, Catholic and Evangelical Churches). The increasing popularity of public religious practice was supported by people's newfound mobility, which in turn facilitated a new market for religious artefacts.

Hence, production and trade of religious artefacts, or goods with religious iconography, became commonplace after the Soviet Union. Consider a village cooperative in Ararat region, which was established in the mid-1990s as a profit-making enterprise. The cooperative produced goods for everyday household use, such as plates, dishes and trays, imprinting on them images of a religious nature like Da Vinci's Madonna, and thus catering to two markets, those who needed the household consumer item, and those who bought the goods for religious purposes, to keep them in their homes as religious artefacts or to donate them to shrines. Such objects (clocks, trays, dishes) can still be found at shrines and provincial churches. Thus, in a short time religious motifs became a popular and sought-after form of iconography. Also, as Melkumyan (2009, 93) has pointed out in his study of the Vernissage market in Yerevan, religious motifs came to be associated with an Armenian national culture. This also led to the emergence of small, informally organized workshops, where a few people worked, making artefacts such as evil eye amulets or crosses.

As the trade in religious sites increased sharply in the 1980s and the early 1990s, the sellers of religious artefacts began attracting the attention of the *militia* (the Soviet equivalent of the police). Although the militia was a formal institution, it relied on rent extraction – an informal mechanism – in exchange for protectionism. Since the end of 1990s, the role of the extortionist, informal networks represented by militia and its successors – police and local authorities – has receded, giving way to the formalized control of the Armenian Apostolic church. Currently, sellers are charged a daily fee by the Church or the local market administrators of approximately 1000 drams (nearly USD 2). Although the process of rent extraction has been decriminalized, this remains an informal, non-contractual rent required by the Church (or market authorities) for cleaning the space and ordering the market. Some vendors also reported that they were allowed to set up their stalls for free, indicating some flexibility.

The religious markets I describe are both stationary and mobile.[3] Stationary markets may be held daily, weekly or seasonally in a particular place. These are usually close to monasteries that are popular tourism destinations. The goods they sell address the religious and tourist needs of buyers. These stationary markets are built structures in the form of a permanent bazaar surrounding a religious site. Mobile fairs, by contrast, are more informally organized; they emerge on the occasion of a religious festival, a traditionally fixed pilgrimage day, or other proper event, and are immediately dismantled once the event is over.

The stationary/mobile dichotomy is also characterized by an infrastructural difference. Stationary markets have fixed infrastructure, such as sheltered stands, paved alleyways, or a permanent awning. The sales outlets are registered under the vendors' names, and administered by some sort of official power, such as the Church or local authorities. They are embedded in local social relations and hierarchies (see e.g. Gell 1982). Outsiders rarely work at these markets, and job opportunities are mostly limited to the inhabitants of the neighbouring towns and villages. Such a market may also be part of a tourism-related infrastructural network, and visiting it may be a part of a tour programme.

By contrast, mobile markets change their configuration whenever they are set up. More often than not, people are free to choose where to sell; place selection is on a first-come basis.[4] The fee is the same for everyone. While stationary markets have their microclimates and social microstructures in which people work side by side for years, the same is not the case with mobile markets. Vendors at mobile markets have their own trajectories of mobility, which may take each of them to different places. The mobile market does not resemble a community structured through reciprocal relations. For example, at stationary markets a trader may borrow money from an adjacent seller when he or she does not have the change to return to a customer. Such everyday transactions become difficult in a mobile market; I have observed a buyer being kept waiting for 15 minutes as a vendor travelled to the other end of the fair to borrow money from a relative to make change.

Mobile markets also tend to have an overtly festive atmosphere, created by music, rope-dancers, and an abundance of special foods for sale. Their function is subordinated to the religious festival. They may start and end differently, depending on the numbers of pilgrims, which can vary greatly. Business may be intertwined with religious practices. Unlike stationary markets, which also can maintain some festive functions, such as musicians or painters to provide entertainment for tourists, the mobile markets *are part* of the folk feast. They do not have the amusers and the amused, but rather everyone is a participant, both vendors and buyers (Figures 1 and 2).

Pilgrimage as ritualized consumption and exchange

The pilgrimage economy in Armenia consists of structured rituals and unstructured folk festivals. Economic transactions are part of both, as pilgrims typically pass through the market twice. They transit the market to go to the shrine to perform the necessary rituals, and after they leave the shrine, they may partake in a festival. Over the course of my fieldwork I noticed how, travelling to the shrine, pilgrims appeared purposeful, purchasing ritual items: sacrificial animals, amulets to be blessed by the priest or presented to the shrine, or candles. But on their return, the same pilgrims frequently participated in the festival, buying food, drinks, souvenirs and presents. Put differently, markets constitute one of the central loci of the pilgrimage process and the pilgrimage topology. Hence,

Figure 1. Market at the Surb Nshan shrine.

irrespective of the structured-versus-unstructured marketplace I described above, there are two separate pilgrimage economies that may operate in the same locale.

Besides the ritual significance of what one brings to the shrine, what one takes away is equally important. Here, as I observed, the market plays an enabling role. According to popular belief, nothing can be taken from the saint. People who take anything, indeed, any object or donated food, from the shrine would be engaging in a religious transgression and become subject to such punishments as misfortune and disease. On the other hand, many pilgrims want a memento of the sacred. The market resolves this contradiction: an object purchased at a pilgrimage site can serve as a sacred fragment. Although it is accompanied by a financial transaction, the purchased item acquires religious significance, and may be seen by the purchaser as imbued with power. As Ian Reader (2014, 144) puts it, the souvenirs from the pilgrimage site 'could be taken back home as reminders of its aura and as means through which they could express their love for their families and friends and connect them to the place itself'.

According to Bajc, Coleman, and Eade (2007), there is a bifurcation in the semantic centre of the pilgrimage space between the shrine and the marketplace. A Christian discourse would see the marketplace as a secular, material space, in opposition to the sacred space of the shrine (Eade and Sallnow 1991, 25–26). This can create tensions. Recently a small market beside the Goshavank Monastery was accused by the Armenian media of 'doing business' in the Church, leading the local priest to argue that commercial transactions were not inconsistent with religious morality (Davtyan 2016).[5] On this topic, I found a diversity of opinions. A few of the pilgrims I interviewed expressed unease with how close the marketplace has become to the shrine. For others, it was a non-issue; they saw the marketplace as a regular market, and would use it to buy goods that had no religious significance, such as toys. This is not just a fusing of shrine and marketplace but a blurring of boundaries between the sacred and the secular. While there is a tension,

Figure 2. Stall at the Poghos-Petros shrine.

this tension is informally negotiated, leading to an integration of the commercial and religious spheres. In fact, the way to the shrine, usually ritualized and mythologized, now is totally overlapped with the market. The practice of travelling to the shrine, previously full of real or symbolic suffering and obstacles to be overcome, now has become a pleasant consumer's walk through market stalls.

Space organization and social hierarchies, power and profit

As I have noted, mobile fairs occupy the space around the shrine; pilgrims walk through the market to the shrine. The use of market space depends on the spatial layout of the territory: the longer the walk to the shrine, the more extended the marketplace. Sometimes, when the shrine is close to the road or within the city borders, as are the shrines in the village of Kotaik and Yerevan's Church of the Holy Virgin, then the amount of territory for market use is determined by local authorities. For example, on pilgrimage days at the Yerevan church, in the district of Nork, police cars block the street leading to the church, prohibiting traffic. This creates a path to the shrine, which serves as a marketplace. But in most cases the limits of the marketplace are not clearly delineated; they tend to be flexible. The odd stall and mobile vendor may be encountered as far as a few kilometres from the main marketplace; at the other end, the first stands and stalls are next to the shrine.

Previously, I described how proximity between market and shrine led to discord over the encroachment of merchants into religious space. This can be resolved through various controlling and limiting mechanisms. For example, when police cars block a road, the police are exercising power over the passage of pilgrims and controlling their mobility in the vicinity of the church or shrine. The police are also in a position to remove retailers they consider to be in the wrong place. In other cases, clergymen limit trade in the immediate proximity of the church, not allowing particular types of goods, like candles, on which the Church itself has a monopoly.[6] In other instances – as one may observe in the shrines of Poghos-Petros, Amenaprkich and others – the control is weak or absent, and marketplaces may expand considerably.

For the last 20 years, the Armenian Apostolic Church has sought (sometimes unsuccessfully) to control even the smallest local shrines that are not on the pan-Armenian (including Diaspora) tourist and pilgrimage routes. This is done within the overall 'reconquista' strategy of the Church, aiming at expansion of institutional Christianity versus its vernacular, grass-roots forms (Antonyan 2011). Previously, ritual at a shrine had been confined to lighting candles, or symbolic acts like binding handkerchiefs around the branches of a wishing tree. But in recent decades, rituals have become more complex; from the early morning, when the priest arrives at the shrine, he conducts a liturgy and then blesses pilgrims throughout the day. This formalization of pilgrimage rituals attracts more pilgrims. One consequence is that the surrounding marketplace has also expanded steadily to respond to this greater traffic.

Unlike stationary markets, mobile markets have few local people selling goods. Being a vendor is a business that entails networking with producers of handicraft goods, usually in significant quantities. Few locals would sell something at a market that is held only once a year, though some of the poorest villagers may come to sell inexpensive and expendable items such as candles and labdanum; however, peddling by locals often takes the form of asking for alms. Locals participate as pilgrims rather than traders.

The vendors at the mobile fairs usually come from other cities and villages, sometimes quite distant ones. For example, I have met traders from Abovyan, Gyumri, Echmiadzin and Yerevan at shrine fairs in the Kotaik region. The traders I interviewed had individual travel itineraries across the country. How do they know about the pilgrimages? Typical answers indicate that this is information constantly shared and transmitted orally by vendors and pilgrims: 'We learn from each other, go to the sites once, and then fix them in our itinerary.' Here is how one of the vendors at the market in the village of Aramus described his itinerary:

> Now we are at Kotaik shrines. The next will be Kaputan and Tsaghkavan, followed by the village of Samo of Tashir [a local oligarch], then three or four other shrines in Tashir, after that a couple of churches in Alaverdi, those of Sanahin, Akhtala, then come three shrines in Gavar and Martuni, and after that the Yerevan shrines, like Kharberd and Dvin. The season will end with shrines in Charentsavan and Aruch. Each of us has his own list.

These circuits are not random but predicated on mobility between the points traders consider conducive for trade. As vendors told me, there are fewer fairs in southern Armenia, and more in the north (Yerevan is considered the geographical centre). They explained this as a result of control and formalization of trade by the clergy in the south; there is less control over community shrines in the north.

Outside of the clergy, merchants and regulatory authorities, there is another group that can exert authority over shrines: people who may be locally acknowledged as 'keepers' of a particular shrine.[7] These are local people who live near a shrine and who have a spiritual association (through dreams or visions) with it that is acknowledged by others in the surrounding area. This association usually takes the form of an earlier family responsibility to take care of the shrine. The function of 'keeper of the shrine' has never been legally registered, but in Soviet times, when all historical and cultural monuments were the property of the state, such people might be officially assigned the position of guard or cleaner (depending on gender) in exchange for a small salary. In years past, the 'keepers' of a particular shrine may have sold candles and labdanum to visitors (in the Soviet period, church candles were difficult to acquire). Currently, as the churches and shrines are being given back to the Armenian Apostolic Church, the clergy do not accept the authority of these people. However, in many cases, the 'keepers' manage to preserve their rights and functions, leading to a prolonged conflict over who controls the shrine, which spills over into market control. One interview with a 'keeper' at a shrine reveals this conflict:

> There was no priest here earlier. He appeared two years ago. My grandmother took care of this shrine, then my mother and now my uncle. The priest has just realized he can make a lot of money here, he comes and blesses and takes money for that. But he never picks up a broom to clean the place after the pilgrimage. Who has to do it? We do it for free. But it is he who takes the money.[8]

Marketplace classifications

There is typically a range of commercial activity at the marketplace, which serves as a map of informal social organization and hierarchies: peddlers who are in fact seeking alms, craftspeople, those who offer ritual services, and retail sellers. In the first three of these categories, people position themselves in relation to the Church and market through claims to a greater moral order.

People seeking alms are not typically beggars but peddlers of candles (or other small items) who put psychological pressure on shrine visitors to buy their wares. Peddlers mix with the crowd, stop pilgrims, narrate their personal tales of misfortune, and ask visitors to buy candles. They tend to be located along the beginning of shrine markets to catch those who have not yet bought candles. Peddlers are lowest in the market hierarchy; they are frequently harassed by the police or clergy and accused of disturbing pilgrims or violating church monopolies. While I observed them to be a cohesive group, coming to each other's defence, they are rarely supported or defended by shopkeepers.

Craftsmen sell their own handmade produce, such as religious symbols and motifs, amulets, statuettes, framed icons, mock-ups of churches and *khachkars* (traditional tombstones), handmade toys and sweets. These tend to be family businesses. They are usually in the centre of the market. Their production corresponds to the religious and festive activities at the fair. Craftspeople typically make claims to piety to emphasize the authenticity of their goods. For example, a vendor may describe themselves as an activist of the church or a conductor of the church choir. Valer, a maker of plaster compositions, said:

> I have been in this business for seven years. I came from Uzbekistan, where I had lived for 27 years. I was a car mechanic there. Here in Armenia I started doing everything that is related to plaster. Ours is a family business. I make plaster figurines, my daughter-in-law makes compositions from them, and my son gets raw materials from shops. We can hardly make ends meet, but I like this job. If I could, I would have done it from the very beginning. Our goods are blessed by a priest, we had them blessed in the morning.

Gevork, vendor of hand-made souvenirs, said:

> This is a family business, I do the shaping and carving, and my wife does the design on the compositions. We have always done this work because we are believers. We believe in God. Previously we did well, but now things have changed, trade is declining, people do not have money, they don't buy as much as before.

The third category is people who provide ritual services, such as slaughtering a sacrificial animal for a small fee.[9] The Armenian sacrifice ritual, *matagh*, assigns the sacrificial function to the eldest male member of the family, the patriarch.[10] In recent years, sacrifice has become a paid service in religious markets. The amount paid is not negotiated: 'Whatever you want to or can give is good for me.' Those offering the service pretend not to demand a fee; ostensibly they will agree to whatever is offered, because of the religious nature of the service, which is not to be sold. The ritual of sacrifice includes not only the act of slaughtering, but also drawing crosses with the sacrificial blood on the foreheads of the family doing the sacrifice. Interestingly, even this very intimate part of the ritual is being done by the men doing the slaughtering. Because of the strong competition among them, the people offering this service tend to be on the lookout for clients; once a potential client has been identified, they follow them and offer their services. Once, during the pilgrimage at the shrine of Poghos-Petros (St. Paul and Peter), in the Kotaik region, I was interviewing a person who had been repairing one of the chapels at the shrine. Our conversation was interrupted by an old woman, who asked us where she could find someone to slaughter her rooster. My informant raised his hand to show the way, but then changed his mind and offered his own services for free. The woman agreed immediately, happy she did not have to climb the hill, and insisted on paying ('No, money is a must'). My informant slit the throat of the rooster, waited until it was quivering, then dipped his finger into its blood and drew crosses on the foreheads of the woman and her granddaughter. The amount of remuneration had not been discussed, but the women stretched out her hand to offer some coins (about USD 1.50 in Armenian drams). The man took them, and looked satisfied.

The last group of people in the religious marketplace are the retailers. Unlike the peddlers, the craftspeople and those offering ritual services, the retailers do not place themselves in relation to the church. Rather, they resell merchandise that has been purchased in wholesale markets in Yerevan, such as Petak, Surmalu or Malatia. They may sell religious souvenirs, amulets, ritual paraphernalia, icons and sacrifice animals, and also toys, jewellery, clothes, sunglasses, food, drinks, trinkets and keyrings. To attract buyers, some shopkeepers even offer lotteries, where the winner gets twice as many goods at the same or a lower price. Most retailers are positioned at the edges of the main arteries, rarely crossing the imaginary line where the sacred space begins. For the retailers, selling in a religious market is a business decision to earn a living. Selling in the vicinity of a shrine is no different from selling elsewhere, and their commercial practice, including tax payment or evasion, is little different from practices elsewhere. Garnik, a retailer, told me that he had been trading in religious markets since *perestroika*. He had started out selling toys and sporting goods, but now sold a variety of goods. 'We used to pay the militia so they would allow us to trade at these sites," he said; 'now we pay into the Church Fund.' For him, payment to the militia or the Church was similar in that it was rent. 'The rest has not changed', he added, before feeling compelled to tell me that when he came to the shrine, he did light candles.

Since the collapse of Soviet Union, the sellers are more diverse in age and gender. In the Soviet period, most were elderly women, reflecting the social and economic marginality of religious markets.[11] Currently, men and women of different ages are represented, which may imply the growing economic and social significance of these markets. Until the early post-Soviet years, the festive character of these fairs was reinforced by street performers, such as clowns and rope-dancers, who were considered to have special magical powers. More recently these have declined in number, and lost their ritual potency.[12]

As we can see from the above, informality can be read into the range of commercial transactions at the religious market. At one level, it is a question of where one locates oneself in relation to the Church. In addition, informal norms, which are widely acknowledged, determine the price of religious services. And finally there is a hierarchy of vendors, from peddlers to retailers. What is common to all of them is that the household economy is being run through work at the religious market. But this work is marked by precarity. With the exception of some retailers, the people I am describing buy and resell (or produce and sell) only inexpensive goods; although I did not quiz my informants about money, it was obvious that none of them would be considered to have surplus money to invest in business. And the market they are catering to is one with marginal purchasing power; it is a market for the poor.[13] This too ends up being an informal mediating mechanism; the 'poverty' of the mobile fairs mediates tension between the sacred and the secular, the church/shrine and the market, the pure and the impure. Purchasing something from religious markets becomes an act of charity ('Let's buy something from these people so they can earn a bit' is frequently heard), reinforced by the lack of bargaining.

While bargaining is intrinsic to bazaar transactions in Armenia, this is not always the case in religious markets. The purchase of ritual goods – sacrificial animals, candles, gifts to the saints – or magical objects is meant to be free from bargaining. If one is buying an animal to sacrifice (a sheep, a rooster) one should not bargain, or the sacrifice will not be accepted. For the same reason, the seller should not ask too high a price. (Thus, sellers at regular, non-religious markets usually ask the reason for purchasing an animal to determine what price to ask.) Over the course of my fieldwork, I never observed anyone trying to bargain down the price of goods. Price negotiation works in other discreet ways. A vendor sensing a buyer's uncertainty after hearing the price may lower the price or offer a better deal, like two for one. This happened to me on several occasions. In our conversations, vendors offered goods at a particular price point. As I was thinking how to politely explain that I did not need any of what they were selling, the price would be lowered. Occasionally, I found it impossible to refuse. Over the course of my fieldwork, I have come to conclude that the silent taboo against bargaining makes the trade in religious markets take the form of symbolic exchange of goods, rather than commerce. In this way, it can be thought of as an informal reconciliation of market and trade with Christian morality.

However, purchasing goods at these marketplaces is frequently accompanied by other types of personalized transactions with the vendor. Vendors typically stress quality (or lack thereof), aesthetic perception and authenticity. This is not a depersonalized marketplace; these are personalized transactions of the kind Clifford Geertz (1978) described in his work on bazaars. One shopkeeper told me, 'People want to buy something. They do not ask price. Rather, they ask: which one is better, more beautiful? We help them.' Another shopkeeper, who explained the differences between crosses to me, explained that the more expensive one was from Lebanon, and the cheaper one was from Iran. He added he would not advise me to buy the cross from Iran, because it was of low quality and might quickly lose its colour. Of course, the more expensive crosses might be more profitable.

Religious goods: a globalized market

In a mobile market, the preference is to sell goods that will sell quickly and not create a backlog of unsold inventory. Such items are inexpensive and include candles, food and sacrificial animals. Higher-priced souvenirs are avoided, as is iconography that appeals only to particular denominations. One of the vendors at the Poghos-Petros shrine market told me that she avoided selling Orthodox icons because only tourists from Russia would buy them. However, one can increasingly find amulets with the identical inscriptions in different languages, mostly Russian, sometimes English. 'They are for migrants', vendors explained. These are Armenians who work in Russia and who are visiting their home village and family. They may buy amulets with Russian-language blessings to gift on their return to Russia.

As we have noted, many pilgrims want to acquire souvenirs at religious markets. Sometimes, exactly what they choose is unimportant, so long as the object corresponds to the sacred journey. It may be something with purported power, like an amulet or talisman to ward off evil or magic. In every case, it serves as a memento of the journey. As one seller told me,

> People buy things to take home and keep them as a memento on this or that sacred place. Everyone who comes here would like to buy something. Most pilgrims buy something at every sacred site they visit. You may see dozens of different souvenirs in their homes.

A nearby woman who was buying several models of churches, all in different colours, explained that she bought them as gifts for her relatives. Some buy sacred images or religious artwork to take them to their local shrines as gifts.

The goods sold at religious markets must include particular signs and symbols for them to be considered religious. Usually, this means a cross, or an image of Christ or the Virgin Mary. Small, hand-made clay or plaster models of *khachkar*s and churches, images of saints and icons are commonly recognized as objects of Christian worship. In other goods, however, the religious character is not so obvious. These include three-dimensional figurines of pomegranate trees (sometimes with images of saints on them), styled like vegetative ornaments from Armenian miniatures; they look like art objects, but may also be associated with the Armenian medieval Christianity.

The item itself is less important, as the correct motif makes even keyrings, necklaces and ashtrays into religious objects. Items that have become popular recently include compositions made of plaster, bag cloth, seeds, plastic flowers, and decorative ribbons. In the centre of these items is a figurine of Christ, the Virgin Mary or a few pigeons. In the absence of book-selling at religious markets, one finds wooden, plaster or cardboard replicas of the holy book in different sizes, shaped as talismans, souvenirs, and even keyrings.

Although this production is done by hand, the craftsmen use printings and models for plaster figurines bought at the Vernissage, the Yerevan art and souvenirs market. They also use other readymade materials such as artificial flowers and fruits, printed images purchased at different markets, and mostly imported from China or Iran. In general, all these hand-made things are of very low quality, easy and fast to make, and priced to sell. One sees many people, especially young women,[14] with a woodcut and burnt tree or a plaster figurine composition in their hands. Thus, the newly emerged fashion for kitsch-styled compositions has transformed into a kind of festive ritual.

A few of the larger retailers travel to the country of manufacture, although most of them buy the goods in Yerevan's wholesale markets. China is the largest exporter of manufactured religious artefacts. Some amulets, especially those offering protection from the evil eye, are imported from India, the Middle East or even Turkey. As Russia is one of the main consumers of the religious goods made in China, among the China-made religious goods on sale at the Armenian markets are a great many Russian Orthodox souvenirs, such as printed icons, religious postcards and talismans, designed for Russian clients. Surprisingly, many of the talismans and souvenirs with Armenian-language blessings and prayers on them are made in Turkey.[15] As one vendor explained to me, Turks download Armenian patterns and inscriptions from the Internet and use them for talismans they export to Armenia. The vendor I was speaking with himself periodically travelled to Istanbul to buy amulets. This is typical of a global market, when an item may be designed in one country and manufactured in another because of the low cost of production. Thus, Starrett (1995, 57), in his study of the religious market in Egypt, describes ritual objects with Arabic inscriptions exported from Japan. Consider another example from Armenia: fashionably designed metal baptism crosses being sold by a retailer at one of the religious markets. The retailer told me that he placed orders with the Armenian diaspora in Lebanon, to whom he forwarded designs.

Mass production and export of religious goods shapes the demand for religious objects. Gradually, forms and designs that have never been traditional in a particular locale are adopted, homogenizing the religious market. For instance, now Armenian images of saints are styled like Eastern Orthodox icons. The gonfalon-shaped talismans used to bless and protect houses, cars and offices were first brought to Armenia from the countries of Eastern Christianity (Eastern Orthodoxy and Catholicism), such as Russia, Syria, Lebanon and Greece, approximately 10 years ago, and now their 'glocalized' Armenian-language analogues are popular in the local market.[16]

Religious goods face a test of authenticity to ensure their sacred property. In ordinary markets sellers may use a set of communication techniques to extol and warrant the quality of goods (Fanselow 1990, 253), but in the religious market a different type of authenticity is being proffered. How are such claims supported? As Zaidman and Lowengart (2001, 15–22) describe, in markets in Jerusalem authenticity is achieved through the mediation of retailers who demonstrate the extent of their personal or inherited proximity and connection to the shrine. In Armenia, the origin of goods is also significant. Thus, in warranting the authenticity of talismans, icons and crosses retailers claim they were bought in Echmiadzin, the spiritual centre of Armenians, where all objects allegedly have been blessed by priests. Goods imported from famous religious centres outside Armenia (for example, Jerusalem) also engender greater trust. Religious objects obviously belonging to other Christian denominations (Orthodoxy or Catholicism) may be given more authenticity and trust than local ones because of common stereotypes of greater piety and devotedness of Orthodox and Catholic Christians.[17] In general, vendors (or at least many of them) feel that they are pilgrims, too. Many try to find time throughout the day to visit a shrine and light candles. The exposed piety may be a part of their marketing strategy to ensure if not the authenticity, then the religious efficiency of their goods.

Conclusion

As elsewhere in the world, the economy of religion includes the formation of markets of religious goods. Mobile fairs of religious goods in Armenia emerged in late Soviet times, when ideological control over religious processes and rituals was weak. The collapse of the Soviet Union allowed the emergence of a new religious market, which adopted forms through multiple informal negotiations: between vendors and the Church, between vendors and local authorities, between vendors and the local elite, and finally between vendors and buyers, and among vendors themselves. In this entire process, meaning was (re)ascribed and maintained even as religious sites were brought under the Armenian Apostolic Church. While the religious market, broadly construed, has become partly institutionalized, it remains largely mobile, which allows a high degree of informality.

Originally considered auxiliary to religious sites, markets have gradually become a constituent part of the ritual of pilgrimage, and the consumption of religious goods has become a part of religiosity. People would not approach a shrine without passing through a fair, which topographically and semantically coincides with the passage up to the sacred place. Trade, the selling and buying of goods, thus transforms religious practice itself. Transaction becomes intrinsic to religious practice, and indeed can stand in for other pious acts. Merely being present in the sacred place and selling or buying something may be enough for someone to have a sense of having accomplished an act of devotion – some do not even try to enter the shrine, because it is crowded, and the entrance is often encumbered by pilgrims.

Being ritualized, the process of consumption at the shrine market has acquired specific features that differentiate an ordinary market from a religious fair. These features include a festive atmosphere, the supposed authenticity of goods and piety of vendors, avoidance of overt bargaining, and the ritual necessity to buy something from the vendors, especially the poor. At the same time, the informal and festive nature of such fairs has much to do with a different type of administrative control, and a spontaneous and self-organized and regulated trading process, and with the free and continuous adoption of new forms of religious materiality and consumption, aided by globalization. Informal mechanisms of import and export, production and mediation lead to a blurring of the boundaries between material and practical manifestations of religion. The transnational market in religious goods in general, and religious markets and fairs in particular, thus becomes one of the effective ways of grass-roots globalized transformation of patterns and models of religiosity, and religious materiality and practice.

Notes

1. The dominant religion in Armenia is the Eastern branch of Christianity, the Armenian Apostolic Church. Although there are other Christian denominations and other religions in Armenia (of lesser extent), the pilgrimage markets I describe are usually identified with the Armenian Apostolic Church.
2. This might be explained by the emergence of small businesses in the 1970s and early 1980s, which were illegally built into the system of Soviet industry and later legalized as cooperatives (collective enterprises) after Gorbachev's *perestroika*.

3. Note that while stationary and mobile markets usually do not exist side by side in urban areas, stationary markets near churches sometimes spontaneously expand during festivals (on Easter and Christmas), enveloping the permanent trading units (Antonyan 2018).
4. There appears to be relative equality between traders at mobile fairs, an unwritten rule by which everyone has a right to get a spot for his or her stand or stall. Everyone pays the same fee. The best spots belong to those who were first in line, though in some cases, when virtually the same community of traders attends the same pilgrimage sites for long enough, each of them may already fix their own places, which are not contested by newcomers.
5. This has resulted in new interpretations of religion and history from within the Church. For example, priests of the Armenian Apostolic Church justified the presence of markets near churches by arguing that when Jesus banished merchants from the Temple he was not opposed to the trade: he was banishing animals that made the Temple impure. Thus, the Armenian Apostolic Church had no objection to the sale of ritually 'pure' objects such as candles and icons (Minasyan 2015).
6. Most shrines do not have a candle and religious goods shop inside or on the surrounding grounds, so the church's monopoly over candles is not effectively maintained. And pilgrims typically prefer to buy candles from retailers (because they are cheaper), unless the Church's control over the candle trade is vigilant.
7. There is no common term for keepers; they may be called *pahogh*, *pahak* (guard), *nayogh* (caretaker), or even *ter* (master), depending on the case.
8. However, the conflict may also be settled through the negotiated division of responsibilities or even the ultimate withdrawal of a priest, as at the Amenaprkich shrine.
9. In some cases, 'bloodless' sacrifices may be encountered. A pigeon's leg is incised, its blood is used for religious manipulations, and the bird is let go.
10. Officially, sacrifice is not part of the religious ritual of the Armenian Apostolic Church. Priests thus cannot interfere in the slaughtering process. But prior to it they are supposed to bless the salt that is fed to the animal. If priests are not supposed to be present during the pilgrimage, then the salt can be blessed beforehand.
11. For more on Soviet and early post-Soviet markets, see Mandel and Humphrey (2002).
12. This happens within the framework of an overall decline of the tradition of vagabond arts, due to many reasons that I don't specify here.
13. Armenia is still a poor country, where over 25% of the population live in poverty.
14. I am not focusing on gender issues here, but according to my observations, women are more involved in gift exchange and feel more responsible for buying something for friends or family members. Once, I overheard a phone conversation in which a woman was making a detailed report on what she would bring to her relatives from the pilgrimage site. Gender norms and relations may also account for other dynamics of the market, including differing roles, religiosity patterns, consumption preferences, and so on. However, due to volume and thematic limitations, these issues are set to one side.
15. Armenia and Turkey, though neighbouring countries, do not have diplomatic relations because of political disputes going back to the Armenian Genocide (1915) and the Karabakh War between Armenia and Azerbaijan (1991–1994). However, the informal economic relationships between small entrepreneurs have been actively developing over the last decades.
16. I used 'glocalized' in narrow business and larger anthropological terms. See Robertson (2010, 334–343).
17. My own field notes contain many utterances about the greater piety of Catholic and Orthodox believers in comparison to Armenians.

Disclosure statement

No potential conflict of interest was reported by the author(s).

References

Abrahamian, L., Z. Hambardzumyan, G. Shagoyan, and G. Stepanyan. 2018. "The Chain of Seven Pilgrimages in Kotaik, Armenia: Between Folk and Official Christianity." In *Sacred Places, Emerging Spaces: Religious Pluralism in the Post-Soviet Caucasus*, edited by T. Darieva, F. Muhlfried, and K. Tuite, 70–96. New York: Berghahn.

Antonyan, Y. 2011. "Religiosity and Religious Identity in Armenia: Some Current Models and Developments." *Acta Ethnographica Hungarica* 56 (2): 315–332. doi:10.1556/AEthn.56.2011.2.4

Antonyan, Y. 2018. "Interplay between the Formal and the Informal: Marketing Religious Festivals in Contemporary Armenia." In *Transnational Trade, Trade Routes, and Local Marketplaces between the Caucasus and Central Asia*, edited by S. Fehlings and H. Melkumyan, 65–77. Tbilisi: Universal.

Askew, M. 2008. "Materializing Merit: The Symbolic Economy of Religious Monuments and Tourist-Pilgrimage in Contemporary Thailand." In *Religious Commodification in Asia: Marketing Gods*, edited by P. Kitiarsa, 89–119. London: Routledge.

Bajc, V., S. Coleman, and J. Eade. 2007. "Introduction: Mobility and Centring in Pilgrimage." *Mobilities* 2 (3): 321–329. doi:10.1080/17450100701633742

Beyer, P. 2007. "Globalization and Glocalization." In *Sociology of Religion*, edited by J. Beckford and N. J. Demerath III, 98–117. Los Angeles, CA: Sage.

Cohen, E. 1992. "Pilgrimage and Tourism: Convergence and Divergence." In *The Sacred Journeys: The Anthropology of Pilgrimage*, edited by A. Morinis, 47–63. Westport, CT: Greenwod Press.

Coleman, S., and J. Eade. 2004. "Introduction: Reframing Pilgrimage." In *Reframing Pilgrimage: Cultures in Motion*, edited by S. Coleman and J. Eade, 1–26. London: Routledge.

Coleman, S., and J. Eade. 2018. "Introduction: Communities, Contracts and Capitalism." In *Pilgrimage and Political Economy: Translating the Sacred*, edited by S. Coleman and J. Eade, 1–20. New-York: Berghahn.

Davtyan, S. 2016. "Tavushi temi arajnord: 'Muraba vacharvum e voch miain Goshavankum, ailev Haghartsnum" [Head of the Tavush Diocese: jams are sold not only in Goshavank and Haghartsin]. *Iravunk*. March 13. https://www.iravunk.com/news/1395.

Eade, J., and M. J. Sallnow. 1991. "Introduction." In *Contesting the Sacred: The Anthropology of Christian Pilgrimage*, edited by J. Eade and M. J. Sallnow, 1–29. London: Routledge.

Fanselow, F. S. 1990. "The Bazaar Economy and How Bizarre is the Bazaar Really." *Man*, New Series 25 (2): 250–265.

Fehlings, S., and H. H. Karrar. 2016. "Informal Markets and Trade in the Caucasus and Central Asia: A Preliminary Framework for Field Research." Working paper no. 1 on Informal Markets and Trade.

Geertz, C. 1978. "The Bazaar Economy: Information and Search in Peasant Marketing." *American Economic Review* 68 (2), Papers and Proceedings of the Ninetieth Annual Meeting of the American Economic Association: 28–32.

Gell, A. 1982. "The Market Wheel: Symbolic Aspects of an Indian Tribal Market." *Man*, New Series 17 (3): 470–491.

Gudeman, S., and C. Hann. 2015. "Introduction: Ritual, Economy and the Institutes of the Base." In *Economy and Ritual: Studies of Postsocialist Transformations*, edited by S. Gudeman and C. Hann, 1–30. New York: Berghahn.

Hann, C. 2010. "Broken Chains and Moral Lazarets: The Politicization, Juridification and Commodification of Religion after Socialism." In *Religion, Identity, Post-Socialism*, edited by C. Hann, 3–22. Halle: Max Planck Institute for Social Anthropology.

Kapustina, Y. 2016. "Rynok islamskikh tovarov i uslug v Dagestane: praktiki potrebleniya i obschestvennye diskussii" [The Market of Muslim Goods and Services in Dagestan: Practices of Consumption and Public Debates]. *Gosudarstvo, religiya I tserkov' v Rossii i za rubezhom* [State, Religion, Church in Russia and Abroad] 2: 176–202.

Karrar, H. 2017. "Kyrgyzstan's Dordoi and Kara-Suu Bazaars: Mobility, Globalization and Survival in Two Central Asian Markets." *Globalizations* 14 (4): 643–657. doi:10.1080/14747731.2016.1201323

Kormina, J. 2017. "Pravoslavnye yarmarki i religioznaya modernost" [Orthodox fairs and religious modernity]. In *Experto Crede Alberto: Collection of Articles Dedicated to 70th Anniversary of Albert Baiburin*, edited by A. Piir, 229–247. Saint Petersburg: European University Press.

Mandel, R., and C. Humphrey. 2002. *Markets and Moralities: Ethnographies of Postsocialism.* Oxford: Berg.
Mathews, G., and C. Alba Vega. 2012. "What is Globalization from Below? Introduction." In *Globalization from Below: The World's Other Economy*, edited by G. Mathews, G. L. Ribeiro, and C. A. Vega, 1–17. London: Routledge.
McKevitt, C. 1991. "San Giovanni Rotondo and the Shrine of Padre Pio." In *Contesting the Sacred: The Anthropology of Christian Pilgrimage*, edited by J. Eade and M. J. Sallnow, 77–97. London: Routledge.
Melkumyan, H. 2009. "Presenting and Re-Shaping Armenian Traditional Culture in Yerevan Vernissage." *Bulletin of Mesrop Mashtots University* 3 (7): 92–96.
Minasyan, M. 2015. "Inch iravunkov ekeghetsum momer ev ajl baner en vacharum?" [Do they have the right to sell candles and other things in the church?]. *168.am*. October 27, http://168.am/2015/10/27/554033.html.
Morinis, A. 1992. "Introduction." In *The Sacred Journeys: The Anthropology of Pilgrimage*, edited by A. Morinis, 1–30. Westport, CT: Greenwod Press.
Muzakki, A. 2008. "Islam as a Symbolic Commodity: Transmitting and Consuming Islam through Public Sermons." In *Religious Commodification in Asia: Marketing Gods*, edited by P. Kitiarsa, 205–219. London: Routledge.
Özcan, G. B. 2010. *Building States and Markets: Enterprise Development in Central Asia.* Hampshire: Palgrave MacMillan.
Portes, A. 1996. "Globalization from Below: The Rise of Transnational Communities." In *Latin America in the World Economy*, edited by W. P. Smith and R. P. Korczenwicz, 151–168. Westport, CT: Greenwood Press.
Pelkmans, M. 2009. "Introduction: Post-Soviet Space and the Unexpected Turns of Religious Life." In *Conversion after Socialism: Disruptions, Modernisms and the Technologies of Faith*, edited by M. Pelkmans, 1–16. New York: Bergham books.
Reader, I. 2014. *Pilgrimage in the Marketplace.* London: Routledge.
Robertson, R. 2010. "Glocalization: Time-Space and Homogeneity and Heterogeneity." In *Readings in Globalization: Key Concepts and Major Debates*, edited by G. Ritzer and Z. Atalay, 334–343. Oxford: Wiley-Blackwell.
Sinha, V. 2008. "'Merchandizing' Hinduism: Commodities, Markets and Possibilities for Enchantment." In *Religious Commodification in Asia: Marketing Gods*, edited by P. Kitiarsa, 169–185. London: Routledge.
Starrett, G. 1995. "The Political Economy of Religious Commodities in Cairo." *American Anthropologist* 97 (1): 51–68. doi:10.1525/aa.1995.97.1.02a00090
Steinberg, M. D., and C. Wanner, eds. 2008. *Religion, Morality and Community in Post-Soviet Societies.* Bloomington: Indiana University press.
Tocheva, D. 2014. "The Economy of the Temples of God in the Turmoil of Changing Russia." *European Journal of Sociology* 55 (1): 1–24. doi:10.1017/S0003975614000010
Watson, S. 2009. "The Magic of the Market Place: Sociality in a Neglected Public Space." *Urban Studies* 46 (8): 1577–1591. doi:10.1177/0042098009105506
Weller, R. 2008. "Asia and the Global Economies of Charisma." In *Religious Commodification in Asia: Marketing Gods*, edited by P. Kitiarsa, 15–30. London: Routledge.
Yalçin-Heckmann, L. 2007. "Openings and Closures: Citizenship Regimes, Markets and Borders in the Caucasus." In *Caucasus Paradigms: Anthropologies, Histories and the Making of a World Area*, edited by B. Grant and L. Yalçin-Heckmann, 273–298. Berlin: LIT.
Zaidman, N. 2003. "Commercialization of Religious Objects: A Comparison between Traditional and New Age Religions." *Social Compass* 50 (3): 345–360. doi:10.1177/00377686030503008
Zaidman, N., and O. Lowengart. 2001. "The Marketing of Sacred Goods: Interaction of Consumers and Retailers." *Journal of International Consumer Marketing* 13 (4): 5–27. doi:10.1300/J046v13n04_02

The bazaar in ruins: rent and fire in Barakholka, Almaty

Hasan H. Karrar

ABSTRACT
Since 2013, there have been multiple fires in bazaars in Almaty, Kazakhstan. Most of these fires have occurred in Barakholka, the largest bazaar in Central Asia, known for wholesaling in apparel, shoes and low-quality household and office supplies. Ownership of Barakholka is opaque. Using recurrent Barakholka fires as my point of departure, this article contributes to scholarship by describing how the clearing of old bazaars is followed by new property developments and the imposition of new rent regimes. In doing so, I argue that fire – a form of ruination that not only destroys property but also severs networks and people's relationship to a place – is illustrative of how the bazaar, as a new institution within an emerging post-Soviet market economy, was moulded by private interests, and repeated, often ruinous assertions of control over property. I also argue that this process was embedded in a larger political economy that sought to 'civilize' the earlier marketplaces. This article is based on ethnographic interviews and repeated visits to the Barakhola between 2016 and 2018, and media accounts of the fires.

> Laissez-faire was not a method to achieve a thing, it was the thing to be achieved. – Polanyi, *The Great Transformation*

Recent years – and in particular 2013 and 2014 – saw a succession of bazaar fires in Almaty, Kazakhstan. The bazaars that have been razed by fire were so-called container bazaars. A common feature across the former Soviet Union, as the name implies, container bazaars were marketplaces where trading took place out of old shipping containers that were clustered together to form markets. Although economic liberalization began under perestroika, the container bazaar remains a marker of the post-Soviet commercial landscape and typical of the trading places that proliferated in the wake of the Soviet Union when citizenry descended on the new markets, either to fulfil their everyday consumer needs or to take up trading to mitigate new economic vulnerability. Barakholka, the bazaar I describe in this article, was one such place.

Most of the recent bazaar fires in Almaty have occurred in Barakholka, today Central Asia's largest wholesale market, where apparel, shoes and low-quality household and office supplies are sold. Bazaar fires are followed by mall construction, multi-storey infrastructure purpose-built for trading. In this article I ask what the bazaar fires in Barakholka – or demolition of container bazaars by other means – might reveal about elite control, not just over just rent-generating urban property, but more broadly about elites' ability to leverage the economy for their own interests. Although there is scholarship on bazaars in Kazakhstan (Alff 2015, 2016; Karrar 2019; Sholk 2018; Spector 2008; Yessenova 2006), I foreground bazaar fires to illustrate how the transition from container bazaar to mall reflects an informal economy embedded within the Kazakhstan polity. I argue that the deliberately opaque ownership of Barakholka makes it a place from which rent can be extracted; and demolition, whether by fire or otherwise, allows the imposition of new rental structures.

Newly constructed malls also reflect Kazakhstan's development aspirations, which cannot be disaggregated from how new infrastructure in the country is meant to generate political legitimacy (Karrar 2019; Koch 2018; Laszczkowski 2011; Sullivan 2017). Certainly, in this, Kazakhstan is not unique; in the last quarter-century there has been ubiquitous mall construction across the global South, where many of the traditional retail spaces have given way to purpose-built infrastructure that is purportedly hygienic and orderly, modern and civilized (Abaza 2001; Brody 2006; Endres 2014).

Yet what is critical here is the process. Bazaar fires, whether accidental or deliberate, are a form of violence: people are put in harm's way, businesses are destroyed, inventories are gutted. The recurrence of fires at Barakholka, the latest of which was in November 2018, soon after this article was first submitted to *Central Asian Survey*, should give pause. In unguarded moments, sellers will describe how fires are immediately followed by new construction projects, the implication being that the fires are a means of clearing container bazaars to make way for malls.[1] This is a critical aspect of the spate of bazaar fires I describe.

In her work on fires in American cities in the nineteenth century, Christine M. Rosen (1986, 71) noted the need for spatial reorganization as the population of American cities increased; coterminous with the increasing population was the need for specialized commercial spaces, or what Rosen described as 'territorial agglomeration of firms and businesses' that benefited society by providing clustering, economies of scale, and proximate production and manufacturing services.

Similar pressures were felt in Barakholka, too, which along with the Dordoi Bazaar in Bishkek was one of the two trading hubs in Central Asia. Certainly, in Barakholka, container bazaars have been cleared by means other than fire, although as traders point out, they do not have the right to fight eviction. Still, between 2013 and 2018, and especially in 2013 and 2014, fires almost appear to have become the preferred way of clearing container bazaars, suggestive of the violence that can be brought to bear on a vulnerable stratum of the population.

Urban fires are anthropogenic. They reflect economic, social and political causes and are usually followed by 'innovation and capital investment' (Bankoff, Lubken, and Sand 2012, 4); in Barakholka, new mall construction marks such innovation and capital investment. But I also find utility in approaching bazaar fires as ruination, and Barakholka as an informal marketplace embedded in a state that perpetuates clientelism by funnelling rent to the elite via discreet networks. Let me discuss both of these further.

By 'ruination' I do not refer only to the destruction of physical infrastructure. Ann Stoler (2013, 11) also describes ruination as political, a process that 'lays waste to certain peoples, relations and things that accumulate in specific places'. Fires that raze a marketplace to the ground not also destroy livelihoods but also erode networks that have emerged in a particular place, among the sellers themselves, and between sellers and buyers. In the disappearance of social ties that were particular to a place, Barakholka shares similarities with now-abandoned Soviet towns in Central Asia, where social networks have unravelled as a consequence of outmigration (Pelkmans 2013).[2]

There is also utility in approaching Barakholka as an informal market. Bazaar fires – or immediate evictions – present an opportunity to peel back the layers of informal practices and relationalities that intersect at Barakholka. Barakholka is an informal marketplace, first, because of the uncertainty about the number of shops and sellers, as well as the amount of money and merchandise that circulates through the bazaar. Academic and policy specialists, as well as journalists, offer varying approximations (Alff 2015; Lillis 2013a; Kaminski and Mitra 2010; Sholk 2018). Put simply, no one can authoritatively answer the most basic of questions, such as how many outlets there are, or what is the rate of turnover, for Central Asia's largest bazaar. This should not be seen as a weakness of the state regulatory institutions; rather, this system is 'engendered from above', to use Yulian Konstantinov's (1996) term. While Konstantinov was describing how Bulgarian traders co-opted customs officials in the 1990s, the point is that an opaque market serves the interests of those who control it. Tellingly, who owns what share or what part of Barakholka is not public knowledge.

But the bazaar is not informal only because there is uncertainty of scale or ownership; it also functions within an economy that has evolved to serve the country's ruling elite. Scholarship on Central Asia tends to see the economy as controlled by elite cliques operating through authoritarian structures (Collins 2009; Cooley and Heathershaw 2017; Engvall 2017; Gleason 2003). Markets such as Barakholka are embedded in an economy that funnels rent to the elite via discreet networks (McGlinchey 2011; Radnitz 2010). As an extension, in Central Asia elite control of the economy manifests through other informal institutions, those that are defined by practices, and that are based on the exchange of goods and services (Collins 2006). These elites, whom Kathleen Collins (2009, 251) describes as patrimonial-authoritarian leaders, 'survive through maintaining personal control and the ability to direct patronage to the informal vested interests that surround them and bolster their regime'. Elite ownership of Barakholka is control of rent-generating property.

Finally, in this process it is important to keep in mind that new malls are representative of the allure of a modern consumer world (Benjamin 1999; Buck-Morss 1989). New mall construction engenders 'powerful imaginaries of the future' (Rao 2013, 292). In Barakholka these appear as newly-built plazas, identical sales outlets, and orderly parking lots, all of which signal development in Kazakhstan. Official criticism of container bazaars is driven by an underlying temporality, namely that these marketplaces are a throwback to the 1990s: through demolishing the bazaars, and building malls instead, that tumultuous decade can be transcended.

This article has two parts. In the first part, 'Rent', I offer an overview of Barakholka's development. I describe how the bazaar, as rent-generating property, was embedded in a political economy from which the elite extracted through control of public assets. Barakholka has provided the same function. The destruction of the old bazaars and the building of multi-storey malls provides more sales units and hence more rent. In the second part, 'Fire', I draw from my conversations with traders about the bazaar fires, and how traders describe fires as being followed by new mall construction. I link this to a broader public narrative, which was propagated by the city administration and which was at its height in 2013: that Kazakhstan urgently needed to shed its 'Third World image'. In part, this was to be achieved by 'civilizing' disorderly marketplaces.

This article draws from fieldwork in Barakholka in 2016, 2017 and 2018. My open-ended interviews in the bazaar were of two types. The majority were short exploratory interviews with sellers across the different marketplaces, in which I would inquire about the nature of the business and motivations. In these short interviews, I was often accompanied by a local university student in the capacity of a paid research assistant. During my initial forays in the bazaar, I also developed a rapport with a few sellers, who I then saw repeatedly. Our conversations, which we had in their sales containers, in teahouses and restaurants, and strolling through the bazaar, were wide-ranging: besides economy and politics we talked about families and friends, work and life in the cities where we live. For these conversations, no research assistant was present. All names are pseudonyms.

Rent

The first time I hailed a car outside my hotel in central Almaty and asked the driver to take me to Barakholka, the driver looked confused. 'Barakholka?' he echoed. The bazaar clearly seemed an unlikely destination for someone like myself, who was clearly an outsider; it was only when I quickly explained my interest in economics and trade that he started nodding his head. His question was justified: Barakholka has a reputation for fakes, cheap consumer goods, and wholesaling. *Barakholka* – the word – is Russian for 'flea market', and has been used for the marketplace since the 1990s, when Almaty residents would gather on the outskirts of the city to buy and sell used household items, or to buy cheap manufactured goods that were being imported by itinerant traders from neighbouring countries, primarily China. At the time, such peddling (or, pejoratively, 'speculation') was looked down on (Fehlings 2018; Kaiser 1998), and it was motivated by need. For the former professional class who were forced into trade by economic necessity, it was a source of unease, if not shame (Armstberg and Boren 2003; Fehlings 2017; Mandel and Humphrey 2002; Melkumyan forthcoming).

At that time, Barakholka had had no infrastructure: that sellers used to simply lay out their wares on blankets is a common refrain in Barakholka, as well as bazaars such as Dordoi in Bishkek and Kara-Suu in southern Kyrgyzstan. Recalling the lack of infrastructure highlights the precarity of the 1990s. It is also a measure of how the marketplaces have developed in the quarter-century since. 'Is *this* Barakholka?' I found myself asking the driver as he pulled up in front of Boutique Maryam, a purpose-built mall, and as I would quickly learn, only the first of the Barakholka malls when one approaches the marketplace from the city centre. I was surprised by how orderly Barakholka appeared at first glance, especially in comparison to the bazaars in Kyrgyzstan where I had previously conducted fieldwork.

The Barakholka I drove up to for the first time in the summer of 2016 sprawls along both sides of the six-lane Northern Ring Road. It includes a series of marketplaces, each prominently displaying its name. Most are purpose-built and take the form of two-to-three-storey shopping malls; the construction is recent, and at the time of writing in 2019, was continuing in different parts of Barakholka. The three container bazaars that remain, Raxhat and Batyr east of the ring road and Bolashak on the western side, have a high frontage that conceals the containers that populate the inside. A wide parking lot runs across the entire length of the bazaar; the cars are parked in an orderly fashion. When turning off the North Ring Road, the initial impression is of order, with the bazaar having the aesthetics of a North American strip mall.

Barakholka has grown gradually. The bazaar of today is at the site of a former of *sovkhoz*, Zarya Vostoka; trading probably began as early as the 1960s, with a small informal weekend market in used goods (Yessenova 2006, 43; see also Roberts 2007; Smagulova 2016). Perestroika, and the break-up of the Soviet Union, served as a rupture. The periodic sovkhoz market became a place for Almaty residents to buy and sell used household goods or inexpensive manufactured goods – *barakholka* was not a name but a category. By the late 1990s containers had begun to appear, and the bazaar began to expand.

Those traders who have been at the bazaar since the 1990s also affirm that all the current marketplace infrastructure appeared after 1991. One trader told me that he had been the first to place a container in Batyr, adding that at the time the vegetation had been so dense that one could not see across to the other side of the road. Given the wide acknowledgement of the economic hardship following Soviet collapse, such public recollections should not be seen as nostalgia. They are an acknowledgement of the transition of the past decades; there is a tacit admission that living conditions in the country improved under President Nursultan Nazarbaev. Whenever I have lengthy conversations with traders about how Barakholka developed over the years, the development of the city is also mentioned: new construction, the number of cars on the road today, or how well-lit the city has become. For the traders, the bazaar is not separate from the city; the two are conjoined, and the development of Almaty's infrastructure is acknowledged as a measure of the progress that Kazakhstan has made; clearly, upgrading of infrastructure has lent legitimacy to the regime. Yet in trader narratives, Kazakhstan *also* appears as a state with authoritarian tendencies; whenever I asked about traders mobilizing collectively – to fight eviction, for example – the response was always a firm no. And in unguarded moments, the same traders will describe how the profits from the country's hydrocarbon resources remain confined to a thin stratum, in contrast to what they perceive to be a more equitable distribution of wealth in oil-rich West Asian countries.

Underlying the development of Barakholka was a circuitous path of how bazaars in Kazakhstan proliferated. Following the Soviet Union, bazaars such as Barakholka appeared for three reasons: the collapse of manufacturing and rising unemployment; the need for goods at a price people could afford; and the fact that bazaars were an institution from which rent could be extracted. According to one estimate, between 1991 and 2000, there was a ten-fold increase in the number of the bazaars in Almaty (Spector 2008, 44). They also continued to multiply in the new century, with the number of registered bazaars in Almaty growing from 66 in 2005 to 85 in 2012 (Sholk 2018, 126). People in Almaty I spoke with corroborate that the new markets changed the cityscape after 1991. One long-term resident said that when she thought back to the Almaty of the 1980s she could recall boulevards, parks, apartment blocks and offices, but not bazaars; instead there were nondescript official shops. Other Almaty residents who recalled the Soviet-era city held a similar view.

While a shadow economy had existed under the Soviet Union, the informal economy – as labour surplus, undocumented exchange and discrete, extractive networks – converged in the bazaar. Traders are cognizant of these convergences. For example, one day Camran, who sells bicycles at Barakholka, asked me whether I had visited a particular mall in Almaty. He then told me that during the Soviet era there had been a factory in the same place, where 1500 people used to work. According to Camran, after the Soviet Union collapsed, the factory was sold off, and eventually a mall was built in its place. According to him, just about the only thing that has consistently been built is bazaars, from which rent is siphoned off to 'the top two percent'.

Arman, another trader at Barakholka, saw a clear line between rent extraction at the bazaar and extractive capitalism in Kazakhstan following the fall of the Soviet Union. 'For ten years after the Soviet Union collapsed, my sole business was exporting scrap from Kazakhstan', he told me. It was a very good business, he recalled.

> In the first ten years after communism, it was like everything in this country was for sale. Millions of tons of perfectly good metal were sold as scrap, primarily to China; the lesser quality stuff we would send to Afghanistan or Pakistan. Running factories were scrapped. As a scrap dealer, I was once asked to inspect a factory. I assumed it would be an old factory, with machinery that was falling apart. But there didn't appear to be anything wrong with the factory. It just wasn't running. There was a crane at this factory, and a pylon was suspended from the boom, hanging in mid-air. I asked, 'What is that?' Do you know what I was told? They said, the day the Soviet Union collapsed, they stopped production in the factory. And that pylon had been suspended there ever since. Nobody had even bothered to lower it. This story I am telling you dates from 2001. So, for ten years after the Soviet Union, that pylon had remained suspended in mid-air.

This story – likely embellished – is allegorical for how many industries ceased to function after the Soviet Union. Beginning in the early 1990s, Kazakhstan embarked on a privatization programme. Although privatization was a drawn-out process, which began with the privatization of apartments in 1991 and continued for over a decade, it was in the second stage, between 1994 and 1996, when 3500 state-owned enterprises were privatized, most of them after being severely undervalued (Gleason 2003, 45–47; Olcott 2002, 136–138). Subsequently, many of the Soviet-era enterprises shut down; between 1991 and 1995, industrial output halved, and went from constituting 30% of the economy to just over 16% (Olcott 2002, 129; Schatz 2004, 89). The story that Camran told me, in which a factory was dismantled and a mall appeared in its stead, is entirely plausible.

Between 1991 and 1998, there was also a proliferation of limited-liability partnerships that transformed state assets into private assets. While limited-liability assets were used primarily to privatize state and collective farms, the mechanism was also used to take control over the newly emerging market spaces, such as parts of Barakholka (Sholk 2018; Spoor 1997; Vakulchuk 2013); thus, the sovkhoz was taken over by the elite. As the earlier economy was dismantled, inflation and unemployment soared, feeding the informal economy. This had dire consequences, many of the newly unemployed resorted to shuttle or bazaar trading, relying on individual clan or kin networks for economic survival. Thus, bazaars such as Barakholka were part of a process of public assets being captured for either short-term gain or long-term rent extraction.[3]

Elite control of bazaars reflects the rapid economic liberalization that began under perestroika and accelerated after 1991. Kazakhstan saw both a wave of privatization, and in the case of Barakholka, the reconfiguration of an older and smaller market as rent-generating assets; this was part of a larger process whereby the elite extended their control over the economy. The building of malls should be seen as part of the same process. When I asked traders what benefits a mall affords to the owners that a container bazaar does not, they were quick to point out that multi-storey malls allow more units. Although the rent for an outlet might not be higher than the rent on a container, there are more such units in a mall. Aside from the fact that the transition from container bazaar to mall is framed in a civilizing narrative (as I discuss in the second part of the article), this transition marks a shift in how bazaar owners come up with new ways of extracting from the economy.

This leads to the question of who might stand to lose in this process; I discuss this also in the next part. But in framing this question, I find it useful to invoke Karl Polanyi ([1944] 2001), who, writing at the end of the Second World War, had warned of havoc if markets were allowed to operate without regulation: new property relations and extractive rent systems could 'annihilate' the people. With the collapse of the Soviet Union, *The Great Transformation* suddenly found new relevance, not least because half a century earlier Polanyi had underscored the importance of institutionalizing the protection of labour and property rights (Brook 1994; Neale 1991). For Polanyi, the market should not be allowed to go unregulated. It needed to be checked by state institutions, and ideally be embedded within a moral order upheld by the community. Failure to do so would mean society would be atomized, and individual interests, particularly the interests of those who wielded power, would take precedence over the collective (Dale 2010; Munck 2004).

But while the dismantling of the Soviet command economy was widely welcomed, in the new economic landscape there was little protection; indeed, newfound economic precarity, and how people were forced to rely on personal, localized networks became characteristic of widespread informal employment across the former Soviet Union (Kaiser 1998; Schatz 2004; Werner 1998; Yükseker 2004). Crucially, as tens of millions of people were funnelled into the informal economy (Humphrey 2002), the law offered little protection for the small traders. When traders in Barakholka complain about the lack of legal security, they are referencing the continuity of this earlier ethos, which dates to a time of political transition and economic vulnerability. The precarity of the 1990s was in contrast to the employment security under the Soviet Union, a time that is sometimes referred to with nostalgia (Pelkmans 2013). Consequently, while the commercial 'sphere of exchange' had expanded after the Soviet Union, it was a 'market transition without the anticipated economic, social, and political transformation' (Burawoy 2001, 270). In Kazakhstan, new opportunities for rent extraction followed widespread selling of state assets.[4]

Fire

For those traders who consider themselves successful, or imagine success to be within reach, Barakholka is a place of aspiration. Multiple traders I spoke with described buying a container, a car or an apartment as a measure of success that could be made possible by work in the bazaar. Consider Yalyan, who was in her mid-30s when we spoke to her in 2018 and was selling Korean cosmetics. She had come to the bazaar 15 years earlier. She had trained as a nurse, but finding nursing work unnecessarily bureaucratic (besides which, it did not pay well), she sought to supplement her income by working in the bazaar. Growing up, she said, she could never have imagined herself working as a trader. But after saving money for the first 10 years, she was able to own her own outlet. Now she cannot imagine doing anything else.

But this is not to suggest that bazaar is not changing. In Barakholka, the fires are remembered as turning points. Yalyan, for example, describes the fire as a transition. Although she was not directly affected, for her, the fire was a temporal break: before the fire, when she came to the bazaar; and after the fire, when a part of the bazaar was gutted, new malls were built, more shops were built and there was more competition.[5]

Most of Barakholka is newly built. Camran described the fire in the wholesale shoe market, after which the present shoe bazaars were built:

> The fire started at three o'clock in the afternoon. It burned non-stop for two days. At that time, Barakholka burned from the far end, all the way down to the middle. We would stand here watching the helicopters fly in and try and douse the fire. Traders lost hundreds of thousands of dollars in inventory. Some people lost everything.

We were strolling through the parking lot, where cars were parked in an orderly fashion. He waved his hand towards the parked vehicles.

> This parking lot you can see is new. A few years ago, this too was a part of the bazaar; there were containers spread out everywhere; you couldn't move. For a long time, we had been hearing that this portion of the bazaar needed to be cleared. But nobody was willing to move. Then, one day there was a fire here. Everything went up in flames. Metal containers don't burn, of course. After the fire, when we came out here, there was nothing but charred containers. Those very containers which people had bought for fifty thousand dollars were being sold for three hundred dollars, four hundred dollars.

The fires were followed by new development projects; containers did not reappear in those parts of the bazaar that were burnt. Instead, shopping malls were built. The number of bazaar fires in Almaty varies in different media accounts, although it does appear that most of them took place in 2013 and 2014.

In those two years, there were at least 10 fires in Almaty bazaars, at least six of which were at Barakholka; on one occasion, two lives were lost (admittedly, the published numbers do not agree: according to another estimate, between September and November 2013, there were eight marketplace fires in the city). Although in one case, two bazaar directors were found guilty of negligence, and sentenced to 'freedom limitation', city officials insisted that the bazaars had been illegally built in the 1990s. The city also refused to compensate the traders, noting that the bazaars were interfering with plans for new road construction. In how these stories are reported in local media, there is a tension between fire-prone infrastructure and irresponsible behaviour (e.g. use of candles or welding equipment) and the need to remove container bazaars *anyway*. Thus, even if accidental, fire serves the purpose of city authorities (Lillis 2013a; Kumenov 2018; RFE/RL 2014a, 2014b; Tengrinews 2014).

The series of bazaar fires that began in 2013 coincided with municipal plans being put into effect to demolish the container bazaars. City authorities had a negative view of the old marketplaces. In 2014, Tengrinews reported the deputy head of city planning in Almaty saying that Kazakhstan wanted to shed its 'Third World image … at all costs'. Consider how the *Times of Central Asia* editorialized the removal of bazaars, with implicit distancing of Kazakhstan from the global South:

> Apart from Zilyoni Bazaar in the centre of the city … [other bazaars] are whirlpools where thousands of petty traders, errand boys and courageous customers swarm in a most disorderly

manner reminding one of similar unstructured sprawling massive market places in South America, Sub-Saharan Africa, and southern Asia.

In this new development schema, the 'disorderly market places' were to be replaced by 'gleaming and clean plazas' (*Times of Central Asia* 2014).

Such views were frequently echoed by the leadership. Kazakhstan's prime minister, Karim Massimov, urged traders to move to a civilized path, saying that there would be a new policy whereby the bazaars would slowly be phased out in favour of shopping complexes (*Kazakhstan and Central Asia Today* 2014). In Kazakhstan modernist aspirations centred on the bazaar go back to the early 2000s. The bazaar was seen as dirty and chaotic; the malls and plazas, clean and civilized (Laszczkowski 2011; Spector 2008).

This view of modernity has a powerful allure. I have even heard traders who believed the bazaar fires were deliberately set admit that the new malls were civilized spaces (see also Alff 2015, 260). Herein lies a tension: on the one hand, fires destroy property worth millions of dollars (and in at least one case, two lives were lost). There is also apprehension about higher rents in the newly constructed marketplaces (Lillis 2013b). And yet on the other hand there is a tacit acknowledgement of the superiority of modern marketplaces. In June 2014, the *Times of Central Asia* cited a poll in which twice as many people were in favour of demolishing the container bazaars than were in favour of retaining them. This is a plausible ratio, and broadly consistent with what I heard outside the bazaar.

Underlying this is the power of commercial modernity, the most eloquent statement on which remains that by the Frankfurt School's Walter Benjamin (1892–1940). In ruminations that were penned between 1927 and 1940, and published posthumously as *The Arcades Project*, Benjamin (1999, 874) described the arcade as the mould in which modernity was cast. For the populace at large, as Benjamin reminds us, enamelled shop signs were wall decorations, as the arcade became a place for a public culture to present itself (879). As places made by nineteenth-century modernity, arcades constituted 'a consumer dream world' (Buck-Morss 1989, 37). Prior to the Bolshevik Revolution, Russia too had the equivalent of the arcade in cities such as Moscow and Odessa (Brumfield 2001; Herlihy 2001). With purpose-built malls in the place of Barakholka, Kazakhstan could safely put enough distance between itself and the chaotic bazaars, which at best were a legacy of transition from communism, and at worst constituted an imaginary of trading places in the global South.

Thus, beyond the catastrophic effects of fire is a story of how Barakholka has continued to serve the economic interests of Kazakhstan's elite. For about three decades it expanded steadily, first as an open-air flea market, then in the 1990s as a container bazaar, and since 2013 as a chain of shopping malls. The latest transformation, by fire, has allowed a top-down – and violent – reassertion of control over rent-generating property. This market economy shared similarities with what has sometimes been described as 'predatory capitalism', in which the social, cultural, and natural environment is 'invaded, degraded and subordinated to criteria of private profitability' (Levitt 2006, 173). In the global South, such predatory capitalism tends to be embedded in the informal economy. This is a result of two factors: first, an extensive labour pool that is unemployed or underemployed; and second, people being forced to operate in an economic landscape where the rules are determined by a self-serving elite (Hedlund 1999; Verhaegen and Vale 1993). Although Polanyi was not writing about small traders like those I have described here, his warning that the elite could make a market economy work for them does apply here. 'The true criticism of a market economy', Polanyi wrote in a different time, but still applicable to Central Asia after perestroika, was that 'its economy was based on self-interest' (257).

Conclusion

Depite all the time I have spent talking with traders at Barakholka, who owns what share in the bazaar has been impossible to determine, although there is occasional public speculation that the former president's immediate family or people close to him have shares (Lillis 2014). Similar claims were made on *Respublika*, the opposition news website, shortly before it was shut down (BBC Monitoring Central Asia 2012). In August 2014, in the wake of a bazaar fire, Almaty's mayor, Akhmetzhan Yesimov, threatened to disclose who had shares in Barakholka (Lillis 2014), but, tellingly, he did not. When I asked traders about bazaar ownership, they claimed not to know; this is unlike Kyrgyzstan, where bazaar ownership is known (Alff 2014, 86–87). Perhaps unsurprisingly, the traders I spoke to never gave the impression that this could be a particularly fruitful line of questioning on my part. This could reflect the opaque power and ownership structures in Kazakhstan, or perhaps I remain someone with whom they do not wish to share this information, or both.

Opaque ownership – and discrete owner networks – are inseparable from the history of Barakholka. In nearly three decades after the breakup of the Soviet Union, the elite in successor states can be seen as the residue of empire and socialism, who remain the 'bedrock of political life' (Heathershaw and Schatz 2017, 11). Elite privilege allowed control over segments of the economy, in the process creating 'private fiefdoms' (Engvall 2017, 77–78). In the case of Barakholka, besides creating a modern marketplace, demolishing and rebuilding allows adjusting property relations by increasing the number of shops (through multi-storey malls) and imposing new rent structures.

The losers in this process are the traders whose inventory goes up in flames, or who, in less extreme cases, are forced to vacate at a short notice. I have been told more than once by traders that if they are asked to vacate their containers, they shall do so at once: failure to do so may result in their property being on fire the next day. Even outside those who lose their inventories in fire, there are those who are forced to move out of containers they may have occupied for a long time. Many of them are unable to return to the bazaar because they cannot afford to relocate. It was such people that Polanyi argued needed to be protected; nearly 30 years since the emergence of sovereign states, such formal regulation remains missing, and the traders remain at the mercy of a market economy serving only a thin stratum of society.

While I have not seen a fire in Barakholka, nor visited the bazaar in the immediate aftermath of one, I have witnessed bazaar demolition and reconstruction. Regular visits over three years have allowed me to track changes in infrastructure; besides field notes, photographs serve as a time-lapse of new infrastructure development. For me, a poignant example of ceaseless change was the demolition of the small garment market sandwiched between Alatau and Dovyn, both newly constructed malls. In both 2016 and 2017 this tiny market, with barely a few rows, had struck me as being the least developed of Barakholka's marketplaces. Its unaligned containers, unpaved floors and narrow, congested aisles were a throwback to an earlier time. When I last visited this market, in 2017, I decided that next time I would speak to traders there; but by my subsequent visit, in spring 2018, the market had been demolished, and scaffolding erected, beyond which excavators were at work. I took a few unremarkable photographs to add to my archive of demolition and mall construction images.

Although there is nothing remarkable about photographs of a demolition site, when placed in the context of Kazakhstan's informal economy, these images of ruination reveal an important story. As Ann Stoler (2013, 9–11) reminds us, ruination is a destructive process, but also one that weighs on the future. In the wake of the gutted infrastructure, Stoler asks, what is being refigured? How are futures being imagined? Charred remains, or what is left after a bazaar fire, invite similar questions. In the case of Barakholka the answer lies in the juggernaut construction across the bazaar, aiming on the one hand to erase all signs of the tumultuous decade of transition, yet remaining trapped in an informal economy that came of age during that same momentous decade.

Notes

1. Bazaar and city administrators explain the bazaar fires as resulting from a lack of building regulations, and unsafe working conditions, in the commercial spaces that emerged haphazardly after the Soviet collapse. The only long-term solution, according to city officials, is first, clearing the container bazaars, and second, building malls (Karrar 2019). Fires serve the first purpose, and enable the second.
2. In the transition from container bazaar to mall, recollections of earlier trading practices constitute a form of public memory. Adriana Petryna (1995, 203) has described 'mobile histories' in the post-Soviet era, which constitute 'relations among citizenry … based on the premise that recollection constitutes an important social bond'. I have frequently witnessed this in my conversations with traders as they recollect the past, especially when I am speaking with more than one person and they begin reminiscing among themselves. Telling a funny story, correcting a date, recalling a name is how memory is preserved in conversations between traders; the minutiae may appear unimportant to the researcher, but among the traders it is important that there is concurrence. I do not read these recollections as nostalgia; besides constituting a social bond, as Petryna noted, it is an acknowledgement of changes in the bazaar.
3. Another example illustrates how new bazaar construction imposed new rent structures. One morning in January 2005 traders at Almaty's Bayanauyl car market arrived to find the market cordoned off; they were prevented from accessing their outlets. The traders were told to move to a new market, where they would enjoy rent exemption for three months, after which they would have to buy containers that cost USD 5000–7000. This market closure, which was reported by the local Khabar TV, was unusual in that it resulted in trader protest and the temporary blocking of the Almaty Bishkek Road (on 25 January 2005, according to BBC Monitoring Central Asia, reported on 2 February 2005). 'The market itself and the food on sale do not meet the safety requirements', a police official told the media on the closure of the Bayanauyl car market.
4. But the elite were not the only ones who were benefitting. In 2017, we were talking with a shoe seller in Bolashak who was originally from Tajikistan. He complained about needing to renew his work permit regularly, despite which he still had to dodge the authorities. Would he consider returning to Tajikistan? No, he said, because in Tajikistan I can't even earn a hundred dollars a month. For him, working at Barakholka was an opportunity to make a steady living. Like him, a vast number of people from outside Almaty find employment in Barakholka or in the scores of smaller feeder markets in other cities in Kazakhstan.
5. The first account of a Barakholka fire I heard was in fact in the Kara-Suu bazaar in southern Kyrgyzstan in 2014. I had been speaking with a Kyrgyz women who used to work in Barakholka

selling garments that had been stitched in Bishkek. She had liked living in Almaty, and her business had been good. But after the fires in Barakholka, the Almaty city authorities clamped down on permits for traders from outside Almaty, and she had no choice but to return to southern Kyrgyzstan. For her, too, the bazaar fire marked a transition, albeit a personal one.

Acknowledgements

The fieldwork on which this article is based was generously supported by the Volkswagen Foundation between 2016 and 2019. Susanne Fehlings was instrumental in helping me identify, understand and work through complex questions pertaining to informality, including those beyond the present study. Edward Schatz and Hermann Kreutzmann invited me to present this research at the University of Toronto and the Free University of Berlin. Two anonymous reviewers patiently and repeatedly provided expert commentaries and challenging suggestions as I veered into areas beyond my expertise. Rico Isaacs offered valuable suggestions on framing and presentation. I am grateful to all.

Disclosure statement

No potential conflict of interest was reported by the author(s).

Funding

The fieldwork on which this article is based was supported by the Volkswagen Foundation.

References

Abaza, M. 2001. "Shopping Malls, Consumer Culture, and the Reshaping of Public Space in Egypt." *Theory, Culture & Society* 18 (5): 97–122. doi:10.1177/02632760122051986
Alff, H. 2014. "Post-Soviet Positionalities: Relations, Flows and the Transformation of Bishkek's Dordoy Bazaar." In *Tracing Connections: Explorations of Spaces and Places in Asian Contexts*, edited by H. Alff and A. Benz, 71–90. Berlin: WVB.
Alff, H. 2015. "Profiteers or Moral Entrepreneurs? Bazaars, Traders and Development Discourses in Almaty, Kazakhstan." *International Development Planning Review* 37 (3): 249–267. doi:10.3828/idpr.2014.28
Alff, H. 2016. "Getting Stuck within Flows: Limited Interaction and Peripheralization at the Kazakhstan-China Border." *Central Asian Survey* 35 (3): 369–386. doi:10.1080/02634937.2016.1210860
Armstberg, K.-O., and T. Boren. 2003. *Everyday Economy in Russia, Poland and Latvia*. Huddinge: Sodertorns hogskola.
Bankoff, G., U. Lubken, and J. Sand. 2012. "Introduction." In *Flammable Cities: Urban Conflagration and the Making of the Modern World*, edited by G. Bankoff, U. Lubken, and J. Sand, 3–20. Madison: University of Wisconsin Press.
BBC Monitoring Central Asia. 2012. "Report Claims Kazakh Leader's Brother Expands Control Over Bazaars in Ex-capital." July 18.
Benjamin, W. 1999. *The Arcades Project*. Translated by Howard Eiland and Kevin McLaughlin. Cambridge, MA: Harvard University Press.
Brody, A. 2006. "The Cleaners You Aren't Meant to See: Order, Hygiene and Everyday Politics in a Bangkok Shopping Mall." *Antipode* 38 (3): 534–556. doi:10.1111/j.0066-4812.2006.00594.x
Brook, D. 1994. "The Great Transformation: Its Relevance Continues." *American Journal of Economics and Sociology* 53 (4): 401–432. doi:10.1111/j.1536-7150.1994.tb02611.x

Brumfield, W. C. 2001. "From the Lower Depths to the Upper Trading Rows: The Design of Retail Shopping Centers in Moscow." In *Commerce in Russian Urban Culture, 1861–1914*, edited by W. C. Brumfield, B. V. Anan'ich, and Y. A. Petrov, 167–179. Baltimore, MD: Johns Hopkins University Press.

Buck-Morss, S. 1989. *The Dialectics of Seeing: Walter Benjamin and the Arcades Project*. Cambridge, MA: MIT Press.

Burawoy, M. 2001. "Transition without Transformation: Russia's Involuntary Road to Capitalism." *East European Politics and Societies: and Cultures* 15 (2): 269–290. doi:10.1177/0888325401015002004

Collins, K. 2006. *Clan Politics and Regime Transition in Central Asia*. Cambridge: Cambridge University Press.

Collins, K. 2009. "Economic and Security Regionalism amongst Patrimonial Authoritarian Regimes: The Case of Central Asia." *Europe-Asia Studies* 61 (2): 249–281. doi:10.1080/09668130802630854

Cooley, A., and J. Heathershaw. 2017. *Dictators without Borders: Power and Money in Central Asia*. New Haven, CT: Yale University Press.

Dale, G. 2010. *Karl Polanyi: The Limits of the Market*. Cambridge: Polity Press.

Endres, K. 2014. "Downgraded by Upgrading: Small-Scale Traders, Urban Transformation and Spatial Reconfiguration in Post-Reform Vietnam." *Cambridge Anthropology* 32 (2): 97–111.

Engvall, J. 2017. "License to Seek Rents: 'Corruption' as a Method of Post-Soviet Governance." In *Paradox of Power: The Logic of State Weakness in Eurasia*, edited by J. Heathershaw and E. Schatz, 73–87. Pittsburgh: University of Pittsburgh Press.

Fehlings, S. 2017. "From 'Chelnoki' to Global Players: Encounters in the Context of Caucasian (-Chinese) Trade since the 1990s." *Paideuma* 63: 183–205.

Fehlings, S. 2018. "Informal Trade and Globalization in the Caucasus and Post-Soviet Eurasia." In *Mobilities, Boundaries and Travelling Ideas: Rethinking Translocality beyond Central Asia and the Caucasus*, edited by M. Stephan-Emmrich and P. Schröder 229–262. Cambridge: Open Book Publishers.

Gleason, G. 2003. *Markets and Politics in Central Asia: Structural Reform and Political Change*. London: Routledge.

Heathershaw, J., and E. Schatz. 2017. "The Logic of State Weakness in Eurasia: An Introduction." In *Paradox of Power: The Logic of State Weakness in Eurasia*, edited by J. Heathershaw and E. Schatz, 3–21. Pittsburgh: University of Pittsburgh Press.

Hedlund, S. 1999. *Russia's 'Market' Economy: A Bad Case of Predatory Capitalism*. London: UCL Press.

Herlihy, P. 2001. "Commerce and Architecture in Odessa in Late Imperial Russia." In *Commerce in Russian Urban Culture, 1861–1914*, edited by W. C. Brumfield, B. V. Anan'ich, and Y. A. Petrov, 180–194. Baltimore, MD: Johns Hopkins University Press.

Humphrey, C. 2002. *The Unmaking of Soviet Life: Everyday Economies after Socialism*. Ithaca, NY: Cornell University Press.

Kaiser, M. 1998. "Informal Sector Trade in Uzbekistan." *Journal of Central Asian Studies* 2 (2): 2–19.

Kaminski, B., and S. Mitra. 2010. *Skeins of Silk: Borderless Bazaars and Border Trade in Central Asia*. Washington, DC: World Bank.

Karrar, H. H. 2019. "Between Border and Bazaar: Central Asia's Informal Economy." *Journal of Contemporary Asia* 49 (2): 272–293. doi:10.1080/00472336.2018.1532017

Kazakhstan and Central Asia Today. 2014. "Kazakh PM urges for Bringing Order at Markets and Bazaars." 25 June.

Koch, N. 2018. *The Geopolitics of Spectacle: Space, Synecdoche, and the New Capitals of Asia*. Ithaca, NY: Cornell University Press.

Konstantinov, Y. 1996. "Patterns of Reinterpretation: Trader-Tourism in the Balkans (Bulgaria) as a Picaresque Metaphorical Enactment of Post-Totalitarianism." *American Ethnologist* 23 (4): 762–782. doi:10.1525/ae.1996.23.4.02a00050

Kumenov, A. 2018. "Kazakhstan: Sun Setting on Almaty's Chaotic Barakholka Bazaar." *Eurasianet*, 21 November. Accessed 11 February 2020. https://eurasianet.org/kazakhstan-sun-setting-on-almatys-chaotic-barakholka-bazaar.

Laszczkowski, M. 2011. "Superplace: Global Connections and Local Politics at the Mega Mall." *Astana. Etnofoor* 23 (1): 85–104.

Levitt, K. P. 2006. "Keynes and Polanyi: The 1920s and the 1990s." *Review of International Political Economy* 13 (1): 152–177. doi:10.1080/09692290500396768

Lillis, J. 2013a. "Kazakhstan: Almaty Market Burns Again, Inflaming Suspicions." *Eurasianet*. 12 December. Accessed 11 February 2020. https://eurasianet.org/kazakhstan-almaty-market-burns-again-inflaming-suspicions.

Lillis, J. 2013b. "Barakholka Burns Again." *Kazakhstan Newsline*. 13 December.

Lillis, J. 2014. "Legendry Almaty Bazaar Goes Upmarket." *Kazakhstan Newsline*. 19 August.

Mandel, R., and C. Humphrey. 2002. *Markets and Moralities: Ethnographies of Postsocialism*. Oxford: Berg.

McGlinchey, E. 2011. *Chaos, Violence, Dynasty: Politics and Islam in Central Asia*. Pittsburgh, PA: University of Pittsburgh Press.

Melkumyan, H. Forthcoming. "From Economic Survival to Lifestyle Choice: Flea Markets in Georgia and Armenia." Forthcoming in *Central Asian Survey*.

Munck, R. 2004. "Globalization, Labor and the 'Polanyi Problem'." *Labor History* 45 (3): 251–269. doi:10.1080/0023656042000257765

Neale, W. C. 1991. "Society, State and the Market: A Polanyian View of Current Change and Turmoil in Eastern Europe." *Journal of Economic Issues* 25 (2): 467–473. doi:10.1080/00213624.1991.11505180

Olcott, M. B. 2002. *Kazakhstan: Unfulfilled Promise*. Washington, DC: Carnegie Endowment.

Pelkmans, M. 2013. "Ruins of Hope in a Kyrgyz Post-Industrial Wasteland." *Anthropology Today* 29 (5): 17–21. doi:10.1111/1467-8322.12060

Petryna, A. 1995. "Sarcophagus: Chernobyl in Historical Light." *Cultural Anthropology* 10 (2): 196–220. doi:10.1525/can.1995.10.2.02a00030

Polanyi, K. [1944] 2001. *The Great Transformation: The Political and Economic Origins of Our Times*. Boston, MA: Beacon Press.

Radnitz, S. 2010. *Weapons of the Wealthy: Predatory Regimes and Elite-Led Protests in Central Asia*. Ithaca, NY: Cornell University Press.

Rao, V. 2013. "The Future in Ruins." In *Imperial Debris: On Ruins and Ruination*, edited by A. L. Stoler, 287–321. Durham, NC: Duke University Press.

RFE/RL (Radio Free Europe/Radio Liberty). 2014a. "Another Fire Hits Almaty Market." 5 February. Accessed 11 February 2020. https://www.rferl.org/a/kazakhstan-market-fires-almaty/25253958.html.

RFE/RL (Radio Free Europe/Radio Liberty). 2014b. "Two Sentenced for Fires in Almaty Bazaars." 10 April. Accessed 11 February 2020. https://www.rferl.org/a/two-sentenced-for-fires-in-almaty-bazaars/25328189.html.

Roberts, S. 2007. "Everyday Negotiations of Islam in Central Asia: Practicing Religion in the Uyghur Neighborhood of Zarya Vostoka in Almaty, Kazakhstan." In *Everyday Life in Central Asia: Past and Present*, edited by J. Sahadeo and R. Zanca, 339–354. Bloomington: University of Indiana Press.

Rosen, C. M. 1986. *The Limits of Power: Great Fires and the Process of City Growth in America*. Cambridge: Cambridge University Press.

Schatz, E. 2004. *Modern Clan Politics: The Power of 'Blood' in Kazakhstan and Beyond*. University of Washington Press.

Sholk, D. 2018. "Barakholka (Kazakhstan)." In *Global Encyclopedia of Informality, Vol. 2, Understanding Social and Cultural Complexity*, edited by A. Ledeneva, 125–129. London: UCL Press.

Smagulova, J. 2016. "The Dungans of Kazakhstan: Old Minority in a New Nation-State." In *Multilingualism in the China Diaspora Worldwide: Transnational Connections and Local Social Realities*, edited by L. Wei, 63–86. New York: Routledge.

Spector, R. A. 2008. "Bazaar Politics: *The Fate of Marketplaces in Kazakhstan*." *Problems of Post-Communism* 55 (6): 42–53. doi:10.2753/PPC1075-8216550604

Spoor, M. 1997. "Agrarian Transition in the Former Soviet Union Central Asia: Stagnation and Progress." Working Paper No. 243. The Hague: Institute of Social Studies.

Stoler, A. L. 2013. "Introduction: 'The Rot Remains'." In *Imperial Debris: On Ruins and Ruination*, edited by A. L. Stoler, 1–35. Durham, NC: Duke University Press.

Sullivan, C. J. 2017. "State-Building in the Steppe: Challenges to Kazakhstan's Modernist Aspirations." *Strategic Analysis* 41 (3): 273–284. doi:10.1080/09700161.2017.1295606

Tengrinews. 2014. "900 Firefighters Quench Barakholka in Almaty." 6 February. Accessed 11 February 2020. https://en.tengrinews.kz/emergencies/900-firefighters-quench-barakholka-in-almaty-25814/.

Times of Central Asia. 2014. "Almaty's Junk Markets: How to Get Rid of the Junk and Keep the Markets." 17 June.

Vakulchuk, R. 2013. *Kazakhstan's Emerging Economy: Between State and Market*. Frankfurt: Peter Lang.

Verhaegen, B., and M. Vale. 1993. "The Temptations of Predatory Capitalism: Zaire under Mobutuism." *International Journal of Political Economy* 23 (1): 109–125. doi:10.1080/08911916.1993.11643856

Werner, C. 1998. "Household Networks and the Security of Mutual Indebtedness in Rural Kazakhstan." *Central Asian Survey* 17 (4): 597–612. doi:10.1080/02634939808401058

Yessenova, S. 2006. "Hawkers and Containers in Zarya Vostoka: How 'Bizarre' is the Post-Soviet Bazaar?" *Research in Economic Anthropology* 24: 37–59. doi:10.1016/S0190-1281(05)24002-7

Yükseker, D. 2004. "Trust and Gender in a Transnational Market: The Public Culture of Laleli, Istanbul." *Public Culture* 16 (1): 47–66. doi:10.1215/08992363-16-1-47

Doing business in Yabaolu Market, Beijing: (inter-)ethnic entrepreneurship, trust and friendship between Caucasian and Chinese traders

Susanne Fehlings

ABSTRACT
Based on ethnographic fieldwork in China and Georgia, this article traces the origins and describes current practices of post-Soviet tourist trading in Yabaolu Market in Beijing. While traders from across the Caucasus visit Yabaolu, my focus is on Georgian traders who today perceive themselves as *biznesmeny*. Focusing on a typical trade visit, the article explores the role of ethnic and kinship ties in the organization of this trade. It questions the notion of ethnic entrepreneurship and the idea that ethnic cooperation itself may serve a basis of trust and underpin traders' activities. Instead, the article illustrates how enduring transnational linkages are built on other forms of reliability and reputation. These are framed in the lexicon of friendship, as well as kinship and pseudo-kinship vocabulary, and facilitate commercial transactions between traders of different ethnic, social and religious backgrounds in an environment where state regulation and legal law enforcement are almost absent.

Introduction

Yabaolu Market, the so-called Russky Rynok (Russian Market) in Beijing, is a popular shopping destination for traders from all over the former Soviet Union. Its development is linked to *glasnost* and *perestroika* in the Soviet Union and the reform era in China. As a consequence of political changes, trade and travel between the two countries became possible in the 1980s. While there was a general shortage of supply in the Soviet Union, China provided cheap merchandise and could meet many consumers' demands for clothes and everyday items. Groups of individuals coming from the Baltic states, the Caucasus, Russia, Ukraine and Central Asia started to make trade expeditions to access Chinese marketplaces and to exploit the new possibilities of a market economy.

The post-Soviet traders of the first generation were called *chelnoki*, from the Russian term for a shuttle, a device used in weaving to carry the thread by moving back and forth.[1] The back-and-forth movement of *chelnoki* going to China started in the Russian–Chinese borderlands. Even traders from the Caucasus travelled to Khabarovsk in Siberia, crossed the Sino-Russian border at Pogranichny, and went shopping in Suifenhe to bring back home little more than two suitcases of merchandise. But in Beijing as well, there emerged an open-air market in the city centre: Yabaolu.

Traders first got involved in trade activity as a response to unemployment in the course of the transition. Many *chelnoki* had worked in factories or were part of the Soviet urban intelligentsia, including engineers, teachers and scientists (Humphrey 2002; Niyozov and Shamatov 2007; Spector 2017; see also Melkumyan forthcoming). Having grown up with Soviet ideology, they perceived trade as a shameful occupation. Therefore, when the economic situation improved in the course of the late 1990s or 2000s, many decided to abandon the shuttle-trade sector as soon as possible (Humphrey and Skvirskaja 2009; Fehlings 2017a, 2017b, 2018).

Others, however, soon joined by a new generation of traders calling themselves *biznesmeny* (businessmen), continued to travel to China (see Schröder in this issue). These people were not suitcase traders anymore. Rather, they began buying much larger quantities, filling one or two shipping containers per trip, several times per year. Today's *biznesmeny* perceive themselves as professionals. They are generally proud of what they do, even though bazaar culture is still associated with chaos, low-status goods and a non-modern lifestyle (see Antonyan in this issue and Melkumyan forthcoming). Despite their bad reputation, it is through these bazaars, which function as trading hubs in the region and have expanded since the 1990s, that many goods arrive in Russia, Central Asia and the Caucasus today (Karrar 2013, 2017; Alff 2014; Spector 2017).

My colleague Zviad Mirtskhulava and I travelled with a group of Georgian businessmen from Lilo Bazroba, the largest wholesale market in the South Caucasus, to Yabaolu in Beijing in the spring of 2017. In this article I describe my observations from this trip, which I supplement with long-term field observations in the region – Armenia, Crimea, Georgia – since 2006. Through conversations and interviews with traders in the Caucasus, I am able to identify some patterns indicative of common practice.

Much of this practice can be classified as informal, as it is not regulated by state institutions but is based on oral contracts and organized through personal relationships (Sassen 2001). A term that appears recurrently in literature on petty trade to capture these practices is 'ethnic entrepreneurship'. According to this body of literature, which includes scholarship on transnational trade activity in post-Soviet Eurasia, Caucasian and Central Asian traders in particular organize their activities along personal ethnic and community lines. The notion of trust plays a central role in this argument. Thus, according to research on the informal economy, trust is vital for smooth economic transactions in face-to-face businesses.

I explore this set of assumptions in the specific context of the China trade. I illustrate that while kinship and ethnicity are indeed important, they are not the basis on which Georgian traders build their businesses. Instead, as I observed in Yabaolu, cooperation based on local notions of friendship plays a key role in ethnic and interethnic contexts. Analyzing these forms of cooperation, on different local and international (global) levels, sheds light on the relationship between economic activity and socio-cultural values.

This article starts with a description of the market setting. I then turn to the idea of trust in relation to the theoretical concept of ethnic entrepreneurship and explain the role of kinship and friendship in the specific context of my research field. Finally, I describe the business code of honour, which establishes new forms of trust as a kind of pragmatic consensus enabling smooth exchange between strangers in an informal economic environment.

Tbilisi and Beijing

Yabaolu Market emerged in 1988, according to Guzei (2015). It developed from a street market into a covered market in 1999, and later became a shopping complex for post-Soviet trade tourism, covering more than 220,000 square metres adjacent to Ritan Park. I have not found an estimate of the number of traders, employees and service providers working in the market, and it is difficult to extrapolate. Besides the trading businesses themselves, cargo companies, banks and warehouses, but also hairdressers, restaurants, tourist agencies and many other service providers settled in the area to profit from the post-Soviet clientele. The merchandise ranges from all kinds of clothing, shoes, and items of everyday use, like kitchenware and electronic devices, to accessories like fake Gucci handbags and sunglasses and Louis Vuitton ties.

Linking markets

Guzei (2015) argues that the development of Yabaolu was tightly linked to the development of Cherkizovsky Market in Moscow, which in the 1990s became a hub for the distribution of Chinese merchandise in Eurasia.[2] Since the 1990s, several such trading hubs have emerged throughout the former Soviet region, mostly in the guise of bazaars. Bishkek's Dordoi in Central Asia (see Karrar and Rudaz in this issue) and Odessa's Sed'moi in Ukraine (Humphrey and Skvirskaja 2009; Marsden 2018; see also Ibanez-Tirado in this issue) are only some examples. Lilo Bazroba (bazaar/market), on the outskirts of Tbilisi, plays this role for the Caucasus region. Characteristically, these markets operate in a grey zone, evading state regulation and tax regimes, which is one reason why they have flourished (Humphrey and Skvirskaja 2009). Tens of thousands of people shop in these bazaars daily, and millions of dollars in merchandise changes hands.

According to Lilo Bazroba's administration, 41% of the imported merchandise sold in this market in 2017 originated in China.[3] A structured survey of 300 respondents conducted by our research team in the same year revealed that 19.5% of the respondents working in Lilo regularly or occasionally travelled to Chinese markets. Many of these traders today travel to Guangzhou. Levan and Ramaz, however, the traders Zviad and I accompanied on their business trip to Beijing, have been buying their goods in Yabaolu since the 1990s.

Yabaolu Market is a Russian – or post-Soviet – enclave in central Beijing. Today, it consists of sidewalks lined with small shops and large trade centres named Goja, Zhitan, Tjanja, Jabao and Czili (Dasha). Signs in the Cyrillic alphabet advertise fur sellers, currency exchanges and SIM card shops. There is a Russian restaurant called Mango, where *salat olivje* and other Russian dishes are on the menu, and in the streets Russian-speaking traders can be observed carrying their merchandise and gathering in groups to chat (Figure 1).

Ramaz, who is probably in his fifties, told me how he had come to Yabaolu for the first time. A friend introduced him to the marketplace. After half a day of walking around, he was convinced that he could manage his business without any further help. Levan, who worked as a miner until the break-up of the Soviet Union, had started his business in a similar way. Levan and Ramaz have travelled together since the 1990s. Their stories exemplify the transformation of traders from *chelnoki* to *biznesmeny*. Giorgi, the third member of our travel group, was coming with them for the first time. He owns a shop in a bazaar in

Figure 1. Sidewalk in Yabaolu Market, Beijing (photo by the author).

Batumi, on the Black Sea coast of Georgia. He had been buying his merchandise in Istanbul. His mother, a friend of Ramaz's wife, asked Ramaz to take him to Beijing and introduce him to the 'Chinese business'.

Linking people

Georgian traders tend to stay abroad for between two and four weeks. To get to China, our group took a flight from Tbilisi via Baku to Doha, Qatar, and from there to Beijing. We stayed for two weeks in a hostel next to Yabaolu. A day after our arrival, we were joined by Lena, a Russian woman from Blagoveshensk in Siberia, who has been a friend of Levan and Ramaz for many years. Once in Beijing, each trader had their own schedule and worked individually. Thus, the group were apart for most of the day, but the men shared their hostel rooms, and in the evening, we had dinner and drinks together. During these social events, the businesspeople shared their knowledge and discussed their strategies and networks. They pooled some of their resources, organized cargo shipping together, and helped each other connect with the 'right people'.

In Yabaolu almost all of the places the traders visited were within walking distance. The first day, all four rushed from trade centre to trade centre and from shop to shop checking the seasonal merchandise. Levan specialized in sneakers, Ramaz and Giorgi in women's fashion, and Lena in men's fashion. But though they checked all the displays and prices in different shops, they finally came back to Chinese business partners with whom they already had long-term relationships and with whom they had worked regularly.

As a rule, conversation took place in Russian. I could observe that little presents were exchanged between trusted long-term partners and that the Chinese businesspeople supported their partners in organizing their stays. Chinese business partners exchange money, give travel advice, mediate between factories and traders, translate documents, help negotiate with cargo companies, buy local train and airplane tickets, and even manage day trips, sightseeing and leisure time for their 'friends' from abroad. They take over many of the tasks of 'cultural brokers'. Such brokers, according to Mathews (2015, 139–140), are becoming ever more important in an age of globalization, as 'people are increasingly thrust into parts of the world of which they may know little'. 'It is cultural brokers who provide them an anchor of cultural knowledge':

> This is particularly true within the world of low-end globalization, where there are few formal institutional structures – everything is based on trust and human relations rather than contracts and laws, and cultural brokers are brokers exactly because they have acquired such trust.

Trade activity

Generally, business proceeds along the same sequence. First, traders try to get an overview of the market. They try to get a sense of the latest fashions. This is important because, as a Chinese businesswoman who works with Lena put it:

> You have to feel the trend before the others do. You have to buy it before everyone else. Otherwise, you will have the same goods as everyone else. And then, after a while, people understand that there is a new trend and buy new stuff. But then it is too late. Again, everyone will have it.

Or:

> Competition is big! [*Konkurentsia bol'shaya!*]

Then, traders start their inquiries, which always include the same questions: 'What is the *optom* [wholesale] price?'; 'How many is a *patchka*?' – that is, how many pieces are in a 'batch', the minimum purchase for the wholesale price (usually 4, 8, 12, or 24 pieces per *patchka* for clothes, shoes and similar items); and 'By when can you deliver it?' – that is, will the goods be available within the next few days, and will the trader be able to check the goods before they are ordered and sent to the cargo shipping company? The answer to the latter, I was told, is usually positive, and goods are delivered within two to five days.

It can take several hours, and many discussions, before traders make their decision. Thanks to the internet and phones, they can connect with their family and colleagues in Georgia or Russia to discuss their choices and shopping plans. If necessary, details of the designs can normally be changed. Chinese factories tend to be flexible and work fast. They can adapt the materials and colours and add or omit details within a few days.

Once the traders have decided what to buy, they order the goods from their Chinese partner, who, in turn, orders the goods from the factory. The quantity ordered depends on the nature and price of the *tovar* (merchandise). Lena told me that she usually buys merchandise worth about USD 30,000 per trip. It mainly consists of shirts, which cost between 28 and 45 renminbi (USD 4–7), ties, which cost about 50 renminbi (USD 7–8), and coats, which cost between 150 and 300 renminbi (USD 22–45). She also buys equipment for her shop, accessories (like belts, sunglasses and scarves), and some special orders for clients and acquaintances who have asked her to bring back a specific item or design.

Levan bought approximately 1500 pairs of sneakers. In total, he usually spends about USD 50,000 per trip. Giorgi only bought 15 furs, at about 300–400 renminbi (USD 45–50) each, as he was not satisfied with the business opportunities in Beijing. Ramaz never told me how much he had spent or bought. He kept his transactions secret.

Payments are made in cash (renminbi), which is typical for this kind of informal exchange.[4] I was surprised to learn that Lena's plastic bag, which she was walking around with all day, contained several thousand dollars. When traders decide to place an order, they first leave a deposit. The rest of the money is paid in a second round of negotiations, when the order and invoice are finalized. These invoices have to be shown to customs officials when the goods clear customs in Georgia. After payment, the goods are delivered directly to the trader's cargo terminal.

Larger shops, which have a more distant relationship with their clientele (in these shops, traders establish relationships with the salespeople, not with the shop owner), register their buyers in their books and computers. They keep records of previous orders, which entitle the client to ask for *skidki* (price reductions). In small shops managed by a single shop owner, deals are managed on a more personal level. Sometimes this works *bez deneg* (without money), which means that the money can be handed over later, for example by some friend or acquaintance (a fellow trader) who travels to China within the next few months. The delays enable traders to sell some of the goods and accumulate some money before paying their debts. Working *bez deneg* is a synonym for 'working on trust'.

Levan's and Ramaz's cargo terminal in Beijing was in the basement of one of the major trade centres. Here, traders count the ordered items after they arrive from the factory. It is important to save space during packing, as it can save money, and the traders monitor the process so as not to be cheated (Figure 2).

If the quantity and bulk of the merchandise is less substantial, traders may buy goods and take them directly from the shop. The entry of our hostel was constantly occupied by these bulging packages, and Lena and I once found ourselves dragging such a package to the cargo station, a small garage elsewhere in the district. Each package is then weighed and measured to determine transport costs, paid for, and tagged with a number, the receiving address, and the trader's contact information (phone number).

Figure 2. Cargo terminal in Yabaolu Market, Beijing (photo by the author).

Levan's and Ramaz's merchandise would be brought by truck to Urumqi in western China, then to Almaty in Kazakhstan, then across the Caspian Sea to Baku, and finally to Tbilisi. Such pathways are responsive to the political situation and border regimes, and they may change at any moment (Marsden 2016; Zhang and Saxer 2017). Both traders had travelled along this route to get to know the people who handle the transport of their merchandise. Giorgi, who wanted to avoid tax payments, asked each of us to take two to five furs in our luggage. Everyone (including me) resented him for this, but there was no way to refuse. Complicity, when it comes to tricking the state, is a moral obligation and taken as natural.

From golden age to crisis

Business with China suffered in the economic crisis of 2008 and has not recovered since. There was a lot of nostalgia about the good old days before the crisis. Lena told me:

> In the past, there were a lot of people from all over the former Soviet Union. We had a lot of fun. We went dancing, and there was always a lot of laughter.... Now, we have the crisis. People don't come anymore. The time of our business is over.

Levan mentioned several times that Yabaolu used to be a much more vibrant place: 'People had to step aside, and you could hardly walk without pushing someone.' There are several reasons for this decline. First, Turkey has become an alternative destination, where almost the same merchandise is available for the same price. For many traders, the long trip to China does not pay off anymore. Second, other places in China (e.g., Guangzhou) are competing with Yabaolu. And third, the economic crisis has depressed business overall.

Since the development of Yabaolu and that of marketplaces in post-Soviet Eurasia are interconnected, they experience the same boom-and-bust cycles. As a result, the declining profitability of marketplaces like Cherkizovsky in Moscow and Lilo Bazroba in Tbilisi also affected Yabaolu. During our visit, the decline in sales was on everyone's lips.

Interestingly, when I talked to non-traders in Georgia or Armenia, most people would assert that flourishing shuttle trade is an indicator of a poor national economy. Bazaars are expected to disappear in favour of shopping malls and Western-style brand-name shops (even if the latter are supplied from the same Chinese factories). Street, shuttle and bazaar traders are perceived as a remnant of the transition economy. They do not fit the Western image of a modern citizen and entrepreneur. Paradoxically, then, while on the one hand traders would claim that they are suffering from the economic crisis, in their countries, on the other hand, they are perceived as a consequence of it.[5]

Indeed, the *chelnoki* mentioned above were pushed into trade because of the economic collapse (crisis) of the 1990s. Still, profits in trade were immense in those years, which is why those times are perceived as a golden age by traders.[6] Even small amounts of goods were worth a long journey.

In the 1990s many women played the role of pioneers in this emerging trade activity, but today's business is mainly in the hands of men. Although their profits are comparatively meagre, they have become a more or less permanent source of income and the foundation of the men's status. Business has become an aspect of professional identity, rather than merely representing an easy opportunity for survival.[7]

The question then is whether buying at Yabaolu in Beijing is *still* profitable. Giorgi, at the end of his trip, concluded that it makes no sense for him to go to China. At least in his branch of trade, the same merchandise is cheaper in Turkey. Also, post-Soviet trade activity in China seems to have shifted to Guangzhou, where factories are closer to the marketplace, which is why goods can be had for a lower price.

Levan, Lena and Ramaz explained that they continue to go to Yabaolu for two reasons: first, because they are used to it; and second, because it is here that they have trust-based contacts, which are essential for their business. It is therefore important to take a closer look at the informal social relationships that determine traders' decisions and strategies. I will focus on two categories of contacts: first, within the mobile community of traders from Georgia and other post-Soviet countries; and second, between Georgian/post-Soviet traders and Chinese businesspeople.

Ethnic entrepreneurship and trust

In regard to the first category of contacts, the current literature on shuttle trade – and on post-Soviet trade and bazaars in particular – frequently evokes the concepts of 'ethnic entrepreneurship' and 'ethnic markets'. Guzei (2015, 170), for example, classifies Yabaolu as an ethnic market because

> For the salesmen of Yabaolu, ethnicity is an intangible good. Decorating and advertising the market as 'Russian', its administration intends to attract a larger number of buyers. Precisely the commercial advantage forces the staff to mark the space in Russian style; that is why does Yabaolu's ethnic aureole not merely exist: it is also actively maintained and marketed.

Research on ethnic entrepreneurship can be traced back to classic works such as those of Weber (1993), Sombart (1914 [2001]) and Simmel (1992). In the contemporary literature, ethnic entrepreneurship is usually discussed in the framework of migration and diaspora studies. Hence, current research is mostly concerned with migrant entrepreneurs who are self-employed and establish a business in a host country or host society. Usually, the migrant entrepreneurs studied belong to a larger migrant community and respond to a niche demand resulting from this community's consumption habits and specific tastes. External factors in the host environment, cultural predispositions favouring self-employment, and cultural resources are the main topics debated in this field (Zimmer and Aldrich 1987; Aldrich and Waldinger 1990; Waldinger 1994; Volery 2007).

Ethnic entrepreneurship, like entrepreneurship in the classic sense, intends to combine resources 'in novel ways so as to create something of value' (Aldrich and Waldinger 1990, 112). In the common understanding, this should go along with innovation, processes of discovery, and the evaluation and exploitation of opportunities (Shane and Venkataraman 2000). But 'rather than breaking new ground in products, process, or administrative form', according to Aldrich and Waldinger (1990, 112; compare Rudaz in this issue), most ethnic businesses 'simply replicate and reproduce old forms', something that 'is especially likely in the retail and services sector, where most ethnic enterprises are found'.

The success of ethnic entrepreneurs is expected to be built on or influenced and formed by ethnic factors. Much of the literature emphasizes the importance of networks built on ethnic or kinship ties as a principle of organization and solidarity (Waldinger 1994; Volery 2007; Yalcin-Heckmann 2014). In some exceptional cases, trade is even described as a tool – a kind of pretext – to establish or deepen social ties among relatives and community members (Steenberg 2016, 2018).

In the context of Central Asian and Caucasian long-distance trade in particular, the importance of kinship networks and diaspora communities has been highlighted and described as providing a basic infrastructure connecting producers, drivers, traders and – sometimes – mafia or corrupt state officials (Holzlehner 2014; Yalcin-Heckmann 2014; Marsden 2016; Bram 2017). The advantage of such networks, it is argued, is that in a sphere of uncertainty, where the state is absent or perceived as an enemy, they provide social trust and control, thus serving as an informal alternative to state regulation (Gellner 1988).

In the social sciences, trust, as Humphrey (2018) summarizes, is usually associated with political forms: democracy, good governance, perceived political freedom, and public safety (Hosking, 2010; Mishler and Rose, 2005; Putnam, 1993; Rosanvallon 2008). A lack of trust, on the other hand, is perceived as a problem, the reason for or the outcome of crisis (Corsín Jiménez 2011). For Luhmann (2014 [1968]) trust was a precondition for everyday acts and thus human existence; for Simmel (1992) and Giddens (1990) it was necessary for the functioning of society; and for Habermas (1981) it was the basis of societal understanding and consensus, prerequisites for modernity (Mühlfried 2019, 10–11). It is an established perception that while 'high-trust societies' are politically and economically stable, 'low-trust societies' are not (Fukuyama 1995).

In the economy, according to Dasgupta (1988) and as summarized by Humphrey (2018, 11), 'Trust rests on the existence of a background agency, usually the state, that reliably enforces contracts and provides credible and impartial punishment for errant behaviour.' If the state fails to create this trust, as argued in research on informality and globalization from below, forms of interpersonal trust must replace it to create some kind of stability. Such forms of trust are usually explained as being backed up, as mentioned above, by social control through, for example, mafia-like or kinship networks (or both).[8]

Brednikova and Pachenkov (1999), who have conducted research among Caucasian traders in open-air markets in Saint Petersburg, criticize scholars' emphasis on kin and ethnicity. They argue that cooperation among members of the same ethnic group should be explained not by a shared socio-cultural identity but by pure pragmatism. In their view, ethnic entrepreneurship is based on rationality and a choice of simplicity: traders of the same ethnic and kin group cooperate because they can communicate in the same language, move and live in the same space, and have the tools of social control.

In the end, the two approaches explain the same phenomenon: the use of kin-based networks to guarantee and enforce agreements, which are said to be based on trust. One could of course also emphasize common ethics and culture rather than social control as a ground of trust and argue, with Humphrey (2018, 13), that

> If trust is the outcome of culturally specific performances, it will be doubly problematic in trans-border situations where there are radical differences in social strategies and ideas about what should be revealed and what hidden.

My observations, our survey data from Lilo Bazroba, and research on trade in other parts of the world (Hart 1988; Marsden 2016; Nikolotov 2019) challenge these assumptions. In the context described above, ethnic unity and social control do not by themselves result in trust. With Hart (1988, 187), I argue that while kinship is about obligations, trust is based on emotions, which stand 'in the middle of a continuum of words for belief mixing extremes of blind faith and open-eyed confidence'.

To participate in the long-distance trade described here requires that entrepreneurs – at least at the beginning of a trading relationship – risk trusting trade partners or fellow traders with whom they have no relationship other than an economic one. Without a minimum of credit or trust, this kind of economic activity simply does not work. Thus, using Humphrey's (2018) definition, trust means 'an intention to accept uncertainty and risk based on a positive expectation of others' (10), and it only then becomes 'a product of experience and … is constantly updated on accordance with calculations about probability of default or satisfactory completion of a given partner' (12). Mistrust and caution are therefore a natural part of the process of trust-building. As Marsden (2016, 40, 133), Carey (2017), and Mühlfried (2019) argue, mistrust can be a good strategy. Thus, for example, low expectations concerning the trustworthiness of others can result in positive relationships that can be trusted for their predictability (see also Broch-Due and Ystanes 2016).

Kin

In my work on urban life, city planning and social order in Yerevan, I observed how important the nuclear and extended family in Armenia was (Fehlings 2014, 2015). Its place there is comparable to its socio-cultural value in Georgia (Dragadze 2016) and Azerbaijan (Pfluger-Schindlbeck 2005; Roth 2013). The house is the ultimate symbol of the family (and kin in general) and family values, which are reflected and represented in home construction. It thus fits well with this perception of Caucasian societies that Levan and a significant number of survey respondents admitted that they – doing just what any other Georgian would do – put most of their profits into buying, renovating and building flats and houses, instead of reinvesting them, and that Levan, Ramaz and Giorgi emphasized that they 'do what they do for their families', which was an important topic during the dinners and drinking sessions included in our trip and in the toasts made during these social events. Family was a core factor and value that motivated the activities, decisions and behaviours of the Caucasian traders who travelled to Beijing.

However, unlike what is described in the literature on ethnic entrepreneurship mentioned above, the business activity I observed in Yabaolu itself was *not* based on kinship (or purely ethnic) networks. Fully 55% of the survey respondents from Lilo stated that they worked alone. Only 19% received help from family members living in Georgia, and only 3.4% could count on family members living and working abroad. Although this survey is far from representative, it aligns with my observations. For instance, Levan runs his booths in Lilo Bazroba with his nephew. Giorgi works with his mother, sister and wife, which is not surprising, because, as noted by Bechhofer and Elliott (1981), dependence on family labour is a feature of the petty bourgeoisie everywhere.[9] But neither relies on extensive kin networks – either in Georgia or abroad. In most cases, bazaar business is simply too small to involve and feed more people. Badri, a trader from Lilo Bazroba whom I visited several times and who owns three or four booths and could thus be considered relatively wealthy, employs several other salespeople, including his wife and his godchild's aunt. But that is it.

Certainly, the businesses I describe in this article are different from the businesses described by the mentioned authors, who studied traders who permanently work in marketplaces abroad and organize the whole market chain, from production to transport and sales. The traders from Lilo who deal in Chinese merchandise go to China to shop, essentially. They are sojourners. They use public infrastructure and need contacts. But instead of building on pre-existing kin- or ethnic-based structures, they build contacts *in the course of doing business*, as I will detail presently. Such observations are not necessarily surprising. Many trader communities apply similar strategies. The Afghan traders described by Marsden (2016, 57), for example,

> say that trust is central to their work; few, however, talk about trust as deriving from ties of kinship or of ethnic or national 'sameness'. Trust … requires hard work on the part of those in relationships with one another and this work must be consistently performed over extended periods of time.

Friendship

If some of the 'new' contacts can be framed as 'ethnic', they are based more on a concept of friendship than on the idea of a common origin. 'Friendship', more precisely friendship among male peers, is part of Caucasian sociability. Ramaz and Levan exhibited such a relationship, as did Levan and his partner Goga, who was not with us but was constantly mentioned and contacted by phone. Lena, even though she was Russian and a woman, was included in this circle, and Ramaz even mentioned an Azerbaijani trader who had become close to them.

Ramaz called this kind of relationship in Georgian *dzmakatsoba*, which he translated into Russian as *mushskaya lyubov* (male love). He emphasized that this love has nothing to do with homosexuality, and that it is 'one of the most important things in life, because men need each other'. When I asked him in a joking tone whether this was about his *birzha*,[10] which could be translated as neighbourhood or street gang, he answered very seriously: 'This is not the same. You can take something from the street as well. At some point in life. But this is different. I am talking about real friends.'

In Armenia, as well as in Georgia, these 'real friends' are called 'brothers' (Armenian: *aper*; Georgian: *dzma*) and together constitute a 'brotherhood' (Armenian: *aperuthjun*; Georgian: *dzmakatsoba*). Giorqi, because he was a friend of Ramaz, also became part of Levan's *dzmakatsoba*, because they got to know each other *cherez-dzmaktsi*, which is a compound combining the Russian *cherez* (through) and the Georgian *dzmakasi* (brother-men).

It is interesting that traders conceptualize their relationship as 'brotherhood' in the context of trade, as these local terms are generally linked to a very specific social and local environment.

Caucasian brotherhoods, unlike other forms of friendship,[11] usually emerge in neighbourhoods and their courtyards (Armenian: *hajat, bak*; Georgian: *ezo*). Male bonding in this milieu is built starting in childhood. There may be small differences between the Armenian *aperuthjun* and the Georgian *dzmakatsoba*,[12] but both concepts are related to notions of morality, trust, honour, honesty and masculinity and characterize the type of friends who are partners in all situations of life – be they personal or business-related. Hart (1988, 186) suggests, 'Trust has been historically associated with the notion of friend.' Indeed, trust and honour are particularly emphasized in this context and belong together. As stated by Mars and Altman (1983, 549): 'A man, who is not trusted has no honour: a man without honour cannot be trusted.' A brother-man can ask another brother-man for money – something for which some men would not even ask their relatives (Zakharova 2010; Frederiksen 2012, 2013; Fehlings 2014, 2015; Curro 2015).

These relationships are exclusive, which is why it is surprising that individuals who got to know each other in the context of business (sometimes only recently) and sometimes do not even share the same ethnic background (or gender) think of each other in these terms. One reason for the emergence of these sentiments, as was explained by my interlocutors, is the experience of travelling together. Marsden (2018) makes similar observations about Afghan traders, for whom travelling together is a method of testing the possibility of friendship and future economic partnership. Ramaz, Levan and Lena all remember stories about sickness, about feeling lost and lonely, and about getting help from strangers who became close friends just because they travelled with them.

Social trust in the Caucasus is relatively low (Paturyan 2011). Commonly, all three South Caucasian republics are classified as 'low-trust societies', to use Fukuyama's (1995) term. Indeed, as I witnessed during my fieldwork, interactions with strangers who do not belong to one's own network or community – 'one's own people' – are usually marked by caution and mistrust. It is thus a noteworthy story when Ramaz and Levan say that they once helped an Azerbaijani trader 'just because there was nobody else to help him'. As Ramaz explained, 'We are all abroad. It doesn't matter who you are and where you come from. Here, we need to help each other.'

Once, Levan had to take Lena to hospital. He thought she would die: 'It's horrible, if you know nobody and you don't understand a word.' In such circumstances, traders team up. Some teams, such as, for instance, the international groupings emerging in Moscow's peripheral markets described by Nikolotov (2019), are rather volatile, and their members disperse quickly. Others can be long-lasting. Levan, Lena, Ramaz and Goga eventually became *dzmakatsebi*. Back home, they established relationships between their families and, as they said, 'became family to each other'.

In summary, this means that business, in this case, is not built on ethnic or kinship ties as a principle of organization and solidarity. It is the other way around: relationships established in the course of business between members of the same ethnic or cultural background are afterwards buttressed by framing them in terms of kinship.

In anthropology, such relationships have been conceptualized as pseudo-, fictive, or para-kinship, as forms of relatedness founded on a broader understanding of kinship not based on biology (Carsten 2004, 2000). However, I would be reluctant to frame them as kinship at all. Friendship in the Caucasus, although related to notions of kinship, is a distinct category. As I have shown above, it is contrasted to that of kinship. Analytically, as Killick and Desai (2010, 5) argue, 'By subsuming friendship under a general category of relatedness, we miss what friendship does differently to kinship for the people who practice it, and the different ways in which the two general forms of relationship might be constituted in a particular society.'

Interethnic cooperation

In the environment of Yabaolu, to run a business, one has to establish trust not only with fellow countrymen or other post-Soviet people but also with Chinese mediators and business partners. Given the many racist prejudices I have heard in Russia, Ukraine and the Caucasus about the Chinese, I was rather surprised to observe close relationships between post-Soviet and Chinese traders in Yabaolu. Of course, relationships of trust are exclusive and do not necessarily dispel prejudices. As Ramaz put it, 'We know good people here. But there are also people you should not even talk to.'

The Chinese partners the traders trust have been working with them for many years. A Chinese woman going by Sofia,[13] for example, became Levan's friend. They joked with each other, exchanged little presents, and chatted about their families and holidays. Apparently, they were regularly in touch via Skype and WhatsApp and sent each other birthday wishes and greetings for the major holidays. There was affection.

Allies

Communication across ethnic lines is relatively easy. Many Chinese businesspeople in Yabaolu are fluent in Russian. Some of them, like Sofia, grew up near the Russian–Chinese border; others studied in Russia or Ukraine, like Lena's partner and friend Alisia; still others, such as some salespersons and cargo workers, learned Russian working for Russian companies or in the market. These Russian-speaking Chinese have adopted not only the language itself but also its timbre and the Russian way of speaking – of arguing and bargaining. There is little exotic in these interethnic interactions. The common language promotes the development of trust, perhaps because, as Habermas (1981, 398) argues, 'We cannot distrust our mother tongue. For it is through the mother tongue that cultural traditions run, as well as social integration.' The Chinese businesspeople also seem quite familiar with Russian (or post-Soviet) culture – and apparently easily adapt to their clients' and partners' expectations.

Besides the common language, common goals create closeness within interethnic Caucasian–Chinese business pairs, who form alliances against their competitors. Competitors are traders who work in the same marketplace and compete for the same clients. For the Chinese, these are other Chinese; for the Georgians, these are other Georgians; and for Lena, these are Chinese and Russians who have shops in Heihe or Blagoveshensk, close to her own catchment area. Levan's fiercest competitor sold shoes in Lilo Bazroba and bought his merchandise from a competitor of Sofia in Yabaolu. Generally, Chinese traders were afraid that other Chinese would copy their designs. Alisia, Lena's Chinese business partner, confidentially told her that she would like to come with us to have a look at the merchandise of the neighbouring shop, but then stayed away, saying, 'Better I don't come with you. Perhaps they will recognize me, and then this will be bad for you.'

Based on these observations, I want to suggest that interethnic cooperation is both built on mutual understanding and affection, and business-oriented. Even in business contexts, which are less 'personal', face-to-face interaction and a minimum of confidence lie at the basis of any interaction. Lena, for example, told Alisia that she would not order much from another, very well-established shop, because they had changed their staff. Lena explained that she did not want to work with different people all the time: 'You go there, and there are only strange faces. No one wants to work like this.' She also was very angry that the same shop had started to cooperate with another female trader from Blagoveshensk. Lena took it as a betrayal. We could see from the shop's register that the other woman had ordered considerable quantities of many designs, which ultimately forced Lena to choose from the remainder, since the market in Blagoveshensk would already be saturated. Trust and loyalty thus characterize good (business) relationships, not only among compatriots but also between business partners from different ethnicities and countries.

Business code

In the literature on ethnic entrepreneurship, it is social control that is described as a major tool to ensure trust. More precisely, kinship and ethnic networks are seen as being used to put pressure on their members, who may profit from them but are equally bound by obligations, rules and moral codes imposed by the network communities. If they do not fulfil the community's expectations, individuals may lose their status, be expelled and suffer ostracism, which goes along with the loss of support and social capital and the loss of access to social, political and economic resources. Failures are forgiven to some degree, but fraud is punished immediately.

But what happens if this mechanism of pressure does not work, as in the case of inter-ethnic international exchange? My answer to this question is relatively straightforward: common economic interests and the informal nature of the businesses described here have the same effect as the ethnic ties described in the context of ethnic entrepreneurship and 'family business'. Although the state – that is, the Georgian state – regulates trade within the country's borders (to some degree), the activity of Georgian traders abroad is based on face-to-face interaction and oral and written agreements that are unregulated and unprotected by state institutions. In this sense, this transnational business sphere is part of a 'globalization from below' or 'grassroots globalization' (Appadurai 2000, 2003; MacGaffey and Bazenguissa-Ganga 2000; Mathews 2011; Mathews and Alba Vega 2012; Portes 1997), which contrasts with globalization from above, usually understood as functioning through formal bodies such as nation-states, international financial institutions and regulated firms (Fehlings and Karrar 2016). The Chinese state seems to care even less about shuttle trade and small business than the Georgian officials.

Traders, on both sides, do not perceive the state (as a structure) as necessary at all. They try to avoid it and to solve all problems among themselves. The Chinese traders in Yabaolu thus invent and polish invoices for their clients from abroad, who have to show these bills at customs back home and are obliged to pay taxes when selling in local markets. In the transnational sphere, the market economy creates its own rules – its own culture.

A revealing incident occurred during my work with the traders in Beijing. My colleague Zviad and I were accompanying Levan, who was involved in noisy bargaining, when a Chinese shopkeeper from a neighbouring booth approached him. This person, who traded in gloves, remembered that he had seen Levan a few years ago, together with another Georgian trader, who left without paying a debt of USD 1000. He showed Levan a photograph of this man on his cell phone, and Levan recognized him. Levan was really embarrassed. He quickly explained that his fellow countryman was not his friend but just an acquaintance and tried to call him on his phone to remind him that he should pay his debt to the Chinese creditor. The Chinese trader was extremely polite and full of gratitude. He and Levan were completely in agreement on this topic: things like this should not happen! When I asked Levan whether he believed that his phone call would resolve the situation, he replied that the Georgian trader had not been lucky with his business in recent years, but that he should not have left without settling his bill.

It is shameful not to pay one's debts. Sometimes people pay if you put pressure on them, because they do not want to lose their good reputation. It is important that your name is clean. Otherwise you can't do business.

The pressure Levan was talking about is exercised from within one's own community (shaped by ethnic, kinship, and other local networks, but first of all by being a Georgian trader). Thus, Georgian traders will urge other Georgian traders to pay their bills. On the other hand, this pressure is linked to obligations incurred outside the local community. This story foregrounds a specific business code that guarantees smooth and effective transactions between traders of diverse ethnic, social and religious backgrounds in an informal international context for the good of the business of all.

As in community networks, the informal business world has its own sphere of gossip and rumours. If too many incidents of fraud occur in a marketplace, clients will simply avoid this place. If conditions in China get worse or too unpredictable, the flow of traders shifts towards Turkey or other less expensive locations. As Giorgi and Lena told me, 'We go where there are good conditions.' Equally, if a Georgian trader does not pay his bills in China, he threatens the business of his local comrades, as Chinese traders will be reluctant to cooperate with them in future. Building up good, reliable and long-term relationships is a rational decision and important for the future. Therefore, not surprisingly, the content of this business code of honour is articulated in local moral expressions.

Business friends

I do not think Levan, Ramaz, Giorgi or the other Georgian traders I met in Beijing or in Tbilisi would go as far as speaking of their Chinese business partners as *dzmakatsebi* or 'family'. If they did, they would certainly be joking. But they conceptualized economic partnerships as personal relationships and applied behaviours and codes of conduct sufficient for friendship in a broader sense, thus extending considerable trust. As in partnerships between Hindu traders and Muslim Afghans in the trade business between Odessa and Yiwu, cooperation 'arises from the pragmatic concerns of hard-nosed traders whose lives are caught at the cusps of multiple forms of co-dependencies' (Marsden 2018, 136). At the same time, partnership (friendship) with individuals from outside one's own group is a conscious and voluntary choice.

The concept of friendship in anthropology[14] has frequently been associated with Western societies and economic transformations connected to the rise of capitalism since the eighteenth century. According to this view, the increasing importance of friendship was a result of a new concept of the person linked to an ideology of individualism and a focus on sentiment. For Carrier (1999), the focus on sentiment based on unconditional affection and free will was a reason to reject friendship as a universal category. According to him, for example, Melanesians are people who cannot be friends. Still, I agree with Killick and Desai (2010, 2) that the notion of friendship is not bound to Western modernity. 'While economic change', as I have shown, 'may affect the way in which different relationships are constituted ... the idea of a clear progression from an emphasis on kinship to one of friendship is clearly simplifying a complex reality.'

Rather, it makes sense to broaden the definition of friendship and consider aspects of this relationship other than sentiment, some of which might contradict Western definitions of what friendship should be. One such aspect, contradicting the emphasis on emotion, is the instrumentality and pragmatism illustrated in the examples above. Here, material benefits are perceived as one of the core advantages of friendship, not excluding affection and good feelings (compare Killick and Desai 2010).

Another characteristic of the cooperation described above, which has been identified as a defining feature of friendship in anthropology, is equality. Unlike many social relationships, which involve 'opposed pairs' (father–son, employer–employee, husband–wife), friendship is based on 'persons paired in the same role' (Paine 1969). Issues of hierarchy are rather neglected, and gifts and debts, like those between business partners such as Levan and Sofia, are perceived not as creating uneven power relations but as establishing and confirming trust.

I had no chance to look at this complex interaction from the Chinese perspective. Whatever that perspective might be, it was compatible enough for them to work with the post-Soviet traders. Naturally, there is still a lot of mistrust and prejudice. But in the end, as Lena put it, business brings people together:

> Have you seen how they have become in Turkey? Now women have to wear those chadors and all this. But this does not harm business. Business runs as usual. They earn money, we earn money. That's good. What is bad about it? We ordinary people have to live.

One could conclude from all this that, although trade is socio-culturally embedded, it is, to some degree, trust in the market principle that, in the end, creates a common ground and level of trust in each other.

Conclusion

In this article I have outlined the development of informal post-Soviet trade with China. To outline mechanisms of trust-building, I then focused on a business trip by contemporary Georgian traders who travel to Beijing to buy their merchandise in Yabaolu. Trust is vital to transnational trade in the informal sphere of so-called globalization from below. I then turned to discussing the role of ethnicity and kinship. My analysis leads to the conclusion that – unlike in other trader communities – the Georgian businessmen who work in Yabaolu do not organize their businesses on the basis of ethnic or kinship ties. Instead, social relationships with colleagues from the same Caucasian and similar post-Soviet cultural backgrounds are created in the course of doing business and afterwards legitimized by framing them in terms of pseudo-kinship. Equally, relationships with Chinese business partners are based on personal ties that are built in the context of business but framed as friendship. The informal business environment stimulates the creation of such alliances, which are based on trust, reliability and reputation. Good behaviour with respect to these virtues forms a (business) code of honour, which guarantees smooth and effective transactions between traders of any ethnic, social and religious origin, replacing state regulation and legal law enforcement. Certainly, my observations apply to many different transnational contexts of small-scale bazaar and shuttle trade.

> The Himalayas, the Caucasus, and the Sahara are all historic regions that are comparable to one another not least because of the ways in which they are defined by internal heterogeneity, political fluidity, and forms of mobility and trade that bind their diverse populations together. (Marsden 2016, 22)

It would be interesting to compare the mechanisms of trust-building across these different contexts for a more general understanding of the mechanisms of long-distance small-scale trade.

Notes

1. Unlike the English term 'shuttle traders', the Russian term is associated with the specific historical context of the late 1980s and early 1990s. It is connected to so-called suitcase trade and part of the post-Soviet experience. There is some literature on this activity; see, e.g., Zabyelina (2012), Konstantinov (1996), Konstantinov, Kressel, and Thuen (1998), Werner (2004), Cieślewska (2014), Niyozov and Shamatov (2007), Fehlings (2017a, 2017b), Sasunkevich (2014), Polese (2006), Stammler-Gossman (2011), and Holzlehner (2014).
2. According to Nikolotov (2019, 879), Cherkizovsky was demonized starting in the early 2000s as a centre for 'ethnic criminal gangs, drug trade, trafficking, disease, and especially as a space representing the state's weakness in assuming control over these enormous monetary flows'. For this reason it was closed, and its traders moved to other marketplaces in Moscow.
3. Another 46% of imports came from Turkey, 6% from the United Arab Emirates, 4% from Azerbaijan, and 2% from Iran.
4. Payments are made in the local currency but calculated in USD.
5. This assessment is widespread in post-Soviet countries.
6. Nikolotov (2019, 901) speaks about a 'nostalgic Golden Age of lost futures', which is remembered as a time of solidarity.
7. In our survey in Lilo Bazroba in 2017, 36.1% of 300 respondents answered that they do their job because they see no alternative. Half of them (50.7%) indicated that they would stop doing what they do for the same fixed salary as an employee. Thus, this statement must be qualified accordingly.
8. The role of mafia-like structures in post-Soviet small-scale and bazaar trade has been extensively described (e.g., Holzlehner 2014; Kupatadze 2011; Light 2014; Mandel and Humphrey 2002; Slade 2009).
9. Likewise, 'personalistic and familistic ties are part of business operation in all capitalist societies' (Aldrich and Waldinger 1990, 126). The fact that researchers have not compared their findings on ethnic entrepreneurship to nonethnic business operation may have resulted in an overemphasis on the ethnic component of the former.
10. The Armenian brotherhood contains characteristics of *birzha* but is closer to *dzmakatsoba*. Birzha in Russian means 'stock exchange', but in Georgian slang it indicates identification with the peer group of one's *ubani* or *quartali* (neighbourhood) (Zakharova 2010).
11. E.g., among classmates and colleagues.
12. The Georgian *birzhas* have a strict hierarchy. This hierarchy and the *birzhas*' moral code parallel and are connected to the structure of the criminal world.
13. As it is difficult for foreign clients to pronounce Chinese names, Chinese businesspeople introduce themselves with Russian names like Dima, Sasha, Sofia and Alica.
14. See Killick and Desai (2010) and Bell and Coleman (1999).

Acknowledgements

I thank Hasan Karrar for making this special issue possible, Zviad Mirtskhulava for assistance during fieldwork, my research team for support and a first round of comments, the reviewers for their suggestions, and the proofreader and Martin Fotta for the careful editing. Last but not least I would like to express my gratitude to the Volkswagen Foundation for supporting this research.

Disclosure statement

No potential conflict of interest was reported by the author.

Funding

This work was supported by the Volkswagen Foundation.

References

Aldrich, H. E., and R. Waldinger. 1990. "Ethnicity and Entrepreneurship." *Annual Review of Sociology* 16: 111–135. doi:10.1146/annurev.so.16.080190.000551

Alff, H. 2014. "Embracing Chinese Modernity? Articulation and Positioning in China-Kazakhstan Trade and Exchange Processes." *Crossroads Asia Working Paper Series* 21.

Appadurai, A. 2000. "Grassroots Globalization and the Research Imagination." *Public Culture* 12 (1): 1-19.

Appadurai, A. 2003. *Modernity at Large: Cultural Dimensions of Globalization*. Minneapolis: University of Minnesota Press.

Bechhofer, F., and B. Elliott, eds. 1981. *The Petite Bourgeoisie: Comparative Studies of the Uneasy Stratum*. London: Macmillan.

Bell, S., and S. Coleman, eds. 1999. *The Anthropology of Friendship*. Oxford: Berg.

Bram, C. 2017. "Moscow Azerbaijani-Juhuro 'Oligarchs' and the Eurasian Trade Networks." *Caucasus Analytical Digest* 96: 5–8.

Brednikova, O., and O. Pachenkov. 1999. "Ethnicity of 'Ethnic Economy': Economic Immigrants to St. Petersburg." In *Ethnicity and Economy: Proceedings of the Seminar Held in St. Petersburg (9—12 September 1999), Vol. 8*, edited by O. Brednikova, V. Voronkov, and E. Chikadze, 108–115. St. Petersburg: CISR.

Broch-Due, V., and M. Ystanes, eds. 2016. *Trusting and Its Tribulations: Interdisciplinary Engagements with Intimacy, Sociality and Trust*. New York: Berghahn Books.

Carey, M. 2017. *Mistrust: An Ethnographic Theory*. Chicago: HAU Books.

Carrier, J. G. 1999. "People Who Can Be Friends: Selves and Social Relationships." In *The Anthropology of Friendship*, edited by S. Bell and S. Coleman, 21–31. Oxford: Berg.

Carsten, J. 2004. *After Kinship*. Cambridge: Cambridge University Press.

Carsten, J., ed. 2000. *Cultures of Relatedness: New Approaches to the Study of Kinship*. Cambridge: Cambridge University Press.

Cieślewska, A. 2014. "From Shuttle Trader to Businesswomen: The Informal Bazaar Economy in Kyrgyzstan." In *The Informal Post-Socialist Economy*, edited by J. Morris, and A. Polese, 121–134. London: Routledge.

Corsín Jiménez, A. 2011. "Trust in Anthropology." *Anthropological Theory* 11 (2): 177–196. doi:10.1177/1463499611407392

Curro, C. 2015. "Davabirzhaot! Conflicting Claims on Public Space in Tbilisi between Transparency and Opaqueness." *International Journal of Sociology and Social Policy* 35 (7/8): 497–512. doi:10.1108/IJSSP-12-2014-0122.

Dasgupta, P. 1988. "Trust as a Commodity." In *Trust: Making and Breaking Cooperative Relations*, edited by D. Gambetta, 49–73. Oxford: Wiley-Blackwell.

Dragadze, T. 2016. *Rural Families in Soviet Georgia: A Case Study in Ratcha Province*. London: Routledge.

Fehlings, S. 2014. *Jerewan: Urbanes Chaos und soziale Ordnung*. Berlin: LIT.

Fehlings, S. 2015. "Intimacy and Exposure: The Armenian 'Tun' and Yerevan's Public Space." *International Journal of Sociology and Social Policy* 35 (7/8): 513–532. doi:10.1108/IJSSP-02-2015-0028

Fehlings, S. 2017a. "The Chinese Connection: Informal Trade Relations between the Caucasus and China Since the Early 1990s." *Caucasus Analytical Digest* 96: 2–5.

Fehlings, S. 2017b. "From 'Chelnoki' to Global Players: Encounters in the Context of Caucasian (-Chinese) Trade Since the 1990s." *Paideuma* 63: 183–205.

Fehlings, S. 2018. "Informal Trade and Globalization in the Caucasus and Post-Soviet Eurasia." In *Mobilities, Boundaries, and Travelling Ideas: Rethinking Translocality beyond Central Asia and the Caucasus*, edited by M. Stephan-Emmrich, and P. Schröder, 229–262. Cambridge: Open Book.

Fehlings, S., and H. Karrar. 2016. "Informal Markets and Trade in the Caucasus and Central Asia: A Preliminary Framework for Field Research." *Working Paper Series on Informal Markets and Trade* 1. urn:nbn:de:hebis:30:3-415163.

Frederiksen, M. D. 2012. "Good Hearts or Big Bellies: Dzmakatsoba and Images of Masculinity in the Republic of Georgia." In *Young Men in Uncertain Times*, edited by V. Amit and N. Dyck, 165–187. New York: Berghahn Books.

Frederiksen, M. D. 2013. *Young Men, Time, and Boredom in the Republic of Georgia*. Philadelphia, PA: Temple University Press.

Fukuyama, F. 1995. *Trust: The Social Virtues and the Creation of Prosperity*. New York: Free Press Paperbacks.

Gellner, E. 1988. "Trust, Cohesion and the Social Order." In *Trust: Making and Breaking Cooperative Relations*, edited by D. Gambetta, 143–157. Oxford: Wiley-Blackwell.

Giddens, A. 1990. *The Consequences of Modernity*. Cambridge: Polity Press.

Guzei, I. 2015. "The 'Russian' Market in the Center of Beijing." In *Ethnic Markets in Russia: Space of Bargaining and Place of Meeting*, edited by V. Dyatlov and K. Grigorichev, 159–170. Irkutsk: Publishing House of ISU.

Habermas, J. 1981. *Theorie des kommunikativen Handelns (Vol. II)*. Frankfurt am Main: Suhrkamp.

Hart, K. 1988. "Kinship, Contract and Trust: The Economic Organization of Migrants in an African City Slum." In *Trust: Making and Breaking Cooperative Relations*, edited by D. Gambetta, 176–193. Oxford: Blackwell.

Holzlehner, T. 2014. *Shadow Networks: Border Economics, Informal Markets and Organized Crime in the Russian Far East*. Münster: LIT.

Hosking, G. 2010. *Trust: Money, Markets and Society*. London: Seagull Books.

Humphrey, C. 2002. *The Unmaking of Soviet Life: Everyday Economics after Socialism*. Ithaca: Cornell University Press.

Humphrey, C. 2018. "Introduction: Trusting and Mistrusting across Borders." In *Introduction in Trust and Mistrust in the Economy of the China-Russia Borderlands*, edited by C. Humphrey, 9–35. Amsterdam: Amsterdam University Press.

Humphrey, C., and V. Skvirskaja. 2009. "Trading Places: Post-Socialist Container Markets and the City." *Focaal: European Journal of Anthropology* 2009 (55): 61–73. doi:10.3167/fcl.2009.550105.

Karrar, H. 2013. "Merchants, Markets, and the State." *Critical Asian Studies* 45 (3): 459–480. doi:10.1080/14672715.2013.829315.

Karrar, H. 2017. "Do Bazaars Die? Notes on Failure in the Central Asian Bazaar." *Working Paper Series on Informal Markets and Trade* 4. urn:nbn:de:hebis:30:3-431138.

Killick, E., and A. Desai. 2010. "Introduction: Valuing Friendship." Introduction In *The Ways of Friendship: Anthropological Perspectives*, edited by E. Killick, and A. Desai, 1–19. Oxford: Berghahn Books.

Konstantinov, Y. 1996. "Patterns of Reinterpretation: Trader-Tourism in the Balkans (Bulgaria) as a Picaresque Metaphorical Enactment of Post-Totalitarianism." *American Ethnologist* 23 (4): 762–782. doi:10.1525/ae.1996.23.4.02a00050

Konstantinov, Y., G. M. Kressel, and T. Thuen. 1998. "Outclassed by Former Outcasts: Petty Trading in Varna." *American Ethnologist* 25 (4): 729–745. doi:10.1525/ae.1998.25.4.729

Kupatadze, A. 2011. "Similar Events, Different Outcomes: Accounting for Diverging Corruption: Patterns in Post-Revolution Georgia and Ukraine." *Caucasus Analytical Digest* 26: 2–6.

Light, M. 2014. "Police Reforms in the Republic of Georgia: The Convergence of Domestic and Foreign Policy in an Anti-Corruption Drive." *Policing and Society* 24 (3): 318–345. doi:10.1080/10439463.2013.784289.

Luhmann, N. 2014. *Vertrauen: Ein Mechanismus der Reduktion sozialer Komplexität*. Konstanz: UVK.

MacGaffey, J., and R. Bazenguissa-Ganga. 2000. *Congo-Paris: Transnational Traders on the Margins of the Law*. Bloomington: Indiana University Press.

Mandel, R., and C. Humphrey. 2002. *Markets and Moralities: Ethnographies of Postsocialism*. Oxford: Berg.

Mars, G., and Y. Altman. 1983. "The Cultural Bases of Soviet Georgia's Second Economy." *Soviet Studies* XXXV (4): 546-560.

Marsden, M. 2016. *Trading Worlds: Afghan Merchants across Modern Frontiers*. London: Hurst & Company.

Marsden, M. 2018. "Islamic Cosmopolitanism out of Muslim Asia: Hindu–Muslim Business Co-Operation between Odessa and Yiwu." *History and Anthropology* 29 (1): 121–139. doi:10.1080/02757206.2017.1359587

Mathews, G. 2011. *Ghetto at the Center of the World: Chungking Mansions*, Hong-Kong. Chicago: University of Chicago Press.

Mathews, G. 2015. "African Logistics Agents and Middlemen as Cultural Brokers in Guangzhou." *Journal of Current Chinese Affairs* 44 (4): 117–144.

Mathews, G., and C. Alba Vega. 2012. "Introduction: What is Globalization from Below?" In *Globalization from Below: The World's Other Economy*, edited by G. Mathews, G. L. Ribeiro, and C. Alba Vega, 1-15. London: Routledge.

Melkumyan, H. Forthcoming. "From Economic Survival to Lifestyle Choice: Flea Markets in Georgia and Armenia." Forthcoming in *Central Asian Survey*.

Mishler, W., and R. Rose. 2005. "What are the Political Consequences of Trust? A Test of Cultural and Institutional Theories in Russia." *Comparative Political Studies* 38 (9): 1050-1078.

Mühlfried, F. 2019. *Misstrauen: Vom Wert eines Unwertes*. Stuttgart: Philipp Reclam jun.

Nikolotov, A. 2019. "Volatile Conviviality: Joking Relations in Moscow's Marginal Marketplace." *Modern Asian Studies* 53 (3): 874–903. doi:10.1017/S0026749X1700107X

Niyozov, S., and D. Shamatov. 2007. "Teaching and Trading: Local Voices and Global Issues From Central Asia." *Toronto Studies in Central and Inner Asia* 8: 281–300.

Paine, R. 1969. "In Search of Friendship: An Exploratory Analysis in 'Middle-Class' Culture." *Man* 4 (4): 505–524. doi:10.2307/2798192

Paturyan, Y. 2011. "(Dis)Trusting People and Political Institutions in Armenia." *Caucasus Analytical Digest* 31: 6–9.

Pfluger-Schindlbeck, I. 2005. *Verwandtschaft, Religion und Geschlecht in Aserbaidschan*. Wiesbaden: Reichert.

Polese, A. 2006. "Border-Crossing as a Strategy of Daily Survival: The Odessa-Chisnau Elektrichka." *Anthropology of East Europe Review* 24 (1): 28–37.

Portes, A. 1997. "Globalization from Below: The Rise of Transnational Communities." WPTC-98-01.

Putnam, R. 1993. *Making Democracy Work*. Princeton: Princeton University Press.

Rosanvallon, P. 2008. *Counter-Democracy: Politics in an Age of Distrust*. Cambridge: Cambridge University Press.

Roth, S. 2013. "The Making of Home, the Making of Nation: Cultural Notions of Conflict and Displacement in Post-Soviet Azerbaijan." In *Caucasus Conflict Culture: Anthropological Perspectives on Times of Crisis*, edited by S. Voell and K. Khutsishvili, 169–194. Marburg: Curupira.

Sassen, S. 2001. *Global Cities: New York, London, Tokyo*. Princeton: Princeton University Press.

Sasunkevich, O. 2014. "'Business as Casual': Shuttle Trade on the Belarus-Lithuania Border." In *The Informal Post-Socialist Economy*, edited by J. Morris and A. Polese, 135–151. London: Routledge.

Shane, S., and S. Venkataraman. 2000. "The Promise of Entrepreneurship as a Field of Research." *Academy of Management Review* 25: 217–226.

Simmel, G. 1992. *Soziologie: Untersuchungen über die Formen der Vergesellschaftung*. Frankfurt am Main: Suhrkamp.

Slade, G. 2009. "The Georgian Mafia." *Caucasus Analytical Digest* 19: 5–8.

Sombart, W. 1914. *The Jews and Modern Capitalism*. Kitchener, Ontario: Batoche Books.

Spector, R. A. 2017. *Order at the Bazaar: Power and Trade in Central Asia*. Ithaca: Cornell University Press.

Stammler-Gossman, A. 2011. "'Winter-Tyres-for-a-Flower-Bed': Shuttle Trade on the Finnish-Russian Border." In *Subverting Borders: Doing Research on Smuggling and Small-Scale Trade*, edited by B. Bruns and J. Miggelbrink, 233–256. Wiesbaden: VS.

Steenberg, R. 2016. "Embedded Rubber Sandals: Trade and Gifts across the Sino-Kyrgyz Border." *Central Asian Survey* 35 (3): 405–420. doi:10.1080/02634937.2016.1221577

Steenberg, R. 2018. "Accumulating Trust: Uyghur Traders in the Sino-Kyrgyz Border Trade after 1991." In *Routledge Handbook of Asian Borderlands*, edited by A. Horstmann, M. Saxer, and A. Rippa, 294–303. Bilton Park: Routledge.

Volery, T. 2007. "Ethnic Entrepreneurship: A Theoretical Framework." In *Handbook of Research on Ethnic Minority Entrepreneurship: A Co-evolutionary View on Resource Management*, edited by D. Léo-Paul, 30–41. Cheltenham: Edward Elgar.

Waldinger, R. 1994. "The Making of an Immigrant Niche." *International Migration Review* 28 (1): 3–30. doi:10.1177/019791839402800101

Weber, M. 1993. *Die protestantische Ethik und der "Geist" des Kapitalismus*. Frankfurt: Athenäum Hain Hadenstein.

Werner, C. 2004. "Feminizing the New Silk Road: Women Traders in Rural Kazakhstan." In *Post-Soviet Women Encountering Transition: Nation-Building, Economic Survival, and Civic Activism*, edited by C. Nechemias and K. Kuehnast, 105–126. Baltimore: Johns Hopkins University Press.

Yalcin-Heckmann, L. 2014. "Informal Economy Writ Large and Small: From Azerbaijani Herb Traders to Moscow Shop Owners." In *The Informal Post-Socialist Economy: Embedded Practices and Livelihoods*, edited by J. Morris and A. Polese, 165–186. London: Routledge: Taylor & Francis Group.

Zabyelina, Y. 2012. "Costs and Benefits of Informal Economy: Shuttle Trade and Crime at Cherkizovsky Market." *Global Crime* 13 (2): 95–108. doi:10.1080/17440572.2012.674185

Zakharova, E. 2010. "Street Life in Tbilisi as a Factor of Male Socialisation." *Laboratorium* 1: 350–352.

Zhang, J., and M. Saxer. 2017. "Introduction: Neighbouring in the Borderworlds along China's Frontiers." In *The Art of Neighbouring: Making Relations across China's Borders*, edited by J. Zhang, and M. Saxer, 11–29. Amsterdam: Amsterdam University Press.

Zimmer, C., and H. E. Aldrich. 1987. "Resource Mobilization through Ethnic Networks." *Sociological Perspectives* 30 (4): 422–445. doi:10.2307/1389212

Business 2.0: Kyrgyz middlemen in Guangzhou

Philipp Schröder

ABSTRACT
Among the many 'businesspeople' whom the promise of commercial success has drawn to southern China in recent years one can find a small number of Kyrgyz middlemen. Working mostly with Russian-speaking clients, their job is to organize buying trips, coordinate with local manufacturers, translate, and oversee cargo shipments. Based on ethnographic fieldwork since 2013, this article examines in detail the careers, work routines and business model adopted by Kyrgyz middlemen in Guangzhou. I argue that in contrast to the early bazaar or shuttle traders, who have been operating across Eurasia since the 1990s, these Kyrgyz middlemen constitute a next kind of economic actor within more diversified, service-oriented and formalized value chains across post-Socialist Eurasia (referred to here as Business 2.0). One of these middlemen's most salient contributions is to translate between the informal and formal domains of national economies as well as within cross-border economic transactions.

Introduction

The history of Guangzhou in foreign trade dates back to the Qin dynasty, 221–206 BC. Located along the Pearl River, the city's port has also remained vital for economic development and urbanization, and as a gateway to the outside world, throughout later periods. Since these origins of the maritime Silk Road, this included the colonial era of British influence after the First Opium War (1839–42; van Dyke 2005), and the years 1949–1978, when trading activities of the People's Republic of China focused on brother countries in the Communist Bloc (Guo and Liu 2012, 66).

In 1978, the post-Mao leadership under Deng Xiaoping announced its new economic policy of 'reform and opening up'. In the 1980s, to advance 'socialism with Chinese characteristics', measures were implemented to decollectivize agriculture, attract foreign investment, privatize state-owned industries, lift price controls, and permit citizens to start their own private enterprises. Guangdong Province, including its main city, Guangzhou, was chosen by the Party leadership to be at the very forefront of this restructuring towards a socialist market economy. From then on, the region evolved into China's prime base for light and textile industries, and a commercial infrastructure with special economic zones, wholesale markets, warehouses and logistics services was established (Zhou, Xu, and Shenasi 2016, 6).

Relocating to this new 'factory of the world' was especially attractive for China's rural populations, whose internal mobility was made possible by a relaxation of the state's migration controls. Many followed the promise of better income from working on a factory floor than in the traditional agricultural sector (Fan 1996, 28). As a result, the main cities of the Pearl River Delta, Guangzhou, Shenzhen, Foshan and Dongguan, are now among the most densely urbanized areas of the world. Shenzhen, for example, experienced a 'feverish' growth rate of 27% annually between 1980 and 2006 (Bach 2010, 422). And by 2020 China's 'floating population' of rural-to-urban migrants is projected to reach 291 million.[1]

Chinese nationals aside, since the early 2000s Guangzhou was also identified by all sorts of foreign business venturers as an appealing destination to make a good profit. Among them are about 20,000 traders from sub-Saharan Africa who currently reside in the city (Mathews 2015). Topics such as their local community life, exposure to racial discrimination, involvement in transnational commercial systems, and function as 'cultural brokers' between Africa and China have been well researched (e.g., Yang 2009; Bredeloup 2012; Gilles 2015).

But as far as the relations between China and the post-Soviet world are concerned, the primary subject of scientific inquiry has been the Middle Kingdom's westward reach across its national border. This has included, for example, an emerging Sinophobia alongside Chinese attempts to establish 'soft power' influence, to reach deals on resource extraction and energy delivery, and to make investments in infrastructure and business development as part of China's Belt and Road Initiative (Laruelle and Peyrouse 2012; Peyrouse 2016; Nursha 2018). Beyond such larger-scale matters, the daily lifeworlds and economic activities of citizens from neighbouring Central Asian countries who moved to China have attracted academic attention only recently. In particular, research has focused on commodity traders from Tajikistan who are active in the city of Yiwu (Ibañez-Tirado 2018; Ibañez-Tirado and Marsden 2018). The main objective of the present article is to discuss ethnographic insights on the career paths and work routines of another ethnic trading group with a different occupational profile that is operating in a different environment: ethnic-Kyrgyz middlemen in Guangzhou. Fieldwork for this article was conducted during multiple research trips to southern China between 2013 and 2015.

Following this introduction, the first empirical section (Chinese Careers) outlines the 'softer' entry these middlemen made into their line of business as compared to the earlier bazaar or shuttle traders of the 1990s. The latter were post-Socialist 'pioneers' navigating in a free market environment and usually had neither prior knowledge about capitalist practices nor professional training in the economic sphere. The second section, The Middleman Game, describes the practical details of the services my interlocutors provided. This included organizing buying trips to China for their Russian-speaking clientele, coordinating meetings with local manufacturers, translating during negotiations, and finally handling cargo shipments and quality control. The third section contrasts the business model adopted by the Kyrgyz middlemen in Guangzhou with that of their bazaar trading predecessors. Highlighting values such as reliability, politeness and professionalism, I argue that these middlemen represent a next kind of economic actor, referred to here as Business 2.0, within Eurasian value chains that have become more formalized, service-oriented and diversified since the post-Socialist 1990s.[2] I conclude with some comparative observations on the social positioning of the Kyrgyz within the multi-ethnic fabric of Guangzhou and reflect on the middlemen's own prediction that their business model could only be a temporary one, and that their longer-term economic future would be 'at home'.

Chinese careers: soft market entries

Marat's journey from Kyrgyzstan to Guangzhou

'In my case', says Marat, 'everything related to China started with *wushu* [a form of martial arts] once my uncle decided to train me and other boys in the village of my parents.' This was in the remote district of Kara Kulja, in southern Kyrgyzstan, in the middle of the 1990s. At that time, Marat's home country was no longer a member of the Soviet Union but an independent republic. Its economic system had been largely deregulated, privatized and geared to facilitating trade across more permeable borders. Marat remembers that in his youth, 'We were already flooded with all kinds of goods from China: toys, rubber sandals, CD players and construction materials.'

Alongside this merchandise, the first credible eyewitness reports on current life in China reached Kyrgyzstan's periphery. Marat's uncle had become fascinated with *wushu*, a full-contact sport developed in China after 1949, while he studied to be a teacher in Osh, the biggest city in southern Kyrgyzstan, in 1991. Some years later, the first of his pupils returned to Marat's village after he had spent a year learning Mandarin in China's Shandong Province (supported by a Kyrgyzstani government programme called Cadre of the Twenty-First Century). Marat was impressed by this young man:

> He was dressed well. . . . And he told us about China, how it is modernizing. Of course, in a small village like ours, there were not many such people. So I wanted to be like him already then. Yes, you can say that he was my stimulus.

About 15 years later, Marat and I sit in his rented apartment, close to the Zhongshanba metro station in Guangzhou. He tells me that after finishing village school he began studying in Osh in 2000. At that time, Marat was part of only the third cohort at this local university that was offered classes in Mandarin. 'But back then there were only five students in our group, and Chinese was generally still unpopular.' Following his graduation in 2005, Marat remained at the university for one more year to teach beginning Mandarin. His salary was stable, but never more than 3000 Kyrgyzstani som per month (about USD 70 at the time).

Dissatisfied, Marat tried for a career in trading. For that he could rely on experience and contacts from when he had translated for Chinese traders when he still was a student. This had already earned him about 5000 som (USD 120) per month. His side job usually took him to the Kara-Suu Bazaar, which is southern Kyrgyzstan's primary import-export site for merchandise 'made in China' and elsewhere. About 20 kilometres from Osh, the Kara-Suu Bazaar began as a *kolkhoz* (state farm) market in 1983. But in the 2000s it grew to feature 3000–7000 selling spots and serve as an essential hub in the regional economy, particularly with Uzbekistan (Karrar 2017).

In this period in post-Soviet Kyrgyzstan, being involved in commerce was no longer shameful, which in the 1990s was still driven by more general Socialist convictions about 'criminal speculation' (Mandel and Humphrey 2002; Hohnen 2003), or by the more particular ethno-historical reference that the Kyrgyz always used to be non-profit-seeking nomads (Schröder 2018). Many Kyrgyz had begun to associate the world of trading not primarily with personal, financial and cultural uncertainties, instead seeing it as the most promising route to middle- or upper-class success. This was even more apparent given the limited income that could be achieved in other careers, such as employment in the service industry or the public sector (unless one turned to bribe-taking – Engvall 2016).

'Therefore, I decided to make my own attempt at trading', recalls Marat. Together with an aunt who already rented a container in Kara-Suu, he began selling shoes. Some of them Marat bought and then resold from a Chinese business partner, for whom he had earlier worked as a translator. He also flew regularly to Urumqi, in the neighbouring Xinjiang region of China, to purchase other models directly. But it soon became obvious to Marat that his first business endeavour was about to fail:

> It just did not work out for us. Sometimes we could add only one som to the price we paid, at most maybe 10 or 15 som. The competition was big, and we were not set up properly, so we could not sell enough to survive.

Next, Marat relocated to Urumqi, where on his previous visits he had become acquainted with the owner of a Chinese company that exported pesticides to Kyrgyzstan and Kazakhstan. For the next four months, it was Marat's job to translate manuals and safety instructions from Mandarin to Russian. He remarked that although he was 'bored' by this monotonous task, his language skills improved in this environment where there was 'nothing else for me than to communicate in Chinese'.

In 2006, Marat managed to be hired for a trip to Guangzhou, where he translated for 'friends of my relative', who were in the typography business and looked to buy new equipment from a local manufacturer. This was Marat's first glimpse of the middleman game. He remembers: 'Back then, I had met only two or three other Kyrgyz in Guangzhou. And all of them I had already known from Urumqi. But only one did this job of being a middleman.' Marat still had fond memories of this one friend, who supported him once Marat finally decided to move from Urumqi to Guangzhou. Though this fellow Kyrgyz had arrived only half a year earlier, he offered Marat a job in his start-up company, and the two young men also shared an apartment.

Marat's tasks were to identify good-quality merchandise in local markets and build up a relationship with these manufacturers. He went out on his first own job with the representatives of a Russian wholesale shoe dealer, who on the successful completion of the business paid Marat 1500 yuan [USD 212] as a fee. Still, during his first half year in Guangzhou Marat struggled to make ends meet. In 2007, he tried a new approach. To find employment during the famous (biannual) Canton Import-Export Fair and other exhibitions, when Guangzhou was frequented by foreign buyers, Marat just stood outside the airport gates and handed out business cards that detailed his services.

> That is actually how I found my first clients, most of them Russians. My very first one was simply helpless, because the person who was supposed to meet and work with him just did not show up. . . . I still work with this particular client today, almost 10 years later.

Only in 2009 Marat could afford to take a first trip back home to Kyrgyzstan. In 2010, he already earned enough to sponsor language courses for his little brother, who first studied for a year near Shanghai but then moved to Guangzhou to be closer to Marat. A little later, Marat chose to leave his Kyrgyz friend's company, because of disagreements about the sharing of profits. 'Since then I have been working on my own. When I left my friend's company, some of our former clients decided to come with me, but mostly I had to find new partners.'

When Marat and I had this conversation in 2013, he could already look back at some quite profitable years as a freelancing middleman in Guangzhou. He had established a solid client base and a good reputation and usually was in such high demand that he even outsourced some work to his little brother. In great years he could earn up to USD 100,000. This enabled him to travel home whenever he wanted, and he owned and rented out several apartments in Kyrgyzstan's capital, Bishkek.

This close-up look at Marat's life trajectory illustrates some of the individual twists and turns in becoming a middleman in Guangzhou. But juxtaposing his biography with those of the other Kyrgyz I was in touch with in this city, a common pattern clearly emerges. First, they had exposure to China's commercial vitality in their 1990s' youth, which especially manifested itself in the massive inflow of consumer goods into local bazaars and from there into even the remotest villages. Second, they made a conscious choice to learn Mandarin, based on the conviction that it would be a profitable skill for future business-making. Marat took up Chinese studies in the southern Kyrgyz city of Osh, but some of his peers did so in Bishkek, or Moscow, or on-site in China. Third, during their days as students or shortly after, all of these young men had made their first attempts at trading with Chinese merchandise, often as junior partners of older relatives who were already active in that domain. Marat did so in Kara-Suu, while others gained their experiences in Bishkek's Dordoi Bazaar or in smaller or bigger markets between Moscow, Siberia or Russia's Far East (if family members had migrated there to trade). Fourth, all these later Kyrgyz middlemen had first gained experience somewhere else in China, as a student, translator or trader, before arriving in Guangzhou. In most cases, the starting point for this professional journey was the city of Urumqi, which is closest to Kyrgyzstan, and has a sizeable Muslim population, and where living costs are more affordable than in the Chinese metropolises further east.

Contrast: Kyrgyz trade pioneers in Russia

Taken together, I would call the career path of Marat and other such Kyrgyz middlemen a 'soft market entry'. My point of comparison is the first generation of Kyrgyz bazaar traders in the post-Socialist era, who relocated to other countries, usually Russia, with the same hope of increasing their earning potential. Yet the introduction of those pioneers to the capitalist world was rapid and unmediated, and the vast majority of them were entirely unprepared for it. Those young men and women, who were in their twenties and thirties in the early 1990s, had prepared for a communist future, not one in private trading (also because the resale of purchased goods at a profit had been criminalized as 'speculation' and 'parasitism' in the Soviet era – Stephan 1991; Fitzpatrick 2006). But with the collapse of salaries in the public sector during the 'dark years' of transformation, whoever had dreamed of becoming a scientist, medical doctor, nurse, engineer or teacher faced uncertainty in how to provide for a family.

Elzat is a typical case of such 'accidental trader' (Sahadeo 2011), that is, someone who unexpectedly needed to leave her original profession and become a *kommersant* (merchant). The recollections of Elzat about the days until she finally settled as a wholesale trader in Novosibirsk's main market offer quite a contrast to Marat's development. Instead of taking her place in a PhD programme in biology in Tashkent (Uzbekistan), Elzat embarked on her first trip to Poland in 1991, trying to sell cotton bed linens she had purchased from the 'famous *kombinat* [plant]' in her native city of Osh. 'But we were all economically ignorant', she commented, just after telling me that she had chosen to go to Warsaw 'only because my close friend heard from someone else that it would be a good market there. She convinced me that it would be worth it, and so we went there together.'

This brief quote reveals not only the large degree to which Elzat and other early traders had to rely on their existing social network and the word-of-mouth information circulating within it, but also that their trial-and-error process entailed significant other risks, both financial and personal (Cieslewska 2014). After her unsuccessful trip to Poland, which barely broke even, it took her much time and effort to identify more profitable sites and 'establish a channel' to sell the cotton products she had cheap access to at the time. Furthermore, a talent for improvisation was in high demand in those days of 'wild capitalism' to 'agree' on customs tariffs or bribes with border officials, or to escape the violent racketeers of post-Soviet bazaars and keep one's merchandise (Humphrey 2002). 'When going to Novosibirsk', Elzat remembered,

> we knew that the racketeers would be waiting for us at the train station. So we arranged with the train conductor that he would stop some hundred metres before the station. It was night, and so we could quickly get off and run away with our goods into the dark.

Such improvisations did not always work out. Elzat shared many stories with me in which aspiring trading careers were ended and families were left heavily indebted because whole bundles of goods got 'burnt' at border crossings (i.e., they were confiscated by uncompromising officials) or because some merchandise simply did not match the clients' taste or asking prices in a particular period. But if someone navigated these imponderables skilfully, the hunger for consumer products in post-Soviet Russia could mean enormous profits. Already in 1993, Elzat sometimes sent home up to USD 10,000 per week to support her family. Soon she would fly three times a month between Osh and her long-standing base in Novosibirsk, bringing in merchandise by air cargo. Elzat and her sisters, who she gradually introduced to the trade business in Novosibirsk, sometimes stored up to 3000 bathrobes or bed linens in one room of their rented apartment. 'More storage was not needed,' she says, 'because we sold such quantities within two or three days.'

Based on such experiences, pioneer traders such as Elzat quickly got used to investing all of their personal money all of the time, to relying on their gut decisions and to adjusting to an environment that they often referred to as 'chaotic' and 'as if among wolves'. Furthermore, they needed to handle such constant all-or-nothing scenarios within only one or two years of market acclimatization. Later on, Marat and the other Kyrgyz middlemen of Guangzhou could 'move into business' more gradually and thus enjoyed a softer market entry. They had acquired first-hand trading experience with Chinese merchandise, but in the comfortable capacity of a helping hand and not with their own livelihood permanently on the line. They obtained a significant part of their professional skills from education, especially Mandarin-language training, and did not have to cancel a previous career plan. Their first phase of 'learning by doing' commonly occurred from the salaried position of a translator, or even an employee of a company involved in China business, and thus did not have the grave financial risk of a self-employed trader. Elzat made her Poland trip within months of choosing not to pursue a PhD in biology, but in Marat's case 13 years elapsed between his first lesson in Mandarin and his becoming a freelance middleman in Guangzhou.

In that way, Elzat and Marat represent different generations of Kyrgyz capitalist actors. While my main point here was to use a glimpse into the first generation's entry into business to demonstrate how that of the second one was 'softer', the careers of Elzat and Marat also provide evidence of the formation of a post-Socialist market beyond that: first, the regional expansion of Kyrgyz economic involvement in regional value chains, from trading in goods 'made in China' in Russian bazaars to facilitating deals with manufacturers in China for third parties; second, the diversification of professional roles, which added to the bazaar traders the service-oriented job of the middlemen. I will discuss in which ways the latter is based on an entirely different model and perception of how to conduct business properly and successfully in the section Business 2.0. But we first need to understand the everyday work routines of Kyrgyz middlemen in Guangzhou.

The middleman game

Aziz's 'furniture tour' with clients from Azerbaijan

Aziz is a friend of Marat and fellow Kyrgyz middleman residing in Guangzhou. During our one-hour taxi ride to Foshan, which hosts one of world's largest furniture exhibition centres, he remembers the first assignment that took him there. 'I had to organize a furniture tour for clients from Azerbaijan. After I met them at the airport, we drove straight to Foshan. There, I showed them around so they could see the local supply and meet the manufacturers.' While Aziz guided his clients through the main wholesale market, which extends for more than 5 kilometres and features about 3500 businesses, he shared insights with them on the latest trends in furniture design, materials and pricing, but also on pitfalls to avoid.

'Among what they sold in Azerbaijan was rattan outdoor furniture. We first focused on this. Well, and that's how we ended up at Mr. Fang's [exhibition] stand and also got to know him personally.' Mr. Fang's company made a good first impression on the clients of Aziz, handing out an informative brochure with a presentable corporate design and offering good-quality furniture for a competitive price. 'But, of course it never stops there', explains Aziz. 'No professional client coming to China would be satisfied and make a contract until he saw the actual production site.' Aziz describes this as a delicate point in basically all similarly evolving business partnerships: the foreign buyer wants to ensure that negotiations occur directly with the actual manufacturer and not only with some Chinese middleman, who would unnecessarily inflate costs to provide their own profit, and who could not guarantee a durable partnership built on same-quality goods at a steady price.

The next day Aziz and his clients drove to Mr. Fang's factory in an industrial district of Foshan. Aziz depicts the tour they were given in detail:

> Mr. Fang explained the manufacturing process to the Azerbaijanis. They could also inspect the equipment, talk to some of the workers, and finally were brought to another showroom which had the same furniture as before in the exhibition centre. Then we moved to Mr. Fang's office and negotiations began. The Azerbaijanis were served tea and then we went through every item that they were interested in, bargaining about the price, the quantities and the delivery time.

According to Aziz, the two parties eventually concluded a 'satisfactory deal', and usually met right in the middle between the original asking price of Mr. Fang for a particular item and the counteroffer by the Azerbaijani businessmen.

For Aziz himself, this was an assignment with a 'below-average profit'. In total, he spent 10 days with his two clients from Azerbaijan, browsing through the exhibition halls in Foshan for other (non-rattan) furniture deals. His basic compensation was USD 100 per day for translation and guide services, plus expenses for food and accommodation. But Aziz had also negotiated percentages of the total order value from both parties on the successful completion of the deal. He elaborates:

> Our profit [that of middlemen] depends on ourselves, meaning on how well we agree with the Chinese manufacturer at the very beginning. So, once I notice that my clients like a certain product at an exhibition stand, I either quickly say a number to the Chinese guy [in Mandarin], for example 10, or I show it to him using the hand gesture for 10 [crossed index fingers of two hands or a closed fist of one hand]. This means that I demand 10% as a fee, which the Chinese manufacturer will add on top of his actual asking. That way, the client never gets suspicious about my individual interests, even if he and the Chinese partner put numbers down on paper later on.

Although at USD 5000 the order the Azerbaijanis placed with Mr. Fang was rather small, Aziz still earned USD 1050 for three days of work from just that one deal (USD 300 for translation, USD 500 as 10% from Mr. Fang and USD 250 as 5% from his clients).

Beyond that, the encounter with Mr. Fang proved to be a fortunate one for Aziz. Ever since Aziz guided the two Azerbaijanis through Foshan in 2012, he and Mr. Fang have remained in touch and further developed their relationship. In the following years, Aziz brought many more clients from all over the post-Soviet space to Mr. Fang's exhibition stand and his factory. The two even aimed to expand their business partnership. Aziz invited Mr. Fang to visit Kyrgyzstan when the latter began considering an investment there to escape the ever-rising labour costs in Guangzhou. In that regard, the tie between Aziz and Mr. Fang was considered by other Kyrgyz middlemen in Guangzhou 'particularly deep'.

The 'furniture tour' Aziz organized for the two traders from Azerbaijan illustrated especially the need for a middleman to walk a fine line between pushing deals towards a maximum value, because his service fee is based on this amount, while still giving the impression of acting in the clients' best interest and matching them with reliable Chinese counterparts. With this strategic approach, Aziz, Marat and other Kyrgyz middlemen in Guangzhou arranged for the export of Chinese-made goods as diverse as clothes and shoes, pharmaceuticals and medical supplies, toys, shower cabins, tractors, and parts of assembly lines.

Middleman tasks

The basic tasks in each of these middleman assignments were similar, including client communication, preparatory research, translation or consulting, and cargo handling. Depending on the particular merchandise, however, more or less effort was necessary to prepare, conduct and finalize a transaction (which then was reflected in the service fee charged). In one case, Marat needed to travel to five cities across different provinces of China to preselect the three most suitable manufacturers of larger sewing equipment. He also acquainted himself with the respective ISO standards this client wanted the equipment to comply with and learned the specific technical vocabulary in both Russian and Mandarin. Following the purchase, Marat did not risk sending such a high-value and sensitive good with just any cargo company: 'In this particular case of course I turned to the most reliable one there is in Guangzhou, even though this eventually cut some of my personal profit from that deal.'

The handling of a client's cargo emerged as a key task that separated the successful from the average middleman. To take care of the shipment from Guangzhou to the final destination, Marat and Aziz relied on individual ties each had developed with local cargo companies. For the middlemen themselves, this was an additional source of income, because for 'bringing goods' to a particular cargo company they could demand that the client be charged an additional fee based on weight or volume, such as USD 1 per kilogram. Furthermore, the middlemen could offer different price options to their clients according to various 'models of shipping'. The first choice to be made was between air, ship, train and truck, which significantly differed in speed: from three days with direct 'express air cargo' to Moscow to 18 days or longer by land through Urumqi (Xinjiang) and Central Asia. The next decision was whether to send the cargo the white, black or grey way. According to Aziz and other Kyrgyz middlemen, 'white' described a shipment of original goods with proper declaration papers, and 'black' as a shipment of knockoff or copy goods (Mathews, Lin, and Yang 2014, 226). In 2014, sending something the black way was significantly cheaper, at USD 5–10 per cubic metre, compared to USD 50 per cubic metre for the white way, but also stood a larger risk of being confiscated at border crossings (and thus depended on 'reliable contacts' with bribable customs officers). The grey way was a mixed shipment of original and knockoff/copy goods, for which the price was USD 25–30 per cubic metre.

Cargo handling was considered a matter of trust between a middleman and a client regarding two elements crucial in any trade: product quality and money. It was among the responsibilities of Aziz or Marat to thoroughly check that the merchandise that left the Chinese production site was in fact of the same standard, specification, colour, and so on, as the samples the clients had inspected during negotiations. This was meant to counter the fraud scheme practised by some Chinese manufacturers, who would fill the order with unsold inferior goods from their storage and then claim that the 'misunderstanding' could only be resolved if the goods were shipped back to them. Given that the usual arrangement between foreign buyers and Chinese manufacturers was that 30% of the total amount was paid up front and 70% after the completed shipment, the clients' loss from such a failed deal could be substantial (and they were then better advised to keep and try to sell these unwanted goods).

Clients usually entrusted the middlemen with their investment money and coordinated the release of payments with them. The funds were either deposited in cash with the middleman or sent via bank transfer. At the time of my fieldwork, the more established Kyrgyz middlemen of Guangzhou had their business registered as a service agency in Hong Kong. There they usually also kept their bank accounts, because transfers to mainland China via financial service providers such as Western Union were limited to USD 5000 (see also Gilles 2015, 39). If necessary, money was sent from Hong Kong by online banking to a branch or cooperation bank in Guangzhou and then could be cashed out there. In 2014, some of the Kyrgyz middlemen had also just begun to accept payments and deposits in bitcoin or other peer-to-peer cryptocurrencies.

A Kyrgyz niche?

Aziz, Marat and other Kyrgyz middlemen of similar standing had a diverse portfolio of permanent clients from all over the former Soviet Union. Some of the traders they worked for were from Kyrgyzstan as well. But there was general agreement that a decent middleman's livelihood would be impossible to accomplish with, as Aziz described it, 'only our own people and our small national market' (Kyrgyzstan had 5.8 million inhabitants in 2014). But why would a businessman from Azerbaijan, Kazakhstan or Russia rely on an ethnic Kyrgyz, and not on a fellow countryman, if obtaining merchandise 'made in China' involved equally large amounts of money and massive uncertainties? From talking to transnational traders who would have been potential clients of Aziz or Marat, but were not their actual clients, I learned that Kyrgyz middlemen were considered a good choice because of their language skills, their specific 'cultural behaviour', and their emplacement in a 'small nation'.

In contrast to the situation in neighbouring Uzbekistan and Tajikistan, in Kyrgyzstan the Russian language has maintained much of its high functionality since the dissolution of the Soviet Union. In Article 10 of the current Kyrgyzstani constitution, Russian is still referred to as the 'official language', next to Kyrgyz as the 'state language'.[3] Furthermore, Russian has remained integral to many domains of everyday life in Kyrgyzstan, such as mass media, popular culture and interethnic exchange, but also is prevalent in higher education and the urban business environment (Korth 2005; Schröder 2017, 163–67). This early and continuous exposure to Russian, as Marat remarked, proved to be an asset when enlarging one's network beyond Kyrgyz clients:

> When businessmen from Russia contacted one of us for the first time, they were often quite surprised that we basically speak Russian like a mother tongue, though we are from Central Asia. And then they appreciated the easy communication with us even more.

Language abilities aside, transnational entrepreneurs often remarked that middlemen from Kyrgyzstan would have a typical *mentalitet*, a mentality or a mindset, which was understood to positively distinguish them from that of other 'Central Asians'. As summarized by one ethnic Russian clothes-trader from Novosibirsk:

> Our own guys are very demanding and rude, without any idea of what service is. Several Tajiks I worked with, they were too shy to tell me about any difficulty or misunderstanding during our trip in China. Compared to that, I liked the mentality of the Kyrgyz middlemen. All of them were very polite and flexible when we needed to change something. But also, they were open about what they thought of the negotiations, the counterparts and the deals as such.

The Kyrgyz middlemen themselves happily agreed with this (primordial) essentialization of their collective identity, which was inspired by a Soviet ethnogenetic template

(Schröder 2018, 269–70). After acknowledging that 'such cultural differences in behaviour certainly help us', a fellow Kyrgyz middleman of Aziz and Marat then pointed to a rather strategic thought, which he considered not less important for foreign entrepreneurs: 'I know that they also like us because we cannot threaten their business at home. We cannot copy it.' In brokering a deal between them, a middleman usually gained deep insights into both their clients' venture and the manufacturing process of the Chinese counterparts. Yet afterwards the Kyrgyz middleman would usually lack the legal status, investment capital, network of buyers and political-administrative protection to duplicate that line of business in the national setting of the client. 'We cannot seriously compete with a Russian entrepreneur in Russia, because this market is too big and difficult to access for us', explained Marat. 'By choosing us, they also protect themselves, because a Russian middleman, for example, could open the same venture as one of his clients in Russia more easily than I ever could.'

In that way, the Kyrgyz middlemen in Guangzhou occupied a certain niche within the regional value chain of the China-export trade across Eurasia. Their attractiveness to businessmen from the former Soviet Union originated in a well-balanced relationship that incorporated various elements of closeness and distance: shared Russian language, the Kyrgyz 'open mentality', and the fact that these middlemen would be weak competitors outside their own small national market. At the same time, this shows that 'enough' cultural intimacy and trust to engage in business deals with Kyrgyz middlemen does not exclusively rest on the same ethnic background, shared citizenship, or even regional origin (Mathews 2015, 132).

Business 2.0: participating in a post-bazaar economy

Updated values: reliability, politeness and professionalism

Aziz, Marat and other Kyrgyz middlemen operating in Guangzhou remarked on the decisive role of online communication in their daily business routines. On the one hand, this referred to the technical functionality of Internet-based information exchange. The middlemen easily stayed in touch with their clients across multiple national borders through application services such as WeChat, instantly sending or receiving text and voice messages with their mobile phones or exchanging picture and video files of particular merchandise. They browsed Chinese e-commerce platforms such as taobao.com and alibaba.com to identify new potential manufacturers, to inquire about their product lines, and to get a first impression of their professionalism and customer friendliness (Schröder 2018, 277–81).

Internet infrastructure, mobile devices and software aside, the social reputation one could gain or lose online was of key concern to the Kyrgyz middlemen. It was something they understood to be directly convertible into good assignments. Some middlemen maintained their own websites in Russian, where they advertised the quality of their work (e.g., 'The services of our company – this means faster growth for your business') and documented in detail crucial steps of the workflow (e.g., a series of more than 70 pictures to show the disassembly and packaging of chandeliers prior to transport). The middlemen posted price lists for their services (e.g., 'conducting business negotiations – from USD 80') and provided contact details, with a postal address in Guangzhou and mobile phone numbers in Russia and China. Whereas the personal website was a nice tool for self-presentation, there also existed specific Internet forums through which clients could exchange their experiences with middlemen and leave comments about the quality of their services. This presented a more participatory, interactive setting than a website for following how the performance of middlemen was assessed and their professional reputations negotiated in regard to key skills and personal qualities.

The motivation to establish long-term client relations based on a good standing in the business community also carried over to the offline world. Beyond the quality of their own work input, the Kyrgyz middlemen of Guangzhou also took responsibility for other service providers they included in a deal, even if this cut into their own profit. Marat told me:

> In one case, the cargo company I chose made a mistake. They just send the wrong equipment to my client, but did not admit it. So eventually I paid for the right cargo to be shipped, because a client should not suffer from this mistake, and then maybe choose someone else next time or give me a bad review.

Whether online or in face-to-face encounters, the impression management of the Kyrgyz middlemen in Guangzhou was geared towards transparency and professionalism. More precisely, when asked about the core values that would carry their business model, Marat and his peers emphasized reliability (*nadezhnost*), politeness (*vezhlivost*), competence (*gramotnost*) and accuracy (*tochnost*).

Certainly, these are rather commonplace ingredients in the modern-day, global recipe of commercial success. But in the context of post-Socialist economies, such values contrast significantly with earlier ways of conducting business. Again, this can best be illustrated by the example of Elzat, the 'accidental trader' I introduced earlier. In the emerging capitalist market of the 1990s, Elzat's competitive advantages obviously could not have included years of practical experience in trading or any theoretical knowledge gained from a prior economic education. 'But', she argued, 'I was used to taking responsibility and deciding quickly. These have been my strengths since I, as the oldest child in the family, had to raise most of my eight siblings when we were younger.' In 2013, when I first inquired about Elzat in the bazaar of Novosibirsk, she was still famous for the decisiveness (*reshitelnost*) and fearlessness (*besstrashie*) she had developed in her childhood experiences. One fellow Kyrgyz trader, who had known Elzat for two decades, recalled: 'Yes, we always called her Lenin. That was her nickname from the beginning, because she marched forward no matter what, and she could not be stopped.'

Given her personal qualities, the early post-Soviet bazaar appears to have been the right place at the right time for Elzat. She and other 'pioneers of trade' depicted the market situation in the 1990s and early 2000s as strongly supply-oriented. 'After the [Soviet] Union fell, people were so hungry for goods that they were interested in anything', remembered Elzat

> If you somehow managed to bring your goods to the bazaar, past the borders and the racketeers, and if you had just a little feeling for what people could need, then you got rich easily. ... Once, for example, I made almost USD 50,000 just from selling candles before the New Year season.

In such a sellers' market, success depended less on satisfied and returning customers or retail buyers. The primary focus was on quick profits, even if this meant overcharging, or reselling defective merchandise (Geertz 1963, 35). In the operations of present-day traders in bazaars across the former Soviet Union, it is noticeable that such tactics have vanished since then. With a bazaar clientele that is more knowledgeable and selective than before, and with stronger competition among the wholesale traders themselves, the supply–demand relationship now appears to rather favour the buyers. Furthermore, as Fehlings (2017, 192) notes for current traders in Georgia and Armenia, they 'have to operate in a much more official framework and on a more visible level' ever since 'the state' has permeated bazaar economies with formalities such as licensing, taxation and import declarations.

I made the same observation during my fieldwork on bazaars in Russia and Kyrgyzstan, but none of the traders I encountered there had the service orientation of the Kyrgyz middlemen in China. In fact, Marat, Aziz and their peers self-consciously defined themselves as a 'new generation in business' and distinguished their approach from the one dominant in earlier post-Socialist capitalism. 'We are very different from shuttle traders [*chelnoki*] or market people [*baraholchiki*]', Marat pointed out. 'We are a modern version of them, an update, you could say.' Aziz framed the same thought as one of 'civilizational progress', referring to the still commonplace understanding of bazaars as chaotic, loud and dangerous locales (Spector 2017). Since the emergence of the first such markets in the 1980s Soviet era, the verb *bazarit* (literally 'to bazar') also came to be associated in Russian colloquial language with 'to argue', 'to swear', 'to scandalize' or 'to demand' (Belovinskiy 2015).

To capture the (perceived) evolution since the bazaar beginnings of Elzat and other pioneering traders, I want to refer to the 'anti-bazaar' business model advocated by Kyrgyz middlemen in Guangzhou as Business 2.0. Elzat and her contemporaries did not oppose this categorization or seem to be offended by it. Unlike the narratives told by the Kyrgyz middlemen around 2013, their recollections about the 1990s did not mention any 'joy' or 'freedom' they might have felt in their new post-Soviet occupation, and only a few traders of Elzat's generation admitted to a feeling of pride in the eventual material success they had achieved. Instead, the representatives of Business 1.0 foregrounded the overcoming of stigmatization and personal disdain after being forced to take up the bazaar life. As a friend of Elzat put it: 'It was an unavoidable necessity to survive and to struggle through the dark years [of post-Soviet transformation] for the sake of our children's future.'

Adjusting to a diversified, formalized market environment

Business 2.0 also points to further changes in market environments that have occurred since the former Soviet Socialist Republics gained independence and needed to integrate their national economies into an expanding capitalist system. Elzat still had to navigate the bazaars of Warsaw, Novosibirsk and Urumqi on her own, which took more time, faced language barriers, and eventually turned out to be more of a trial-and-error approach. More than 20 years later, the Kyrgyz middlemen are an embodiment of a growing labour division within regional value chains and the growing importance of specialist service providers. In Kyrgyzstan, Marat and his middleman peers belong to a recently emerging segment of white-collar professionals, which also include business consultants, PR and marketing specialists, and representatives of private-interest lobbying organizations (Schröder and Schröder 2017).

A related development concerns the growing relevance of formal institutions in the post-Socialist economic landscape across Eurasia. Multilateral efforts to regulate and harmonize policies such as export regulations, customs tariffs and sanitary standards are usually associated with (aspiration to) membership in bodies such as the World Trade Organization (WTO) and the Eurasian Economic Union.[4] Looking at Marat's work realities as of 2013 showed that a middleman needed to be aware of formal matters such as an equipment's exact technical categorization in order to have it smoothly shipped across multiple borders, and to ensure that his client could manufacture in compliance with international norms (which ideally would allow export to high-profit, Western European consumer markets). From that point of view, a story about an economy 'radically informalized' (Hann and Hart 2011, 115), such as the following one shared by a long-term fellow trader of Elzat, seems to be truly from another time and impossible today:

> I arrived at the border of northern China and [Russian] Siberia with all my goods. Desperate, and not knowing what to do, I walked along the tracks of the local train station. Finally, I spotted a cargo train that would be running along the Transsib [Trans-Siberian Railway] to Moscow. And I agreed with the conductor, on the spot, that I could load my goods into one of the empty wagons and he would let me off in Novosibirsk. Back then everything was possible for the right price.

For all the sellers, buyers, traders, middlemen and manufacturers involved, operating within a regional economic environment that nowadays is more diversified, more saturated and more strictly regulated generally means less personal and financial risk, but also lower profit margins. On the individual level, it appears that in a time of Business 2.0, the fearlessness and improvisational skills of a trader such as Elzat would be less in demand than the advanced language abilities and convincing professional demeanour of a middleman such as Marat.

Situated at the centre of Business 2.0 exchanges, these middlemen had become more than translators in the literal sense, such as from Russian or Kyrgyz to Mandarin and back. In fact, they were essential for processes of translating and brokering between the informal and formal domains within national economies, as well as along transnational value chains. In the present article, this became most apparent when Aziz first needed to build up a relationship with a future customer informally, through social networking or online forums, before he could later serve as a trusted advisor on whether a formal purchase agreement should be made between his customer and a Chinese manufacturer. In other instances, middlemen used their informal ties to get better deals for their clients from local cargo agents, to reliably bring this cargo across a border post between China and Kyrgyzstan through their 'guys', or to widen their clients' customer base by getting them in touch with their own friends or relatives who were active in a complementary line of business somewhere in the former Soviet Union. At the same time, the middlemen were handling a wide spectrum of formalities, from registering their own companies and striving to obtain longer-term business visas, to filing customs declarations and checking the ISO standards for their clients' equipment.

For these reasons, I argue that the Kyrgyz middlemen in Guangzhou do not typically represent 'globalization from below', which is primarily characterized by informality, small amounts of (cash) capital, low-priced merchandise and illegal or semi-legal transactions (Mathews and Vega 2012, 1). Judging from the business model and daily

Table 1. Comparing Business 1.0 and 2.0.

	Business 1.0: (accidental) bazaar traders	Business 2.0: business middlemen
Starting point	From belief in Soviet future to the 1990s' 'dark years' of transformation	From exposure to inflows of Chinese merchandise in the late 1990s to attraction to becoming businessmen
Entry	Rapid, only self-employed; market economy as unknown territory	Gradual, first as employee; market economy as the familiar system
Preparation	None, 'jumping into the sea'	Study of Mandarin, junior trader experiences
Environment	'Wild capitalism': high risk, high gain; informal agreements; one-(wo)man show	Formalizing (standards); diversifying (more actors); less risk, less profit; new white-collar professionalism
Model	Fearlessness, improvisation, quick profit	Reliability, professional services, partnerships

operations of Marat and his fellow middlemen, they could be said to engage in 'globalization from the middle'. This notion reflects their main economic functionality: translating and mediating between the various informal and formal aspects of regional value chains. It also underlines that these Kyrgyz middlemen commonly brokered deals that involved recently emerged (or still emerging, post-Socialist) middle classes: a middle-sized Chinese manufacturer; a midlevel trader or entrepreneur from somewhere in the Caucasus, Russia or Central Asia; and middlemen who self-identified as belonging to a 'Kyrgyz upper-middle class'. This insight, again, supports the argument of Morris and Polese (2014, 295) that informality is not exclusively a resource of social resilience for the marginalized or dispossessed, but also might be 'used by better-off segments of a society to achieve their goals' (Table 1).

Conclusion: leaving 'home' soon?

This article has examined the careers, work routines and business model of ethnic Kyrgyz middlemen who resided in Guangzhou. I contrasted the professional biographies of these freelancing middlemen, the first of which had arrived in southern China in 2006, with those of Kyrgyz 'trade pioneers', who began operating in post-Socialist bazaars in the 1990s.

My first observation was that the middlemen enjoyed a 'softer market entry' than the early traders, because they had more time to grow into their occupation and develop a particular skill set through education, while having the security of working in hired capacities (such as that of a translator). The second observation was that the attractiveness of Kyrgyz middlemen for clients from other post-Soviet republics emerged from their good command of the Russian language, their 'mindset' of being equally polite, flexible and candid, and their low (threat) potential to become a competitor in their clients' own national markets. The third observation was that the contemporary Kyrgyz middlemen presented reliability, politeness and professionalism to be at the core of their business model, whereas among the trade pioneers quick intuition, decisiveness and fearlessness had been considered to promise good profits in the bazaar economy. In the 20+ years of evolution from Business 1.0 to Business 2.0, this shift in conduct corresponded to a growing relevance of service providers and formal institutions (e.g., export regulations and international standards) in the diversifying value chains across Eurasia.

In both Business 1.0 and Business 2.0, we can generally detect practices of 'muddling through' – an experiential approach to deal with situations of uncertainty through flexible adaptation (Lindblom 1959). But considering that 'muddling through' commonly refers to changes that are 'slow, incremental and relatively cheap' (Donahoe 2009, 7), this would be more associated with Marat's informed, careful market entry and with his gradual professional trajectory leading to freelancing as a middleman in Guangzhou. In contrast, Elzat's career took a rapid turn at high speed into largely uncharted territory, namely from science to trade, within some months, during the 1990s' 'wild capitalism'. Therefore, it rather resembles the experiences of many post-reform Chinese entrepreneurs, who framed their beginnings in a socialist market economy as 'jumping into the sea' (Liu 2001).

Marat, Aziz and their peers shared a general characteristic with other 'middleman minorities' in that they 'functioned as economic and political intermediaries between rulers and populace but were regarded as outsiders by both' (Nyíri 2011, 146–47). For the Kyrgyz middlemen in Guangzhou, it remained true as well that within the Chinese expression 'foreign friend' (*waiguo pengyou*), the 'emphasis is always on "foreign" more than on friend' (Mathews 2015, 137). Yet, comparing their experiences with those of their colleagues from sub-Saharan Africa, the Kyrgyz middlemen's lack of social integration into local Chinese society was not due to racial stereotypes or distancing. None of the Kyrgyz middlemen reported any incident of ethnic discrimination. To the contrary, Marat and his peers understood the 'Asian phenotype and way of behaviour' they shared with the Chinese as increasing their business opportunities. Furthermore, the Kyrgyz flew under the social radar in Guangzhou because they were so few: in a city of more than 11 million there were an unofficially estimated 250 Kyrgyz, and of these about only 50 were middlemen, and the rest university students.

Despite some favourable conditions for a profitable niche in value chains tied to China's global export trade, it seemed unlikely already in 2013 that the group size and cultural visibility of a Kyrgyz diaspora in Guangzhou or other cities of China would increase in the next years. Most importantly, this was because the Kyrgyz middlemen themselves considered their business model in China temporary. During my fieldwork, Marat and others voiced complaints that it had been getting more difficult year by year. First, there was more local competition in Guangzhou, especially from a growing number of Russian middlemen and Russian cargo companies. Then, the acceptance of Russia and Kazakhstan into the WTO and the establishment of the Eurasian Customs Union in 2010 (with Russia and Kazakhstan as inaugural members) had narrowed Kyrgyzstan's comparative trade advantages. When Kyrgyzstan had still been the only WTO member in the region, and its business(wo)men had been supported by particularly trade-friendly national policies, the country had been the main entry point for goods 'made in China' for the wider region. But with these changing institutional affiliations and the continuing investment in transportation infrastructure as part of China's Belt and Road Initiative, alternative trade routes to the ones passing through Kyrgyzstan had gained momentum, for example the one from Xinjiang through Tajikistan to Afghanistan and Pakistan (Peyrouse 2011).

The Kyrgyz middlemen of Guangzhou also remarked that their limited legal status in China would prevent them from 'really settling down'. In particular, they mentioned their always temporary permission to stay, usually not longer than a one-year business visa, and the general restrictions on foreigners acquiring property in China. In that situation, the 'future time orientation' (Bonacich 1973, 585) of Marat, Aziz and their peers remained towards Kyrgyzstan, and during their days in China they aimed to work hard and spend little (which in the classic theory of middlemen minorities is called thrift). Instead of a lavish lifestyle in Guangzhou, they invested most of their profits in Bishkek real estate and prepared for a post-middleman career 'at home'. This strategy included developing a network of reliable Chinese partners and parsing the business models of their most successful clients for applicability to Kyrgyzstan. The aspiration that basically all of the Kyrgyz middlemen in Guangzhou shared around 2014 was either to become a large-scale importer or to get involved in the secondary sector of industrial production. Marat, for example, aimed for a deal with a well-known producer of 'elite shower cabins' to become their exclusive distributor in Kyrgyzstan and so 'create my own local monopoly'. Aziz tried to partner up with his long-time Chinese partner Mr. Fang to start a cement factory close to Bishkek and connect to the construction boom in Kyrgyzstan's capital at that time.

It will be interesting to follow up on whether these are the first indications of another shift in Kyrgyzstan's economic development after 1991, away from the early predominance of trade and the subsequent strengthening of the (middlemen) service sector, and towards a Business 3.0 scenario, with a 'new entrepreneurial spirit' that focuses on textiles, food and other areas of local processing or manufacturing (Schröder and Schröder 2017).

Notes

1. China Daily. "China's floating population to hit 291 million in 2020." Report. 12 December 2015. http://www.chinadaily.com.cn/business/2015-11/12/content_22438127.htm, accessed 25 July 2018.
2. As will become apparent throughout the article, my argument of a market 'evolution' from Business 1.0 to Business 2.0 does not rest on a strict comparison of the 1990s trade pioneers with the post-2005 business middlemen. What needs to be mentioned, however, is that (1) in the 1990s there were no such middlemen around as those depicted in the present contribution; and (2) many of the active Kyrgyz traders I encountered in the fieldwork for this research relied on the services of their ethnic fellow middlemen.
3. Constitution of the Kyrgyz Republic. Available at the website of the Ministry of Justice of the Kyrgyz Republic (http://cbd.minjust.gov.kg/act/view/ru-ru/202913/20?cl=ky-kg&mode=tekst); last accessed: 10 January 2020.
4. The EAEU is a comparatively new body, established in 2015, and is based on the Eurasian Customs Union, which itself was established in 2010. Furthermore, many countries across Eurasia have become members of the WTO rather recently (Kyrgyzstan in 1998; China in 2001; Russia in 2012; Tajikistan in 2013; Kazakhstan in 2015), and the applications of others (such as Azerbaijan and Uzbekistan) are still pending.

Acknowledgment

I thank Susanne Fehlings, Hasan Karrar and three anonymous reviewers for their valuable comments on earlier versions of this article.

Disclosure statement

No potential conflict of interest was reported by the author.

Funding

This work was supported by the Volkswagen Foundation [Grant no. Az. 86870].

ORCID

Philipp Schröder http://orcid.org/0000-0001-5228-0858

References

Bach, J. 2010. "'They Come in Peasants and Leave Citizens': Urban Villages and the Making of Shenzhen, China." *Cultural Anthropology* 25 (3): 421–458. doi:10.1111/j.1548-1360.2010.01066.x
Belovinskiy, L. V. 2015. *Encyclopedic Dictionary of Soviet Everyday Life*. Moscow: New Literature Review.
Bonacich, E. 1973. "A Theory of Middleman Minorities." *American Sociological Review* 38 (5): 583–594. doi:10.2307/2094409.
Bredeloup, S. 2012. "African Trading Post in Guangzhou: Emergent or Recurrent Commercial Form?" *African Diaspora* 5 (1): 27–50. doi:10.1163/187254612X646206.
Cieslewska, A. 2014. "From Shuttle Trader to Businesswomen: The Informal Bazaar Economy in Kyrgyzstan." In *The Informal Post-Socialist Economy: Embedded Practices and Livelihoods*, edited by J. Morris and A. Polese, 121–134. New York: Routledge.
Donahoe, B. 2009. "Situated Bounded Rationality: Linking Institutional Analysis to Cognitive, Processual, and Phenomenological Approaches in Anthropology." Max Planck Institute for Social Anthropology Halle/Saale Working Paper No. 117.
Dyke, P. van. 2005. *The Canton Trade: Life and Enterprise on the China Coast, 1700-1845*. Hong Kong: Hong Kong University Press.
Engvall, J. 2016. *The State as an Investment Market: Kyrgyzstan in Comparative Perspective*. Pittsburgh, PA: University of Pittsburgh Press.
Fan, C. C. 1996. "Economic Opportunities and Internal Migration: A Case Study of Guangdong Province, China." *Professional Geographer* 48 (1): 28–45. doi:10.1111/j.0033-0124.1996.00028.x.
Fehlings, S. 2017. "From Chelnoki to Global Players. Encounters in the Context of Caucasian (-Chinese) Trade since the 1990s." *Paideuma* 63: 183–205.
Fitzpatrick, S. 2006. "Social Parasites: How Tramps, Idle Youth, and Busy Entrepreneurs Impeded the Soviet March to Communism." *Cahiers Du Monde Russe* 47 (1/2): 377–408. doi:10.4000/monderusse.9607.
Geertz, C. 1963. *Peddlers and Princes: Social Change and Economic Modernization in Two Indonesian Towns*. Chicago, IL: University of Chicago Press.
Gilles, A. 2015. "The Social Construction of Guangzhou as a Translocal Trading Place." *Journal of Current Chinese Affairs* 44 (4): 17–47. doi:10.1177/186810261504400403.
Guo, X., and C. Liu. 2012. "Guangzhou's Special Path to Global City Status." In *Aspects of Urbanization in China: Shanghai, Hong Kong, Guangzhou*, edited by G. Bracken, 59–78. Amsterdam: Amsterdam University Press.
Hann, C., and K. h. Hart. 2011. *Economic Anthropology: History, Ethnography, Critique*. Cambridge, UK: Polity Press.
Hohnen, P. 2003. *A Market out of Place? Remaking Economic, Social, and Symbolic Boundaries in Post-Communist Lithuania*. Oxford: Oxford University Press.
Humphrey, C. 2002. *The Unmaking of Soviet Life: Everyday Economies after Socialism*. Ithaca, NY: Cornell University Press.
Ibañez-Tirado, D. 2018. "Hierarchies of Trade in Yiwu and Dushanbe: The Case of an Uzbek Merchant Family from Tajikistan." *History and Anthropology*, 29 (S1): S31–S47. doi:10.1080/02757206.2018.1506776.
Ibañez-Tirado, D., and M. Marsden. 2018. "Perspective: China's Old and New Central Asian Ties." *Current History*. https://www.academia.edu/37498925/Perspective_China_s_Old_and_New_Central_Asian_Ties.
Karrar, H. H. 2017. "Kyrgyzstan's Dordoi and Kara-Suu Bazaars: Mobility, Globalization and Survival in Two Central Asian Markets." *Globalizations* 14 (4): 643–657. doi:10.1080/14747731.2016.1201323.
Korth, B. 2005. *Language Attitudes towards Kyrgyz and Russian Discourse, Education and Policy in Post-Soviet Kyrgyzstan*. Bern: Peter Lang.

Laruelle, M., and S. Peyrouse. 2012. *The Chinese Question in Central Asia: Domestic Order, Social Change, and the Chinese Factor*. London: Hurst.

Lindblom, C. 1959. "The Science of Muddling Through." *Public Administration Review* 19: 79–88. doi:10.2307/973677.

Liu, X. R. 2001. *Jumping into the Sea: From Academics to Entrepreneurs in South China*. Lanham: Rowman & Littlefield.

Mandel, R., and C. Humphrey. 2002. *Markets and Moralities. Ethnographies of Postsocialism*. Oxford: Berg.

Mathews, G. 2015. "African Logistics Agents and Middlemen as Cultural Brokers in Guangzhou." *Journal of Current Chinese Affairs* 44 (4): 117–144. doi:10.1177/186810261504400406.

Mathews, G. n., and C. A. Vega. 2012. "Introduction: What Is Globalization from Below?" In *Globalization from Below: The World's Other Economy*, edited by G. Mathews, C. A. Vega, and G. L. Ribeiro, 1–16. New York: Routledge.

Mathews, G., D. Lin, and Y. Yang. 2014. "How to Evade States and Slip Past Borders: Lessons from Traders, Overstayers, and Asylum Seekers in Hong Kong and China." *City & Society* 26 (2): 217–238. doi:10.1111/ciso.12041.

Morris, J., and A. Polese. 2014. "Conclusion: Agency Strikes Back? Quo Vadis Informality?" In *The Informal Post-Socialist Economy: Embedded Practices and Livelihoods*, edited by J. Morris and A. Polese, 294–299. New York: Routledge.

Nursha, G. 2018. "Chinese Soft Power in Kazakhstan and Kyrgyzstan: A Confucius Institutes Case Study." In *China's Belt and Road Initiative and Its Impact in Central Asia*, edited by M. Laruelle, 135–142. Washington, DC: George Washington University. http://centralasiaprogram.org/wp-content/uploads/2017/12/OBOR_Book_.pdf.

Nyíri, P. 2011. "Chinese Entrepreneurs in Poor Countries: A Transnational 'Middleman Minority' and Its Futures." *Inter-Asia Cultural Studies* 12 (1): 145–153. doi:10.1080/14649373.2011.532985.

Peyrouse, S. 2011. "Tajikistan's New Trade: Cross-Border Commerce and the China-Afghanistan Link." *Ponars Eurasia* Policy Memo 169.

Peyrouse, S. 2016. "Discussing China: Sinophilia and Sinophobia in Central Asia." *Journal of Eurasian Studies* 7 (1): 14–23. doi:10.1016/j.euras.2015.10.003.

Sahadeo, J. 2011. "The Accidental Traders: Marginalization and Opportunity from the Southern Republics to Late Soviet Moscow." *Central Asian Survey* 30 (3–4): 521–540. doi:10.1080/02634937.2011.602563.

Schröder, P. 2017. *Bishkek Boys: Neighbourhood Youth and Urban Change in Kyrgyzstan's Capital*. Oxford and New York: Berghahn Books.

Schröder, P. 2018. "The Economics of Translocality: Epistemographic Observations from Fieldwork in (-between) Russia, China, and Kyrgyzstan." In *Mobilities, Boundaries, and Travelling Ideas: Rethinking Translocality beyond Central Asia and the Caucasus*, edited by M. Stephan-Emmrich and P. Schröder, 263–288. Cambridge: Open Book.

Schröder, P., and E. Schröder. 2017. *Entrepreneurship in Kyrgyzstan: Adjustments to a Changing Economic Environment*. Bishkek: Friedrich-Ebert-Stiftung.

Spector, R. 2017. *Order at the Bazaar: Power and Trade in Central Asia*. Ithaca, NY: Cornell University Press.

Stephan, P. B. 1991. "Perestroyka and Property: The Law of Ownership in the Post-Socialist Soviet Union." *American Journal of Comparative Law* 39 (1): 35–65. doi:10.2307/840670.

Yang, Y. 2009. "African Traders in Guangzhou: Routes, Reasons, Profits, Dreams." In *Pursuits of Happiness: Well-Being in Anthropological Perspective*, edited by G. Mathews and C. Izquierdo, 154–170. New York: Berghahn Books.

Zhou, M., T. Xu, and S. Shenasi. 2016. "Entrepreneurship and Interracial Dynamics: A Case Study of Self-Employed Africans and Chinese in Guangzhou, China." *Ethnic and Racial Studies*, January, 1–21. https://doi.org/10.1080/01419870.2015.1125008.

ᵭ OPEN ACCESS

Trade 'outside the law': Uzbek and Afghan transnational merchants between Yiwu and South-Central Asia

Diana Ibañez-Tirado and Magnus Marsden

ABSTRACT
This article analyses the trajectories of two transnational networks present in the Chinese city of Yiwu: Afghan merchants who trade goods in and out Afghanistan, Tajikistan and Pakistan; and Uzbek traders (citizens of either Tajikistan or Uzbekistan) who commercialize their merchandise in and out Tajikistan, Uzbekistan and Russia. Our aim is to capture an ethnographically grounded understanding of informal markets and economies by analysing the notion of trade 'outside the law', including the contested yet widely used category of the 'smuggler'. By paying attention to the fluidity of trading practices 'outside the law', we also address the uses and limitations of metaphors widely used in scholarly analysis of informal markets: notably those of 'lower' and 'higher' forms of globalization, and the transposition of formal-legal and informal-illegal exchanges onto the notions of economic 'centres' and 'peripheries'.

Introduction

In this article, we explore the commercial trajectories, interactions and activities of traders from South and Central Asia. A key node in the activities of the traders on whom we focus is the city of Yiwu in China's Zhejiang Province – a commercial hub they visit to procure goods for export and subsequent wholesale. More specifically, we document and analyse two networks: one comprising Afghan traders who move goods in formal and informal ways in and out Afghanistan, Tajikistan and Pakistan; and another made up of Uzbek traders who are citizens of either Tajikistan or Uzbekistan, and who transport goods in and out of Tajikistan, Uzbekistan and Russia.[1] The commercial practices (*tijorat* in Dari and Tajik; *business* in Russian) of these networks are highly complex: legal and formal, as well as illegal and informal, mechanisms of procuring, transporting and reselling their merchandise overlap as goods and traders move in and through Asia. We build on anthropological works that rethink informality and illegal forms of trade and exchange as sometimes being tolerated and at other times prohibited by state officials, and as practices that are experienced by those involved as 'simultaneously formal, informal, legal and illegal' (Galemba 2008, 20; see also Anteby 2008; Hartnett and Dawdy 2013; Prentice 2015). Along with other contributions in this special issue on informal economies and markets,

---

This is an Open Access article distributed under the terms of the Creative Commons Attribution License (http://creativecommons.org/licenses/by/4.0/), which permits unrestricted use, distribution, and reproduction in any medium, provided the original work is properly cited.

we seek to capture the fact that most of our informants' activities swing back and forth between practices and goods that are legal and those that various authorities and legal systems render as being 'illegal' and existing in 'the shadows' (*tenevoy, nezakonny* in Russian; *ghaireqanuni* in Farsi/Tajik). This also reflects aspects of the economy that, as Morris and Polese (2013) have argued, are not in straightforward processes of 'transition' from informal to formalized forms of trade but rather are positioned in relationship to these categories in the context of ongoing political and legal transformations.

A central analytical aim of this article is to engage with a range of metaphors frequently deployed by scholars in their analysis of informal markets. Such metaphors tend to suggest that the contributions made by such spaces to the global economy take place in the 'periphery' and are best conceived of as 'globalization from below', as opposed to more 'formal' forms of economic globalization that are driven by major transnational companies and enterprises. We build on the recognition this body of literature has brought to the significance of informal markets (and those who work within and between them) to globalizing processes. Yet we also suggest three distinct ways in which this approach might benefit from empirical and analytical clarification. First, we highlight the need for scholars to continue emphasizing the interpenetration of formal and informal forms of globalization. In so doing, we illuminate the importance of addressing how the actors involved in 'globalization from below' position their own activities in relationship to formal and informal forms of economic life. Second, we bring attention to the active contributions the traders we have worked with bring to economic globalization and at a variety of levels in a manner that reflects but also transcends the oft-made distinction between formal economic globalization and informal 'globalization from below'.

Trade outside the law, including smuggling, is of enduring historic significance in many contexts. As a result, it is analytically unhelpful to treat such modes of trade one-dimensionally, as a response by peripheral economic actors to formal forms of economic globalization enacted by multi-national companies. In a recent study, Mathew (2016) explored the ways in which the trade in counterfeit goods posed a threat to emerging forms of capitalism in the Arabian Sea. Similarly, Tagliacozzo (2002, 192) has suggested that, in South-East Asia, such informal modes of trade arose in the context of 'the political economy of corruption, the functioning of ethnic networks, and knowledge of local geographies'. In the study of Central Asia, Spector (2017) has argued that informal merchants in Kyrgyzstan have sought to tackle illegal practices and thus achieve institutional order and predictability in the local bazaars following the instability of the 1990s by playing an active role in the creation of trade unions. Building on studies that emphasize such historic interpenetrations between formal and informal forms of trade, we argue that the forms of trade outside the law on which we focus are not simply a response to modern and formal forms of economic globalization. Rather, they are of historic and enduring significance, inform important values in relationship to which traders lead their daily lives – including notions of freedom, autonomy and masculinity – and seek to perform and achieve through their labours of moving money, goods and commercial personnel between China and Central and South Asia.

The article deploys the concept of 'freedom of form' or 'formlessness' to illuminate the ways in which marketplaces constantly seek to escape the constraints of clear yet unrealistic structures and boundaries (Gandolfo 2013). Formlessness appeals to the fluidity of the trade outside the law conducted by our informants. At the same time, the fluidity intrinsic to such a mode of operating also questions the relevance of the hierarchies inherently embedded in metaphors such as 'globalization from below' and 'centre vs periphery' for understanding this type of regional and global trade. In her ethnography of markets in Lima, Gandolfo (2013) develops the notion of 'formlessness' to emphasize the ways both traders and state officials subtly challenge the range of institutions that seek to discipline and formalize marketplaces. As we explore in what follows, our informants regard activities 'outside the law' as absolutely necessary to conducting commerce in the contexts across which they work: both groups of traders often remark, 'we have no option other than finding a route around the law' (*roh, ekhtyar* in Dari/Tajik; *variant* in Russian). Although such remarks may suggest these traders' lack of alternatives, our ethnographic material suggests that for the people with whom we have worked, trade 'outside the law' is more than an economy of survival, a coping activity at times of crisis, or a mechanism to maximize profit. Trade outside the law also encompasses moral values and aesthetic standards that our informants invest in the ability to engage with formlessness: they find pleasure, risk, achievement and aspiration in their subtle, and at times more direct, modes of challenging institutional and legal trading conventions. An expanding body of literature has brought attention to the aesthetic dynamics of practices that have conventionally been regarded by anthropologists as immoral (e.g., Anderson 2011). In his work on the Mediterranean, Achilli (2018, 92) identifies 'the morality of smugglers' as a shared moral universe that is inhabited by migrants and smugglers. In this universe, illegality and deception involve mutuality and reciprocity: rather than being opposite poles, they work simultaneously with one another along a continuum, and this also fosters strong bonds between smugglers, customers and migrants. Ethnographically, we find a similar interaction between formlessness and our informants' moral universes. This is especially visible in relationship to their modes of enacting masculinity, their attitudes to inter-generational knowledge, and their shifting understandings of the reputational consequences of trading outside the law.

Informality and globalization: the metaphors of below/above and centre/periphery

'Globalization from below' and 'low-end globalization' are concepts that contrast informal and small-scale commerce with 'high-end globalization' in the form of institutionally transnational and affluent corporations. Globalization from below is 'the transnational flow of people and goods involving relatively small amounts of capital and informal, often semi-legal or illegal transactions, often associated with the "developing world", but in fact apparent across the globe' (Mathews and Alba Vega 2012, 1). Forms of commerce associated with globalization from below are widely conceived of as taking place in and across informal markets, mainly through illegal forms of trade such as piracy, the copying of goods, and smuggling (Yang 2012; Mathews, Lin, and Yang 2014; Lan 2017). There is also recognition of the ways in which informal and illegal practices are embedded in the operation of officially registered companies and corporations, as well as in global capitalism more generally (Tett 2010; Phillips 2011; Sanyal and Bhattacharyya 2009; Rajak and Dolan 2016). Informality is integral to the production and reproduction of the global economy, not only to forms of 'globalization from below' (Millar 2008; Zack 2014). Furthermore, states are central to the production of the moments at which illegality and informality is condoned or permitted to openly take place (Schneider and Schneider 2008; Faroqhi 2012; Endres 2014; Rasanayagam, Beyer, and Reeves 2014). Scholars in the social sciences and history have brought recognition to the ways in which the activities of trading networks are rendered illegal or informal as a result of the legal frameworks that have emerged from state-law, and the interpenetration of state-law with multinational corporations (Tagliacozzo 2009; Comaroff and Comaroff 2006; Galemba 2008; Ferradás 2013). The concept of globalization from below has done a great deal of conceptual work in bringing attention to alternative actors in processes of globalization. At the same time, however, it reifies the different levels and hierarchies at which globalizing processes take place.

In sum, scholarship on 'globalization from below' rightly identifies the individuals, networks and communities involved in informal markets as the authors and agents of global interconnectivity. At the same time, however, the term tends to reinforce distinctions between on the one hand illegal, informal, and at times criminal activities, and on the other hand forms of economic globalization that are formalized, large-scale and organized in relationship to stable legal frameworks. As Galemba (2008, 21) argues, 'the continuing portrayal of the state as one cohesive entity tends to ... reproduce the formal/informal dichotomy'.

Scholarship on smuggling networks also tends to reproduce the binary categories of centre/periphery, legal/illegal, and formal/informal. Scholars often conceive of smuggling activities as belonging to 'peripheral' and 'informal' market spaces. Such categories are frequently invested with a spatial definition, as taking place at the borders of the nation-state. Yeğen (1996), for example, argues that the legal distinction is *spatialized* in terms of the practices that are portrayed as happening at the 'centre' (legal), and others that thrive at the 'periphery' or margins of the state (illegal; cf. Bruns and Miggelbrink 2012). Borders are represented as the periphery, and informality and illegality as peripheral and thus secondary if not corrosive to national economies (Galemba 2013; Pınar Şenoğuz 2015). At the global scale, such activities are regarded as marginal, in the sense that national and international law forbid them. Concepts such as 'globalization from below' also spatialize them in reinforcing the idea that this form of economic life is most vibrant in the global periphery, or indeed its underbelly. Such hierarchies also reflect moral evaluations of the agency and identities of the actors: while recognized as contributing to globalization, scholarship confines the implication of their agency to the periphery, defined above all in term of its informality.[2]

Our case studies concerning Uzbek and Afghan trading networks focus on trading practices that are involved in the smuggling of goods across multiple boundaries. We explore how individuals and networks involved in the trade in commodities between Yiwu and Central and South Asia regard themselves as skilled in forging capillary-like routes for their activities that criss-cross formal and informal markets and commercial practices. We also point to their own critical awareness that their activities are regarded by external observers as 'informal', 'illegal' and 'small-scale', documenting the specific ways in which they position themselves morally in relationship to such perceptions, as well as to constant shifts in the legal and political environments across which they work.

After briefly introducing the fieldwork on which the article is based, in the following section, we discuss the inherently oscillating nature of the activities of traders who work 'outside the law'. First, we explore interpenetrations between formal and informal spheres by documenting how the status of merchandise changes from legal to illegal in moving through the commercial chains. Second, we analyse how traders' moral evaluations of the nature of their activities swing between, on the one hand, the notion of being forced by their circumstances to break the law in order to make a profit, and on the other, of deriving forms of pleasure, autonomy and achievement from their involvement in such forms of trade.

A note on the fieldwork

The article is based on ethnographic research with traders from Afghanistan and Central Asia in the officially designated trade city of Yiwu, China, and in the various markets to which traders based in that city export their goods.[3] We initially met most of the traders we discuss in the article during fieldwork in Yiwu and the wholesale markets in which they deal in goods procured in China. But our ability to establish such relations also builds on experiences in the mid-1990s of education in Moscow (Diana) and of fieldwork in northern Pakistan (Magnus), during which time we came to know individuals who went onto become global commodity traders (for more details see Marsden 2016a; Ibañez-Tirado 2019). Magnus communicates with his informants in Dari and Pashto, and Diana in Tajik and Russian. We gathered the data primarily by spending time with the traders in their offices, shops, warehouses and homes, the wholesale markets in which they work, and the restaurants and hotels they regularly frequent. We attended our informants' social gatherings, accompanied them on trips to purchase goods for export, helped load containers, and sat with them in their shops and restaurants while contributing to discussions they had with their fellow traders about trade and life on the move. Diana attended daily lessons in Chinese language for foreign traders and their families in Yiwu (over a period of five months); she interviewed approximately 30 male and female traders from Tajikistan in the city, of both Uzbek and Tajik background. She followed up her research in Yiwu by conducting ethnographic research in a bridal shop in Dushanbe and undertaking semi-structured interviews in wholesale markets in Dushanbe and Khujand. Magnus interacted regularly with approximately 50 traders from Afghanistan in Yiwu, and explored the activities of these traders in the countries in which they work, making a series of visits to Afghanistan (especially Kabul, Herat and Mazar-e Sharif) and Saudi Arabia (Jeddah), and joint fieldwork with Diana in Turkey (Istanbul) and Ukraine (Odessa). We have also conducted structured and semi-structured interviews with foreign traders from a broader range of backgrounds – 35 of these interviews are publicly available as video recordings (Ibañez-Tirado and Wu 2018). To protect the anonymity of the interlocutors in this article, not all of them are included in the publicly available recordings.

Yiwu: trade 'outside the law' and 'freedom of form'

Yiwu is a city of 2 million inhabitants, of which 14,000 are foreign traders, in China's commercially vibrant Zhejiang Province. For a variety of trading networks, diasporas and communities across the globe, Yiwu is a node from which to purchase and transport 'small commodities' mainly available in the city's main wholesale market – Futian. These commodities include items of everyday use, like umbrellas, stationery, socks, toys, souvenirs, lights, tools, cosmetics, kitchenware, bags and sunglasses. In addition to the Futian market, Yiwu also hosts the Huangyuen garment market, a furniture market, and the more recently opened machinery market; many factories are also located in the city or nearby.

Foreign traders in Yiwu can be classified as itinerant visitors or permanent residents. Itinerant traders mostly visit Yiwu for two to three weeks once or twice a year to select goods and place orders, though we also know informants from both the networks studied in this article who visit Yiwu monthly. 'Permanent' traders live in Yiwu, mostly holding renewable one- or two-year visas on the basis of having registered trading and cargo companies with the local authorities. Approximately 3000 foreign companies from around the world operate in the city (Jacobs 2016; Rui 2018). Most of these identify themselves as from North Africa (Belguidoum and Pliez 2015), the Levant and Arabian Peninsula (Anderson 2018), South Asia (Cheuk 2016; Marsden 2016b, 2017), Africa (Bodomo and Ma 2010), or the post-Soviet world (Ibañez-Tirado 2018; Skvirskaja 2018). Most permanent foreign traders run their own businesses (e.g., exporting goods to a wholesale shop in their home country) at the same time as providing services to merchants visiting Yiwu to purchase goods. The networks of traders we analyse here concern a great variety of informal trading practices or intertwined forms of legal, informal and illegal activities conducted in Yiwu and its connected commercial outposts in South-West and Central Asia.

Informal practices involve, for example, the brokerage of merchandise on credit from Chinese suppliers based on face-to-face agreements between local sellers and foreign traders permanently residing in Yiwu, as well as the resulting disputes that frequently arise when such debts are not paid on time. Although there are official channels in Yiwu to mediate this type of commercial dispute, and sellers and buyers can file their cases at the local police station, it is more common that the arguing parties avoid such channels and solve their disputes among themselves. Thus, practices such as naming and shaming debtors in social media, harassing and threatening such actors in their offices, or deploying violence to recover debts are not unheard of. Other common practices in Yiwu that are sanctioned to different degrees by local and international commercial laws include the purchase of merchandise that infringes copyright and trademark laws, the forging of invoices to secure tax returns or pay lower customs clearance fees, and various tax-avoidance mechanisms.

At particular geopolitical junctures, goods that were bought legally in Yiwu can turn into illegal merchandise once shipped from China. In 2016 and 2017 Tajikistan passed laws to encourage citizens (especially women) to wear 'national clothes' (Ibañez-Tirado 2016). As a result, 'Western'-style wedding dresses were banned in the country: one of our Tajik informants ended up with 200 dresses from Yiwu 'stuck' in Tajikistan's customs office. Eventually, these traders managed to import the items to Tajikistan 'informally' – by bribing customs officers (*tamozhny*) – as such dresses continue to be popular among Tajikistan's brides, and state officials oversee the ban. Similarly, military clothing, such as boots, is available for purchase in Yiwu, but it is illegal for such items to be transited through Kazakhstan: Afghan traders mostly send them to Afghanistan using sea routes, though sometimes the goods are rejected by Kazakh customs posts.

In Yiwu our informants are also involved in the wholesale acquisition of goods 'outside the law'. This mainly involves the procurement of counterfeit products: pirated goods, or goods that have been copied from another (original) good with a patent, copyright or trademark and labelled without the authorization of the owner of the copyright/patent (Aguiar 2012). They also purchase counterfeit products, called 'knockoffs', or copies that resemble 'original' goods but which do not bear the exact name or logo (e.g., 'Giorgio

Arnami' or 'Gusci' products). While the wholesale procurement, transport and resale of counterfeit goods is illegal in most countries, knockoffs are usually lawful yet still regarded with suspicion by the authorities because of their low quality or because they are designed to deceive consumers.

Another dimension of products purchased in Yiwu that infringe the law arises from the processes of packaging and marketing by traders in the city. In the city's main commercial streets there are numerous printing companies (mostly run by Chinese nationals) which produce labels, boxes and packages for fabricated goods. Traders can ask such shops to print brand labels and product information details that may or may not be the correct description of the merchandise for sale. Diana accompanied Farhod, a trader from Tajikistan visiting Yiwu, to print labels saying 'Made in Ukraine' for dresses produced in the city of Souzhou, China. The Chinese owner of one such printing shop told Diana that her work was 'printing': she did not question whether the labels and packages were accurate or whether the product itself broke Chinese or international commercial laws. Farhod eventually imported to Tajikistan merchandise with forged labels and packaging by bribing customs officials to cover the service of speeding up the release of the container. Officers in Tajikistan expect to receive such bribes whether the merchandise is lawful or not; in this case it also allowed Farhod to overcome other irregularities concerning the goods he had loaded in that container, including low-quality shoes with the logos of major brands. Farhod and several other informants often argued that producing this type of packaging and labels, as well as the counterfeit brands themselves, represented 'the only way' they could sell and make a profit from products purchased in Yiwu. In Tajikistan, Farhod and other informants told us that only by paying bribes could they import to the country the merchandise they purchased in China – a common dimension of the region's 'informal economies' (see introduction in this issue; Rasanayagam 2011; Morris and Polese 2013; Makovicky and Henig 2017; Ibañez-Tirado 2018).

Although traders such as Farhod portray the payment of bribes and the forging of labels and invoices as resulting from their 'not having an option', trading practices 'outside the law' also carry a subtle aesthetic pleasure and sense of achievement that, at times, has been narrated by our informants as a noteworthy aspect of their working lives. These forms of pleasure and achievement that our interlocutors convey while they narrate their trading strategies recall the notion of 'freedom of form' proposed by Gandolfo (2013, 288). 'Freedom of form' in this context refers to particular aspects of the informal economy and the forms of exchange with which it is entwined. The term suggests an incitement to institutional forms and disciplined arrangements of the market that are particularly evident when traders and shopkeepers display cunningness, creativity and other skills to conduct their commercial activities in a way that allows them to continue navigating around the law. Having 'freedom of form' differs from 'not having an option' because the latter emphasizes the trader's being compelled by various circumstances to break the law in order to make a profit from commercial activities. In contrast, 'freedom of form' involves other aspects of the traders' lives that they value and regard as important: their ability to display autonomy and resourcefulness to make their business thrive in a competitive environment such as Yiwu. Both skills and calculations in the 'freedom of form' also allow our informants to chart routes around the state law concerning customs clearance, to make a profit, and to value their self-sufficiency and autonomy by not working for a fixed salary – the central ethical ambition of Afghan traders (Marsden

2016b). At the same time, the opportunities our informants have to display their trading skills 'outside the law' also allow them the possibility of expanding their trading activities. In the next section, we analyse in more detail the activities and commercial endeavours of Uzbek traders from Tajikistan and Uzbekistan, and how they portray themselves as being forced by the circumstances of their everyday lives to smuggle goods.

Central Asian trading networks: Uzbeks from Tajikistan and Uzbekistan

The number of traders from Tajikistan and Uzbekistan operating in Yiwu is relatively small in comparison to other major trading groups in the city, such as those of Afghan background (described in the following section).[4] In 2016, at the time of our fieldwork, there were three well-established trading and cargo companies and two restaurants from Tajikistan in the city, and three restaurants and approximately 15 trading and cargo companies from Uzbekistan. Diana established contact with approximately 30 male and female traders from Tajikistan in Yiwu. The great majority of Central Asian traders in Yiwu were temporary visitors who stayed on business trips, usually lasting little more than two weeks. Traders from Tajikistan who lived in Yiwu tended to have enough capital to buy goods by the container and export these to their home country; larger-scale traders also exported goods to Russia. We also met traders from Tajikistan who owned factories close to Moscow and were involved in the manufacturing of small commodities, such as toothpicks.

Traders from Uzbekistan tended to have larger and more resilient companies, with the capital to export not only to Uzbekistan and Russia but also to Germany and the US. Like the Afghans, such companies worked through networks of Uzbek traders in Western Europe and North America. According to the owner of an Uzbek company in Yiwu, his business associates in Germany and California left Uzbekistan in the early 1990s. Having acquired US and European passports, they established trading companies in the countries where they had settled. Equally important were traders from Uzbekistan who began their commercial careers in South Korea: we met traders in Dogdaemun Market in Seoul (in 2016) who had initially gone to South Korea to work as labourers and later started to trade in cloth between South Korea and Uzbekistan. Another company owner in Yiwu had once run a partner office in Seoul overseeing trading activities that involved the export of merchandise from both Yiwu and Seoul to Uzbekistan. She closed her office in Seoul to expand her business in China through the commercialization of raw material (especially the import of metals used in construction, and the export of diverse fittings for construction). Trading networks from Tajikistan and Uzbekistan in Yiwu operate on a smaller scale than both those of Afghan background and those connected to Afghanistan; yet among the traders from Tajikistan, those who identify themselves as being Uzbek tend to form networks that cross borders and regions (Ibañez-Tirado 2018). For this reason, we focus on networks of traders from Uzbek background that involve mainly Tajikistan's citizens.[5]

A toy shop in Khujand: *kontraband* across borders

Diana met Aka Ikrom and his brother Aka Farukh in a wholesale container-market in the outskirts of Khujand, the main city in northern Tajikistan's Sughd Province, in 2017. Aka Ikrom (who was in his early fifties) and Aka Farukh (in his early forties) were sitting inside an old container with well-arranged shelves displaying an abundance of plastic toys. Unhurriedly drinking tea, they served their retail customers while sitting behind a small till placed on a time-worn wooden table. After a couple of visits, they eventually explained to Diana that in addition to this 'small' shop, they also owned several shops and warehouses in this market, and three shops in a desirable area on Khujand's main street, which they rented to traders who imported high-end clothes, shoes and perfumes from Turkey.

Together with other members of their extended family, the brothers have been involved in diverse trading activities over the past two decades. From an ethnically Uzbek family based in the city of Istaravshan (south of Khujand), these traders established their profitable businesses in a series of stages. Initially they moved goods and products (legally and illegally) across the Tajik–Uzbek border. They then moved on to import merchandise from Russia and China, including Yiwu, to Tajikistan. Finally, the brothers established a complex network of imports and exports that involved all of these countries. Although they said that they were not directly involved in moving goods to and from Kyrgyzstan, they also reported having plenty of clients in the country.[6] From their unassuming appearance and relatively small retail shop outside Khujand, it was difficult to get a sense of these brothers' businesses, trading experience, travels and aspirations for their children.

Aka Ikrom and Aka Farukh attributed some of their success to having been able to accumulate profit from diverse business ventures over the years, and developing good business relations with their relatives in Tashkent (Uzbekistan), as well as work with their third brother (Aka Timur), who had established a business in Sennoy Market in Saint Petersburg in 2009. The brothers also explained that their trade across different borders depended on the 'friendship' (Rus. *druzhba*) relations they have fostered with border officials in Tajikistan and Uzbekistan, who intermittently facilitated the movement of contraband goods (Rus. *kontraband*; Taj. *qochoq*). Thus, they had been able to establish a trading network that often involved the smuggling of merchandise across regional borders.

'We are not bandits! We do not trade with dangerous goods or drugs or anything like that!' Aka Ikrom told Diana between bursts of laughter. 'When I say *kontraband* I mean things like these toys you see here, or other goods that sometimes are not allowed to cross the border.' Indeed, one of their commercial lines of activity involved toys manufactured in Uzbekistan and Russia. From Uzbekistan they imported colourful sets of building blocks and tool kits for toddlers, while from Russia they sourced balls and other toys made out of rubber. According to the brothers, the quality and price of rubber toys and building blocks was better in Russia and Uzbekistan than in China. But their main imports did come from China: once or twice a year the brothers visited Yiwu to purchase low-grade toys (e.g., balls, cars, dolls, and figures of famous super-heroes), as well as headscarves and leggings.

According to the brothers, their clients in Tajikistan, Uzbekistan and Kyrgyzstan do not tend to buy expensive toys or headscarves, so they made a profit through the volume of goods in which they were able to deal. To sell enough goods to make a profit they had to trade beyond Tajikistan through a complicated cross-border circuit. At the same time as legally importing several containers of toys (some of them pirated in Yiwu and infringing copyright laws) to Tajikistan from China (storing these in their warehouses in Khujand), they also illegally passed some of the merchandise on to Uzbekistan. Aka Ikrom called Uzbekistan's import tariffs and system for such low-grade goods a 'nightmare'

(Rus. *koshmar*) due to legislation that made importing goods that could harm Uzbekistan's internal production 'impossible' (Rus. *nevozmozhno*). This legislation affected the trade in toys and leggings, which they openly referred to as constituting a form of smuggling (Taj. *qochoq*) to 'the other side' (Rus. *na to storonu*).

Yet in Uzbekistan they did not only provide their clients with smuggled and low-priced goods destined for sale in wholesale and retail shops. According to Aka Ikrom, one of their relatives in Uzbekistan ran a textile factory: a large registered company that was supposed to produce, in addition to branded cotton T-shirts and underwear, women's black leggings decorated with hot-fixed rhinestones. Such leggings, however, could not compete with the smuggled Chinese versions, so the factory owner himself was said to buy Yiwu-made leggings from Aka Ikrom, which they then arranged to be smuggled across Tajikistan's border to supply his factory. According to Aka Ikorm, after they had arrived in the factory the goods were labelled with the local brand and with a label saying 'Made in Uzbekistan'. This was not the case for T-shirts and underwear, which the owner of the factory could indeed produce in Uzbekistan at competitive prices; Aka Ikrom smuggled these items of clothing to Tajikistan for sale on a wholesale basis. While most of their activities involved moving goods imported from China to Tajikistan towards Uzbekistan, the brothers also occasionally smuggled domestic appliances such as electric ovens and washing machines from Russia and Uzbekistan into Tajikistan. But the shop and warehouses they operated from in Khujand were legal and paid taxes.

These Uzbek traders have built their networks of partners and customers, as well as their knowledge and skills, through decades of travelling and finding ways to navigate around the law. But their search for business prospects was often narrated as arising from changing geopolitical contexts and other adverse circumstances affecting business which gave them 'no other option'. As we have mentioned, the notion of having no option other than breaking the law also conveyed the potentials, aspirations and forms of pleasure offered by the 'freedom of form' encountered between legal and illegal forms of trade. These traders envisioned expanding their business ventures to Latvia and Western Europe. In the late 1990s and early 2000s, Aka Ikrom had travelled to Germany and Spain to buy second-hand lorries of a renowned German brand to drive back to be sold in the 'East'. He reported to Diana in a proud tone that he had sold one of these trucks to an old friend in Ukraine, and several other trucks to clients in Kazakhstan and Tajikistan. In the following years, he began to travel to Latvia to procure second-hand European cars for export to Tajikistan. During this time, he enjoyed travelling and taking photographs of his journeys. He showed such images to prove, as he put it to Diana, that his story was 'true' and to show how 'clever' he had been. But recently the situation had radically changed, making the procurement of EU visas almost impossible for holders of Tajikistan passports, and the brothers now had no other 'option' than to smuggle goods across Central Asian borders. To continue demonstrating forms of pleasure in trading activities outside the law, Aka Ikrom explained how his eldest son, Makhsudbek, had gained admission to a university in Latvia in 2017 for a preparatory course in English. This was as a prerequisite to pursue a BA in economics. Makhsudbek had been of no help to his father in Khujand's shop over the years (he constantly refused to work there), but was still regarded as the entry of the next generation of family business to Europe. Asked why he had chosen Latvia, Aka Ikrom said that they did not have an option (Rus. *drugova varyanta netu*): 'Latvia is good for us. There are many Russians and

Uzbeks, and the universities are good there. There is also good business there, and after all, Latvia is Europe, isn't it?'

Indeed, Aka Ikrom's intentions were not simply that Makhsudbek study in Latvia but that, with his student visa, he begin exploring opportunities for business there. Latvia was well known to Aka Ikrom through his vehicle trading, when he had made a profit while conducting trade in the 'freedom of form' of previously less regulated visa and border regimes throughout Europe and Eurasia.[7]

In the next section, we analyse Afghan trading networks and how they are involved in trading practices outside the law. In this analysis, we emphasize the importance of the circulation of commercial ideas and practices in the expansive arenas to which Yiwu and Central and South Asia are connected.

Afghan trading networks and inter-Asian commerce

Merchants from Afghanistan constitute an important and increasingly visible trading presence in Yiwu. Traders from Afghanistan in Yiwu identify with a range of ethno-linguistic categories, including most importantly Tajik, Pashtun, Uzbek, Turkmen and Hazara. Some traders in the city also identify with religious minorities that have been long important players in Afghanistan's commercial dynamics, especially Afghan Sikhs and Hindus (Dale 1994; Levi 2002, 2015). While Afghanistan is an important destination for the goods these traders purchase in Yiwu and elsewhere in China, not all traders who identify themselves as being from Afghanistan are principally concerned with the China–Afghanistan trade. Indeed, it is possible to identify different trading networks of merchants from Afghanistan based on the countries in which they do business. Many of the approximately 182 trading offices registered to Afghans in Yiwu arrange the transportation of Chinese commodities to Afghanistan. Yet some of the earliest foreign traders in Yiwu were Afghans who arrived in the city in the mid-1990s from Russia and Ukraine. These traders had purchased goods from Urumqi, in Xinjiang, and from Harbin, until discovering that better deals were to be found in Yiwu (Marsden 2015). Another region with which traders from Afghanistan in Yiwu deal is the Arabian Peninsula. Traders ship commodities (especially ready-made clothing, prayer mats and prayer beads) to Dubai, Saudi Arabia and Oman in particular, mostly to established Afghan trading communities settled in each of these settings (Marsden 2018). Finally, increasing numbers of Yiwu-based Afghans are now also seeking commercial partnerships with their co-nationals who have settled in European countries, especially the UK, the Netherlands and Germany (Marsden 2017).

The traders who make up these networks hold and handle diverse positions regarding the relationship of their activities to the domain of the law. Similar to the Uzbek traders analyzed above, who justify their participation in *kontraband* activities by explaining that their merchandise is mainly toys and textiles and thus not harmful, Afghan traders relate in contrasting ways to the category of the 'smuggler' (*qochoqbar*). But this is currently a loaded and contested term in Afghan trading circles. In the context of the post-9/11 US-led invasion of the country, much public discourse in Afghanistan has focused on the activities of smugglers involved in high-value forms of illegality in the country, notably the trade in narcotics (especially but not solely heroin) and also of arms (*salah*) and of 'black money' (*pul-e siyah*). As a result, identification with the category of smuggler entails significant legal and reputational consequences – locally and internationally – for merchants from Afghanistan. It is therefore an issue of great sensitivity for most Afghan traders. Unlike the Uzbek traders discussed above, it is rare for Afghans to identify with the category in a positive manner, though many do freely admit that intermediaries with whom they work 'smuggle' their goods across international borders.

The sensitivity in how Afghan traders relate to the category of 'smuggler' is most visible in the activities of those involved in the trade in high-value commodities. One of Magnus's long-term informants (Haji Tuki), for example, is a Dubai-based merchant involved in the export of Indian-made cigarettes to Afghanistan. The trader – who, before moving his business to Dubai, was based in Afghanistan and then Pakistan – openly talks about the high-level linkages that allow Afghan companies to play a major role in the cigarette trade. According to Haji Tuki, the biggest and most formal Afghan company in the cigarette trade is the official distribution agent of a brand of cigarettes made in an East Asian country. Having recently been awarded several substantial government contracts, his company is also influential in Afghanistan; the same company was also at the centre of considerable controversy in Afghanistan when it secured access, presumably because of its close connections to high-level state officials, to prime warehouse space in Kabul. Yet according to Haji Tuki, the way this company has been successful is through cultivating relationships with high-level officials in the third countries in which it does business, especially in the Russian Federation. Thus, the company has been supplying countries across the post-Soviet world with branded cigarettes since the collapse of the Soviet Union. 'It is a known secret', Haji Tuki told Magnus, 'that the company bosses enjoy access to major officials in the countries in which they trade. They are able thus to move their products without paying the relevant taxes and duties.' This case shows the importance of informal practices to the activities of influential companies active in formal expressions of economic globalization. The trope of 'globalization from below' is of only partial help in bringing attention to such hybrid forms of commerce, which involve historically evolving interpenetrations between formal and informal economic activities.

The role of Afghan traders in the cigarette business in Russia and Central Asia also reveals interpenetrations between small-scale actors and large companies. Afghan traders have interacted with Central Asian trading networks in the transport and sale of cigarettes since the collapse of the Soviet Union. In the early 1990s, the most lucrative activity for Afghan traders in Central Asia was the cigarette trade. Afghans were involved in the transportation of Bulgarian-made cigarettes from Tajikistan to Uzbekistan; most cigarettes crossed the border between the two countries near Tajikistan's northern city of Khujand. At the time, Khujand was an important commercial node for several hundred traders from Afghanistan. The trade in cigarettes required Afghans to handle and safeguard large quantities of cash, which made them the focus of the security agencies of both countries. In Tashkent, the city in which Afghans sold most of the cigarettes they transported from Tajikistan, Afghan money transfer agents were also active, including Afghan Hindu and Sikhs – ethno-religious minority communities that have been critical to trade between South and Central Asia over the past 200 years. It was in this broader context that the large transnational company discussed was able to rise to prominence in the field.

Central Asia's regimes became increasingly hostile to the activities of foreign traders in the context of attempts to establish monopolies and reinforce the boundaries of the nation-state after the initial years of upheaval following the collapse of the Soviet

Union. Against this backdrop, networks such as those comprising Afghan traders no longer operate as they did a decade or more previously. Haji Tuqi tells Magnus that he only imports the cigarettes from India and Dubai to Afghanistan, and from there

> the smugglers can do with them what they wish: they manage their movement across the borders to the SNG [Commonwealth of Independent States] countries, not me. I can't work in those places; they're all corrupt – it's a headache, and you put your life at risk.

Haji Tuki's remark underscores the point made above about how Afghan traders currently distance themselves from the category of 'smuggler'. The Haji's comments also point to the stigma associated with smuggling in Afghanistan today. Yet he also recognizes that the distinction between 'formal globalization' and 'globalization from below' rests on a binary distinction between formal and informal modes of commerce that bears little relevance to how even established transnational companies work.

There is considerable variation in the extent to which the traders conceive the category of 'smuggler' as suitable in their trade in Chinese commodities for everyday use; the variation often relates to the specific contexts in which the traders work. At one end of the spectrum, traders involved in the export of goods between China and Afghanistan openly admit that for very different reasons – ranging from registration of lower-than-real invoice costs to not paying customs duties at the Afghan border – their activities and those of their companions are 'outside the law' (*ghaireqanuni*). But rather than thinking of such practices as smuggling, they mostly refer to the 'system' in which they work as one in which 'corruption' (*fesod*) is pervasive. Traders argue that this leaves them 'no option' (*digar chara nist*) other than to chart alternative routes (*rah*) around the law and to strike deals with corrupt officials. Importantly, the traders are also aware that the 'system' is itself international and embedded in legal agreements. For example, a trader in Kabul said to Magnus,

> We'd much rather pay our dues as taxes so it could be used for the benefit of my country. But when we tell the government this, they say they have an agreement with the IMF that they will not raise custom duties, so doing so is impossible.

At the other end of the spectrum, Yiwu-based traders make strenuous efforts to publicly distance themselves from illegal activities. For example, a union of transport companies established and registered in Yiwu in 2019 publicly informed Afghan traders using WeChat that their members would not agree to transport fake branded commodities to Afghanistan.

Inter-regional commercial interaction

As mentioned, a specific geographic context in which interactions between traders from Afghanistan and Central Asia is evident is wholesale markets across the former Soviet Union. Traders from Afghanistan are involved in the export-import of commodities between China, Russia and Ukraine. This mode of business is heavily dependent on activities the traders refer to as smuggling, especially the import of goods from China without paying formal duties and taxes. It is also openly recognized that the money used to pay for this trade is 'black', in the sense that it has not been taxed in the Russian Federation. Similarly, the traders are dependent on being able to re-export goods across international borders after 'importing' them from China: commodities are thus smuggled between

Ukraine and Russia.[8] To do so, Afghan traders must work closely with local smugglers and their networks in these countries – they are responsible for the physical movement of commodities across national boundaries.

Afghan traders are ambiguous and self-reflexive in critical ways about their participation in such practices. A trader in his late forties remarked to Magnus in his office in Kabul:

> Often the authorities in Moscow come and raid the markets where the Afghans work, closing businesses and confiscating goods. We complain and say how bad it is. In fact, though, we are wrong [*ma malamat astim*]. We bring in goods the black way [*rah-e siyah*], we don't pay duties, and then we also complain when we are penalized.

Indeed, traders not only highlight the moral failings of how their community conducts business and interacts with the authorities of the countries in which they work – they also dwell on the effects that such modes of work have on their collective well-being:

> We Afghans are bad. We want to sell as much of something as possible. We don't care about the price, just about the volume. We sell lots of stuff at the lowest price. Other communities (like the Yemenis) are happy to sell little at a decent price. They have unity. We are involved in self-destruction.

Traders from Afghanistan not only adapt to the conditions of conducting trade in the former Soviet Union, they also reflect critically on its effect on their collective and individual identities and reputations. The traders also compare their mode of doing business to other models of commercial activity of which they are aware: Afghans regularly encounter Yemenis in Yiwu and also in the Arabian Peninsula, another region in which they are commercially active.

Another specific context that has been important for the commercial interactions between traders from Central and South Asia is the Pakistan–Afghanistan frontier region. Many traders currently based in Yiwu ran businesses in the Karkhano market during the 1990. The Karkhano market emerged in the 1960s in the context of the Afghanistan–Pakistan transit agreement, which allowed goods routed for Afghanistan to pass through Pakistani territory on a transit basis. At the time, duties on many goods imported to Afghanistan were less than in Pakistan, where customs charges were also more regularly enforced. Thus, a substantial business emerged in the smuggling of commodities from Afghanistan to Pakistan. A key market in which such commodities were sold was the Karkhano market, in the Federally Associated Tribal Areas, a specific legal space in which Pakistan's federal laws did not apply (Marsden and Hopkins 2011). In the 1960s and 1970s, some of the trade across the border was organized by companies in Pakistan that purchased goods in Kabul from Afghan importers. In the 1980s and 1990s, an increasing proportion of businesses in the market were run by merchant families from Afghanistan that had relocated to Peshawar in the context of the Soviet invasion (1979). By the mid-2000s, the Karkhano market was in decline because of rising duties on goods imported to Afghanistan, as well as the increasing porosity of Pakistan's markets to Chinese commodities imported directly to the country by Pakistani traders. In this period, Afghan traders who had run businesses in the Karkhano for much of the past three decades increasingly moved their business to Afghanistan, Dubai or Yiwu.

Traders in Yiwu today regularly talk openly about their activities in the Karkhano market over this period as being a form of smuggling. Abid, for example, is now in his mid-forties; based in Yiwu since 2003, he is involved in the export of socks to Afghanistan, and of cosmetics to the UAE, where he is also a partner in a chain of Afghan restaurants. Abid is a respectable figure among Yiwu's Afghans, having invested in a sock factory in a town located near the city. But he talks openly about the role he and thousands of Afghans played in smuggling goods across the Pakistan–Afghanistan border in the1980s and 1990s. Indeed, he told me that his company specialized in high-grade cosmetics and perfumes imported as air cargo to the Jalalabad airfield during the Taliban's rule of Afghanistan (1995–2001). Abid and other traders would arrange for the transportation of the goods across the Pakistan–Afghanistan border – often using horses and mules – before selling them to wholesale buyers from across Pakistan in the Karkhano market.

These traders themselves often talk about the transition they have undergone from cross-border smugglers during the Taliban government to respectable 'international' traders today, with activities in the UAE, the post-Soviet world and China. One such trader is Haji Noorudin, a merchant in his late forties from a province in central Afghanistan. Haji Noourdin traded in Karkhano until the mid-2000s, when he moved to Yiwu. In China, he supplies his family business in Kabul with cosmetics, but he also runs a successful trading and transport company. Haji Noorudin is also increasingly involved in purchasing raw materials that are used in the production of soaps and nappies: he supplies these goods to his elder brother, who in 2016 established a factory to make these goods in Afghanistan's northern city of Mazar-e Sharif, and another factory in Uzbekistan.

Having once worked alongside the Taliban in *smuggling* goods across the Pakistan–Afghanistan border, the photos this trader now posts on his WeChat account demonstrate the important role of ties to influential Afghan politicians in his ability to enter the country's industrial sector today. In Yiwu today, traders such as Haji Noorudin actively distance their activities from the field of smuggling. In the spring of 2019, for example, traders in Yiwu established a Union of Afghan Transport Companies. On the occasion of its launch, the union released documents on WeChat which stipulated that transport companies in Yiwu would refuse to be involved in the transportation of 'branded' goods. While such goods inevitably continue to be transported to Afghanistan from China, this public attempt to distance themselves from such practices reveals an important shift in the traders' relationship to the category of smuggler, from one that was celebrated as a mark of autonomy under the Taliban government, to one of sensitivity today. This shift reflects a tightening of regulations in Yiwu in the context of the city's ambition to 'upgrade' to a centre of formal commerce that is part of the country's Belt and Road strategy. As we discussed above, it also reflects Afghanistan's political dynamics and the focus in the country on the deleterious implications of the informal economy for its economy and state structures in the context of the ongoing international intervention.

As with mobile families in other Asian contexts (Ong 1999), Haji Noorudin and similarly positioned traders emphasizes that the geographic expansion, capitalization, and increasingly formalized nature of their business activities have important implications for his social and familial reputation. Many traders argue that their mode of making a living is morally acceptable because of the circumstances of their lives in Afghanistan: 'We do what we can to make as much as we can because we don't know when we will need money to get our families out of Afghanistan and give them a life elsewhere.' More established traders, such as Haji Noorudin, emphasize the shifts their family lives have undergone over the past two decades and how these have given rise to new ambitions and aspirations. He said to Magnus in January 2018,

> When I was growing up, we had no option other than to help our families in business. There was a war going on in Afghanistan, and life was hard. We started doing business as children because we needed to earn a living. Now we are actively encouraging the education of our children. My own son has studied in an international school in Yiwu, and next year I am sending him to America to go to college.

Conclusion

Illegal trading practices and more particularly smuggling tend to be explored through a discursive approach that dwells on the self-portrayal of smugglers and their actions. Much of this work has sought to understand the types of moral justifications made by smugglers; after all, as Erami and Keshavarzian (2015) suggest, 'smuggling' is a moral-legal category (see also Botoeva 2019). As our interlocutors try to make a living out of illegal activities merged with more formal economic exchange, they seek to justify and build moral hierarchies about what they are doing and why, and who they harm in the process. Such assessments, calculations and circumstances shift. Shifts take place in the context of national and geopolitical dynamics, changes in the form of state and international commercial law, and, more intricately, as goods, money and people move from wholesale shops to warehouses in Yiwu, and from shipping containers to the buyers in the different geographical places where our interlocutors work. The malleability and contextually defined nature of the category 'smuggler' is illustrated across this article. Uzbek traders now positively identify with the term *kontraband*, a concept associated in Soviet times with immoral and corrosive practices. By contrast, Afghan traders distance themselves from the notion of *qochokbar*, a term widely associated in the period before the current intervention with masculine prowess and a healthy degree of autonomy from the state.

By analysing the multi-sited and fluid forms of the trade practices of the merchants of Uzbek and Afghan background, we have underlined the experiential aspects of the traders' moral, economic and geopolitical commercial activities as being 'outside the law'; these include forms of moving merchandise in ways that are referred to as smuggling. The diverse activities these traders undertake 'outside the law' accentuate the 'freedom of form' encountered in the trade and exchange chains in which legal and illegal, formal and informal practices are embedded. Beyond our informants' expressions of 'not having an option' other than discovering routes around the law, smuggling is more than simply a survival activity or coping mechanism deployed in times of poverty and crisis, or a strategy to maximize profit. The concept of 'freedom of form' is analytically helpful in this regard because it recognizes that the discovery of routes around and through the law is a skill that traders value and invest with moral significance. Smuggling and other trading practices that take place 'outside the law' involve a variety of labour embedded in forms of pleasure, aspiration, ambition and achievement.

Another contribution of this article has been to reflect on the extent to which notions of formal and informal globalization are of use for analysing the activities and contributions of the types of traders with whom we have been working. In so doing, we have sought to bring attention to diverse trajectories of global trading networks and demonstrate their active and ongoing contribution to processes of economic globalization and connectivity. We have sought to demonstrate that the dichotomies used in existing metaphors do not fully encompass the ways in which trading practices outside the law and the trading networks of Uzbek and Afghan merchants are also integral to the production and reproduction of the global economy. We have also suggested that work that focuses on the particularities of economic life in the former Soviet stands to benefit from studies that explore interactions between commercial actors operating across regional and geopolitical contexts.

By taking into account how Central and South Asian markets are built on historic trading practices and networks, our concluding remarks also seek to initiate further debate on the globalization of the former Soviet world. Our comparison between Afghan and Uzbek trading networks brings attention to parallels between trading and smuggling across these contexts; equally importantly, it also points to intersections between Central and South-West Asia. Afghan trading networks and their importance to inter-Asian commerce, including Central Asia, have remained obscured by narrow definitions of 'Soviet' and 'post-Soviet' contexts. At the same time, emerging markets and informal practices in the contexts of the collapse of the Soviet Union were vital for Afghan traders to prosper, for example in Moscow, Dushanbe, Khujand, Tashkent and Odessa. There is scope for further research on the ways in which interactions between actors from countries of the former socialist *ecumene*, such as Vietnam, Libya, Yemen and Syria, and those from formerly Soviet societies have played an important role in shaping the distinctively 'post-Soviet' trading economy (Anderson 2018). Such research stands to reveal further aspects of the inter-regional and connective manner in which globalized forms of economic life 'outside the law' have emerged over the past three decades.

Notes

1. This article builds on long-term research as part of the TRODITIES project.
2. Concerning trade in and from China, Marsden (2017) has shown that traders are not marginal actors in the making of the roads and routes currently encompassed by the Belt and Road Initiative. See also Karrar (2013).
3. Our combined research includes 12 months in Yiwu (2013–2018) and short-term fieldwork in Turkey (2016, 2017), Ukraine (2013, 2014, 2016), South Korea (2016) and Russia (2012, 2014, 2015), as well as individual field trips to Tajikistan (Diana 2017) and to Afghanistan, Pakistan and Saudi Arabia (Magnus 2016, 2017, 2018, 2019).
4. For a nuanced analysis of trading networks from the Middle East and North Africa, as well as Russia, in Yiwu, see Anderson (2018), Pliez (2012) and Skvirskaja (2018).
5. For a detailed discussion of the complexities of Uzbek identities in Central Asia see Finke (2014), Fumagalli (2007) and Liu (2012). For an ethno-historical analysis of Uzbek populations in northern Tajikistan, see Abashin (2015).
6. For a detailed analysis of the movements along these borders, see Reeves (2014).
7. Working in trade while holding a student visa is a silent, yet often illegal aspect of the life of the traders with whom we have spoken (Ibañez-Tirado, 2019; Marsden 2016b).
8. The conflict between Russia and Ukraine following from the annexation of Crimea in 2014 has reduced such activities, though commodities do reportedly continue to move along this route.

Acknowledgements

Thanks to Susanne Fehlings and Hasan Karrar for useful comments on this article and their invitation to collaborate with their team of researchers. We also thank Gulzat Botoeva for her input to the initial discussion of this work, and to three anonymous reviewers for their insightful questions and suggestions. We have used pseudonyms to refer to our research participants throughout this article.

Disclosure statement

No potential conflict of interest was reported by the authors.

Funding

The research on which this article is based was supported by the European Research Council under the European Union's Horizon 2020 research and innovation programme (669 132 – TRODITIES).

References

Abashin, S. 2015. *Sovetskii kishlak: mezhdu kolonializmom i modernizatsiei* [Soviet Kishlak: between colonialism and modernization]. Moscow: Novoe Literaturnoe Obozrenye.

Achilli, L. 2018. "The 'Good' Smuggler: The Ethics and Morals of Human Smuggling among Syrians." *Annals of the American Academy of Political and Social Science* 676 (1): 77–96. doi:10.1177/0002716217746641

Aguiar, J. C. G. 2012. "They Come from China': Pirate CDs in Mexico in Transnational Perspective." In *Globalization from Below: The World's Other Economy*, edited by G. Mathews, L. Ribeiro, and C. Alba Vega, 36–54. London: Routledge.

Anderson, P. 2011. "Threads of Virtue: the Ethical Lives of Syrian Textile Traders." Unpublished PhD thesis, University of Edinburgh.

Anderson, P. 2018. "Aleppo in Asia: Mercantile Networks between Syria, China and Post-Soviet Eurasia since 1970." *History and Anthropology* 29 (sup.1): S67–S83.

Anteby, M. 2008. *Moral Gray Zones: Side-Production, Identity, and Regulation in an Aeronautic Plant*. Princeton, NJ: Princeton University Press.

Belguidoum, S., and O. Pliez. 2015. "Yiwu: The Creation of a Global Market Town in China." *Journal of Urban Research* 12: 1–14.

Bodomo, A. B., and G. Ma. 2010. "From Guangzhou to Yiwu: Emerging Facets of the African Diaspora in China." *International Journal of African Renaissance Studies* 5 (2): 283–289.

Botoeva, G. 2019. "Use of Language in Blurring the Lines between Legal and Illegal." In *The Illegal, the Immoral and the Criminal: the Transnational Perspectives on Informality*, edited by A. Polese, A. Russo, and F. Strazzari, 67–83. London: Palgrave Macmillan.

Bruns, B., and J. Miggelbrink, eds. 2012. *Subverting Borders: Doing Research on Smuggling and Small-Scale Trade*. Germany: VS.

Comaroff, J., and J. Comaroff. 2006. "Law and Disorder in the Postcolony: An Introduction." In *Law and Disorder in the Postcolony*, edited by J. Comaroff and J. L. Comaroff, 1–56. Chicago: University of Chicago Press.

Cheuk, K. 2016. "Everyday Diplomacy among Indian Traders in a Chinese Fabric Market." *The Cambridge Journal of Anthropology*, 2 (34): 42–58.

Dale, S. 1994. *Indian Merchants and the Eurasian Trade*. Cambridge: Cambridge University Press.

Endres, K. 2014. "Making law: Small-Scale Trade and Corrupt Exceptions at the Vietnam-China Border." *American Anthropologist* 116 (3): 611–625.

Erami, N., and A. Keshavarzian. 2015. "When Ties Don't Bind: Smuggling Effects, Bazaars and Regulatory Regimes in Postrevolutionary Iran." *Economy and Society* 44 (1): 110–139. doi:10.1080/03085147.2014.909986

Faroqhi, S. 2012. "Trade between the Ottomans and the Safavids: The Acem Tüccarı and Others." In *Iran and the World in the Safavid Age*, edited by W. Floor and E. Herzig, 237–251. London: I. B. Tauris.

Ferradás, C. A. 2013. "The Nature of Illegality under Neoliberalism and Post-Neoliberalism." *PoLAR: Political and Legal Anthropology Review* 36 (2): 266–273. doi:10.1111/plar.12026

Finke, P. 2014. *Variations on Uzbek Identity: Strategic Choices, Cognitive Schemas and Political Constraints in Identification Processes*. New York: Berghahn.

Fumagalli, M. 2007. "Framing Ethnic Minority Mobilisation in Central Asia: The Cases of Uzbeks in Kyrgyzstan and Tajikistan." *Europe-Asia Studies* 59 (4): 567–590. doi:10.1080/09668130701289869

Galemba, R. B. 2008. "Informal and Illicit Entrepreneurs: Fighting for a Place in the Neoliberal Economic Order." *Anthropology of Work Review* 29 (2): 19–25.

Galemba, R. 2013. "Illegality and Invisibility at the Margins and Borders." *POLAR: Political and Legal Anthropology Review* 36 (2): 274–285. doi:10.1111/plar.12027

Gandolfo, D. 2013. "FORMLESS: A Day at Lima's Office of Formalization." *Cultural Anthropology* 28 (2): 278–298. doi:10.1111/cuan.12004

Hartnett, A., and S. L. Dawdy. 2013. "The Archaeology of Illegal and Illicit Economies." *Annual Review of Anthropology* 42: 37–51. doi:10.1146/annurev-anthro-092412-155452

Ibañez-Tirado, D. 2016. "Gold Teeth, Indian Dresses, Chinese Lycra and 'Russian' Hair: Embodied Diplomacy and the Assemblages of Dress in Tajikistan." *Cambridge Journal of Anthropology* 34 (2): 23–41. doi:10.3167/ca.2016.340203

Ibañez-Tirado, D. 2018. "Hierarchies of Trade in Yiwu and Dushanbe: the Case of an Uzbek Merchant Family from Tajikistan." *History and Anthropology* 29 (supl.): S31–S47. doi:10.1080/02757206.2018.1506776

Ibañez-Tirado, D. 2019. "West-Central Asia: a Comparative Assessment of Students' Trajectories in Russia (Moscow) from the 1980s and China (Yiwu) from the 2000s." *Journal of Eurasian Studies* 10 (1): 48–60. doi:10.1177/1879366518814664

Ibañez-Tirado, D., and B. Wu. 2018. *Yiwu: 35 Short Stories* [Video]. https://v.qq.com/x/page/b07312ywyty.html.

Jacobs, M. 2016. *Yiwu, China: A Study of the World's Largest Small Commodities Market*. New Jersey: Homa & Sekey Books.

Karrar, H. H. 2013. "Merchants, Markets and the State: Informality, Transnationality and Spatial Imaginaries in the Revival of Central Eurasian Trade." *Critical Asian Studies* 45 (3): 459–480. doi:10.1080/14672715.2013.829315

Lan, S. 2017. *Mapping the New African Diaspora in China: Race and the Cultural Politics of Belonging*. London: Routledge.

Levi, S. C. 2002. *The Indian Diaspora in Central Asia and Its Trade*. Leiden: Brill.

Levi, S. C. 2015. *Caravans: Indian Merchants on the Silk Road*. New York: Penguin.

Liu, M. 2012. *Under Solomon's Throne: Uzbek Visions of Renewal in Osh*. Pittsburgh: University Press.

Makovicky, N., and D. Henig. 2017. "Introduction: Re-imagining Economies (after Socialism): Ethics, Favours, and Moral Sentiments." In *Economies of Favour after Socialism*, edited by D. Henig and N. Makovicky, 1–20. Oxford: University Press.

Marsden, M. 2015. "From Kabul to Kiev: Afghan Trading Networks in the Former Soviet Union." *Modern Asian Studies*, 49 (4): 1010–48.

Marsden, M. 2016a. *Trading Worlds: Afghan Merchants across Modern Frontiers*. London: Hurst and Company.

Marsden, M. 2016b. "Crossing Eurasia: Trans-Regional Afghan Trading Networks in China and Beyond." *Central Asian Survey* 35 (1): 1–15. doi:10.1080/02634937.2015.1070516

Marsden, M. 2017. "Actually Existing Silk Roads." *Journal of Eurasian Studies* 8 (1): 22–30. doi:10.1016/j.euras.2016.11.006

Marsden, M. 2018. "Beyond Bukhara: Trade, Identity and Interregional Exchange across Asia." *History and Anthropology* 29 (S1): S84–S100. doi:10.1080/02757206.2018.1496915

Marsden, M., and B. D. Hopkins. 2011. *Fragments of the Afghan Frontier*. London: Hurst and Co.

Mathew, J. 2016. *Margins of the Market: Trafficking and Capitalism across the Arabian Sea*. Oakland: University of California Press.

Mathews, G., and C. Alba Vega. 2012. "Introduction: What is Globalization from Below?" In *Globalization from Below: The World's Other Economy*, edited by G. Mathews, G. L. Ribeiro, and C. Alba Vega, 1–16. Oxon; New York: Routledge.

Mathews, G., D. Lin, and Y. Yang. 2014. "How to Evade States and Slip past Borders: Lessons from Traders, Overstayers, and Asylum Seekers in Hong Kong and China." *City and Society* 26 (2): 217–238. doi:10.1111/ciso.12041

Millar, K. 2008. "Making Trash into Treasure: Struggles for Autonomy on a Brazilian Garbage Dump." *Anthropology of Work Review* 29 (2): 25–34. doi:10.1111/j.1548-1417.2008.00011.x

Morris, J., and A. Polese. 2013. "Introduction: Informality – Enduring Practices, Entwined Livelihoods." In *The Informal Post-Socialist Economy: Embedded Practices and Livelihoods*, edited by J. Morris, and A. Polese, 1–17. Abingdon, UK: Routledge.

Ong, A. 1999. *Flexible Citizenship: The Cultural Logics of Transnationality*. Durham, NC: Duke University Press.

Pınar Şenoğuz, H. 2015. "Kilis as 'Little Beirut': Shadow Markets and Illegality in the Southeastern Margins of Turkey." *L'Espace Politique* [Online] 27 (3).

Phillips, N. 2011. "Informality, Global Production Networks and the Dynamics of 'Adverse Incorporation'." *Global Networks* 11 (3): 380–397. doi:10.1111/j.1471-0374.2011.00331.x

Pliez, O. 2012. "Following the new Silk Road between Yiwu and Cairo." In *Globalization from Below: The World's Other Economy*, edited by G. Mathews, G. L. Ribeiro, and C. Alba Vega, 19–35. London: Routledge.

Prentice, R. 2015. *Thiefing a Chance: Factory Work, Illicit Labor, and Neoliberal Subjectivities in Trinidad*. Boulder: University Press of Colorado.

Rajak, D., and C. Dolan. 2016. "Remaking Africa's Informal Economies: Youth, Entrepreneurship and the Promise of Inclusion at the Bottom of the Pyramid." *Journal of Development Studies* 52 (4): 514–529. doi:10.1080/00220388.2015.1126249

Rasanayagam, J. 2011. "Informal Economy, Informal State: The Case of Uzbekistan." *International Journal of Sociology and Social Policy* 31 (11/12): 681–696. doi:10.1108/01443331111177878

Rasanayagam, J., J. Beyer, and M. Reeves. 2014. "Introduction: Performances, Possibilities and Practices of the Political in Central Asia." In *Ethnographies of the State in Central Asia: Performing Politics*, edited by M. Reeves, J. Rasanayagam, and J. Beyer, 1–26. Bloomington: University Press.

Reeves, M. 2014. *Border Work: Spatial Lives of the State in Rural Central Asia*. Ithaca, NY: Cornell University Press.

Sanyal, K., and R. Bhattacharyya. 2009. "Beyond the Factory: Globalisation, Informalisation of Production and the New Locations of Labour." *Economic and Political Weekly* 44 (22): 35–44.

Schneider, J., and P. Schneider. 2008. "The Anthropology of Crime and Criminalization." *Annual Review of Anthropology* 37: 351–373. doi:10.1146/annurev.anthro.36.081406.094316

Skvirskaja, V. 2018. "'Russian Merchant' Legacies in Post-Soviet Trade with China: Moral Economy, Economic Success and Business Innovation in Yiwu." *History and Anthropology* 29 (sup1): S48–S66. doi:10.1080/02757206.2018.1496916

Spector, R. A. 2017. *Order at the Bazaar: Power and Trade in Central Asia*. Ithaca, NY: Cornell University Press.

Tagliacozzo, E. 2009. *Secret Trades, Porous Borders: Smuggling and States along a Southeast Asian Frontier, 1865–1915*. New Haven, CT: Yale University Press.

Rui, H. 2018. "Yiwu: Historical Transformation and Contributing Factors." *History and Anthropology* 29 (sup1): S14–S30. doi:10.1080/02757206.2018.1516654

Tagliacozzo, E. 2002. "Smuggling in Southeast Asia: History and its Contemporary Vectors in an Unbounded Region." *Critical Asian Studies* 34 (2): 193–220. doi:10.1080/14672710220146205

Tett, G. 2010. *Fool's Gold: How Unrestrained Greed Corrupted a Dream, Shattered Global Markets and Unleashed a Catastrophe*. London: Abacus.

Yang, Y. 2012. "African Traders in Guangzhou: Routes, Reasons, Profits, Dreams." In *Globalization from Below: The World's Other Economy*, edited by G. Mathews, G. L. Ribeiro, and C. Alba Vega, 154–169. Oxon: Routledge.

Yeğen, M. 1996. "The Turkish State Discourse and the Exclusion of Kurdish Identity." *Middle Eastern Studies* 32 (2): 216–229. doi:10.1080/00263209608701112

Zack, T. 2014. "'Jeppe': Where Low-End Globalisation, Ethnic Entrepreneurialism and the Arrival City Meet." *Urban Forum* 26 (2): 131–150. doi:10.1007/s12132-014-9245-1

Index

Note: Page numbers in **bold** refer to tables and page numbers in *italics* refer to figures.

Abdukérim, R. 56
Abduwéli 48–9
'accidental trader' 121
Achilli, L. 137
ad hoc marketplaces 34
Afghan traders 135
Afghan trading networks 145–7
Aldrich, H. E. 102
Allies 107–8
Almaty residents 7, 84
Altman, Y. 105
Antonyan, Yulia 5
Armenia 65–7
Armenian Apostolic Church 70, 76
Astana (2017) 7

Baitas, Meiirzhan 5
Bajc, V. 68
bazaars, local vernaculars 4
bazaar trade 12–13, 38
bazaar traders 20
Bechhofer, F. 104
Bellér-Hann, I. 54
Benjamin, Walter 88
Bourdieu, P. 52
Brednikova, O. 103
business code 108–9
businesbs friends 109–10
Business 2.0, post-bazaar economy: diversified, formalized market environment 128–30; reliability, politeness and professionalism 126–8

Caelli, K. 14
Carey, M. 104
Cargo terminal, Yabaolu Market *100*
Carrier, J. G. 109
cash register regulations 17–18
Caucasus and Central Asia, informal markets and trade 28–32
Central Asian Survey 6, 7, 81
Central Asian trading networks 142
Central Eurasian Studies Society (2017) 7

China's rural populations 117
China's Zhejiang Province 135
Chinese careers, soft market entries: Kyrgyz trade pioneers in Russia 120–2; Marat's journey 118–20
Christian denominations 75
Christian discourse 68
Cieślewska, A. 23
city authorities 87
Coleman, S. 68
Collins, Kathleen 82
container bazaars 80–2
craftsmen 71
cultural brokers 98–9, 117
cultural predispositions 102

Dasgupta, P. 103
Desai, A. 106, 109
de-secularization, Soviet Union 63
'disorderly market places' 88
The Dordoi bazaar 18–20

Eade, J. 68
Eastern Christianity 75
Eastern Orthodox icons 75
Elliott, B. 104
entrepreneurial activities, bazaar 13
entrepreneurship 14–15
Erami, N. 150
ethnic entrepreneurship and trust 96, 102–4
Eurasian Economic Union 129
European Research Council 7
European Union's Horizon 2020 research 2

Fehlings, Susanne 5–6
field site and field methods 35–6
fire 86–9
First Opium War 116
foreign traders 140
freedom of formformlessness 136, 141–2
friendship 105–7
Fukuyama, F. 106

INDEX

Galemba, R. B. 138
Gandolfo, D. 137
Geertz, Clifford 34, 52, 73
Georgian/post-Soviet traders 102
Georgian traders 18
Giddens, A. 103
globalization 14–15
'globalization from below' concept 137–9
go-between *(dellal, bédik)* 55–7
grass-roots globalization 15
The Great Transformation 86
Guha-Khasnobis, B. 14, 17
Guangdong Province 116
Guzei, I. 97, 102

Habermas, J. 103
Hart, K. 3, 39, 103, 105
Hemdulla, R. 56
household accessories 15
household economy 18
Humphrey, C. 103, 104

Ibañez-Tirado, Diana 6
informal economy 3–4, 34
'informal entrepreneur' 14
informality 14–15, 17, 49–50
'informality-formality' continuum 23
informal networks 18
informal practices 140
innovation and capital investment 81
inter-Asian commerce 145–7
inter-regional commercial interaction 147–50
intrinsic motives and social networks 39–40

Kaminski, B. 12, 19
Kanbur, R. 14, 17
Karrar, H. 5, 13, 19
'keeper of the shrine' function 70–1
kélishish agreement 53
Keshavarzian, A. 150
Khujand 142–5
Kifaytulla Rehmitulla 52
Killick, E. 106, 109
'knockoffs'/copies products 140
Konstantinov, Yulian 82
Kyrgyz businessmen trading 21

larger shops 100
liberal market economy 11
Lilo and Dordoi markets 22
local authorities 15
'low-end globalization' concept 137–9
Lowengart, O. 75
Luhmann, N. 103

marketplace classifications 71–3
Marsden, M. 1, 04, 106
Mars, G. 105
Mathew, J. 136

Mathews, G. 15, 99
Melkumyan, H. 66
metal pushcarts 33
The Middleman Game 117; Aziz's 'furniture tour' 122–3; Kyrgyz 125–6; tasks 124–5
Mill, J. 14
mistrust and caution 104
Mitra, S. 12, 19
mixed motives and flexible social networks 40–1
mobile fairs 67
mobile markets 67
Morris, J. 130, 136
Mühlfried, F. 104

neoliberal economic development 18
Nikolotov, A. 106
nisi (credit) 54–5
non-state formality 50–3
notion of trust 96

official governance 18
Orthodoxy/Catholicism 75
Ostrom, E. 14, 17

Pachenkov, O. 103
path-dependent process 12
patrimonial-authoritarian leaders 82
peddlers 71
People's Republic of China 116
People's War on Terror 48
'permanent' traders 140
personal financial constraints 37
personalized transactions 73
personal loyalty and social obligation 51
pilgrimage economy, Armenia 67–9
pilgrimages 64–5
Polese, A. 130, 136
political uncertainty 14
Poghos-Petros shrine *69*, 72, 74
Polanyi, Karl 86, 87–9
price negotiation 73
price reductions *(skidki)* 100
private profitability 88
privatize state and collective farms 85
professional identity 101
profit *(payda)* 57

Qorghan, Enwer Semet 51, 54, 57

Ray, L. 14
Reader, I. 68
Rehimtulla, Kifaytulla 54, 57
religions markets 65–7
religious artefacts 66
religious goods 74–5
religious markets 64
religious souvenirs 66
rent 83–6
rent-generating assets 85

retailers 72
revenue scale, Dordoi and Lilo *20*
Rosen, Christine M. 81
Rose Revolution 3
Rudaz, Philippe 4–5, 13
Russian-Chinese borderlands 95
Russky Rynok (Russian Market) 95

Saltanat, extrinsic motives and social networks 38–9
Schröder, Philipp 6
Seifullin and Ualikhanov Streets 33
self-employed bazaar (and shuttle) traders 15
self-employment 14
severance pay/pension 37
Shane, S. 14
Simmel, G. 102, 103
small- and medium-sized enterprises (SMEs) 15
small manufacturers 15
social hierarchies 69–71
social networking 49
Sombart, W. 102
Southern Siberian traders 21
space organization 69–71
Spector, R. A. 51, 136
Starrett, G. 75
stationary markets 66–7
'statist-patrimonial capitalism' 16
Steenberg, Rune 5
Stoler, Ann 81
Surb Nshan shrine *68*
survival and entrepreneurship 19–20, *23*

Tagliacozzo, E. 136
Tbilisi and Beijing: linking markets 97–8; linking people 98–9; post-Soviet trade tourism 97
'Third World image' 83
trade activity 99–101

trade, defined 12
trader responses 19
traders' motivation 36–7
traditional economy 34
traditional retail spaces 81
transnational linkages 16, 20
Tughluq, Yarmuhemmet Tahir 52, 53

'unconditional' social networks 34
University of Tübingen (2014) 7
unpacking bags 33
Ürümchi (2011–2012) 47
Uyghur population: 'informal institutions' 47; traders 47; *ubal, yaman bolidu and haram* 51; Xinjiang 46
Uzbek traders 135

Venkataraman, S. 14
village of Aramus 70
Volkswagen Foundation 2

Waldinger, R. 102
Weber, M. 102
World Bank study (2012) 12
World Trade Organization (WTO) 129

Xinjiang: GDP and value of exports **48**; state violence **58**; Uyghur population 46
Xushtar, S. 56

Yabaolu Market 95, 97
Yang, Y. 15
Yeğen, M. 138
Yivu, trade 'outside the law' and 'freedom of form' 139–42
Yüsüpjan 47–8

Zaidman, N. 75

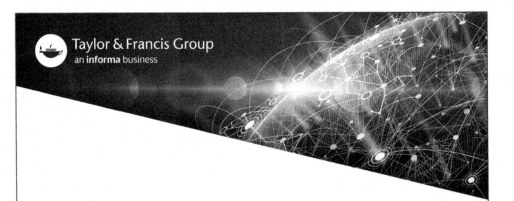